PARROTT • CARLINI • ANGULO

SABAN'S

CO GO POWER RANGERS

VOLUME **FIVE**

BOOM!
STUDIOS

SABAN'S GO GO

SERIES DESIGNER
MICHELLE ANKLEY

COLLECTION DESIGNER
CHELSEA ROBERTS

ASSISTANT EDITOR
GWEN WALLER

COLLECTION ASSOCIATE EDITOR
AMANDA LaFRANCO

EDITOR
DAFNA PLEBAN

HASBRO SPECIAL THANKS
MELISSA FLORES, PAUL STRICKLAND, ED LANE, BETH ARTALE, AND **MICHAEL KELLY**

Ross Richie CEO & Founder
Joy Huffman CFO
Matt Gagnon Editor-in-Chief
Filip Sablik President, Publishing & Marketing
Stephen Christy President, Development
Lance Kreiter Vice President, Licensing & Merchandising
Arur e Singh Vice President, Marketing
Bryce Carlson Vice President, Editorial & Creative Strategy
Scott Newman Manager, Production Design
Kate Henning Manager, Operations
Spencer Simpson Manager, Sales
Elyse Strandberg Manager, Finance
Sierra Hahn Executive Editor
Jeanine Schaefer Executive Editor
Dafna Pleban Senior Editor
Shannon Watters Senior Editor
Eric Harburn Senior Editor
Chris Rosa Editor
Matthew Levine Editor
Sophie Philips-Roberts Associate Editor
Amanda LaFranco Associate Editor
Jonathan Manning Associate Editor

Gavin Gronenthal Assistant Editor
Gwen Waller Assistant Editor
Allyson Gronowitz Assistant Editor
Jillian Crab Design Coordinator
Michelle Ankley Design Coordinator
Kara Leopard Production Designer
Marie Krupina Production Designer
Grace Park Production Designer
Chelsea Roberts Production Design Assistant
Samantha Knapp Production Design Assistant
José Meza Live Events Lead
Stephanie Hocutt Digital Marketing Lead
Esther Kim Marketing Coordinator
Cat O'Grady Digital Marketing Coordinator
Amanda Lawson Marketing Assistant
Holly Aitchison Digital Sales Coordinator
Morgan Perry Retail Sales Coordinator
Megan Christopher Operations Coordinator
Rodrigo Hernandez Mailroom Assistant
Zipporah Smith Operations Assistant
Sabrina Lesin Operations Assistant
Breanna Sarpy Executive Assistant

Licensed by:

POWER RANGERS

WRITTEN BY
RYAN PARROTT

ILLUSTRATED BY
ELEONORA CARLINI
WITH INK ASSISTANCE BY **SIMONA DI GIANFELICE**

COLORS BY
RAÚL ANGULO

LETTERS BY
ED DUKESHIRE

COVER BY
DAN MORA

SEVENTEEN

MARCUS TO WITH COLORS BY **RAÚL ANGULO** | ISSUE SEVENTEEN MAIN COVER

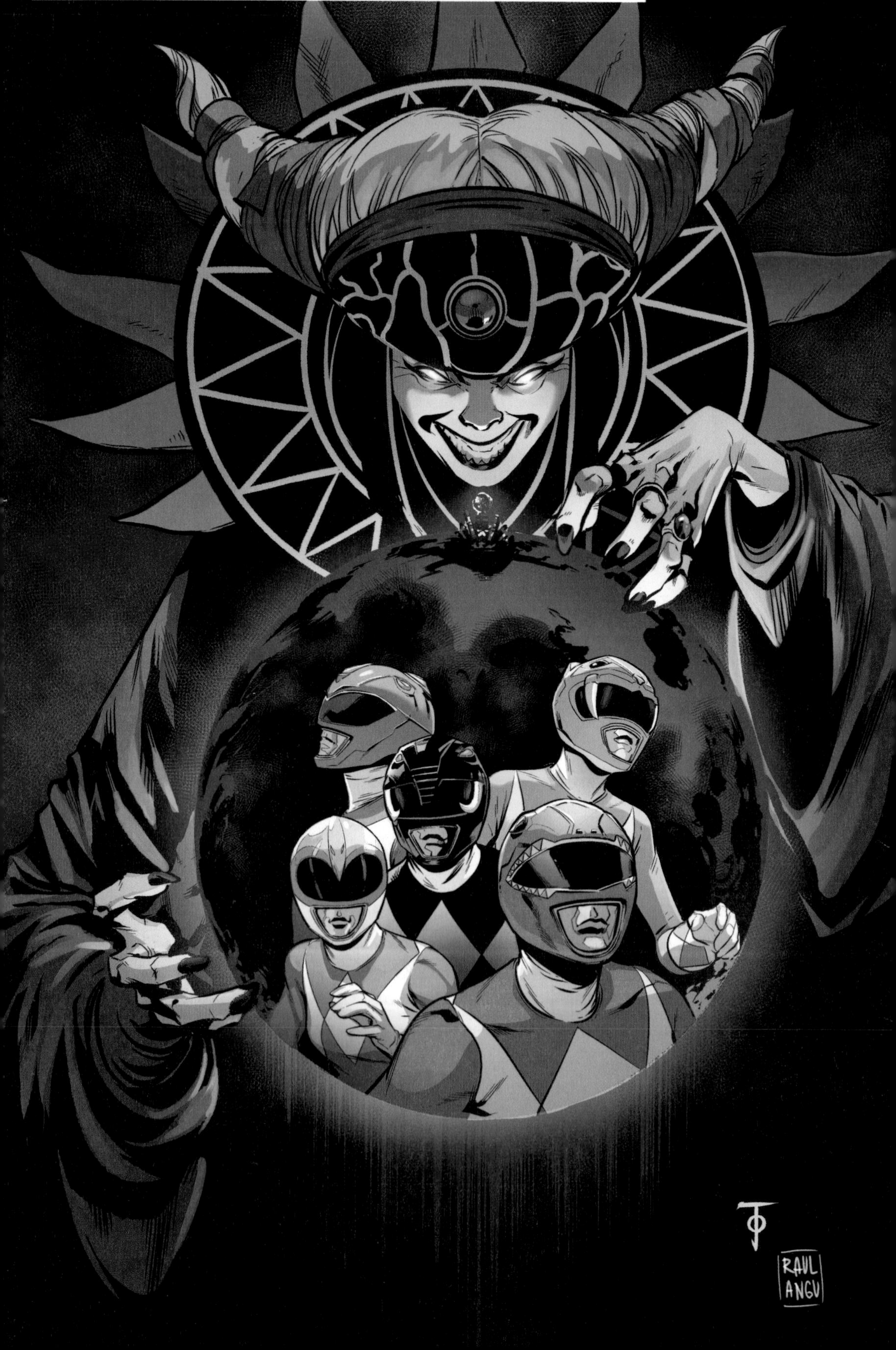
RAUL
ANGU

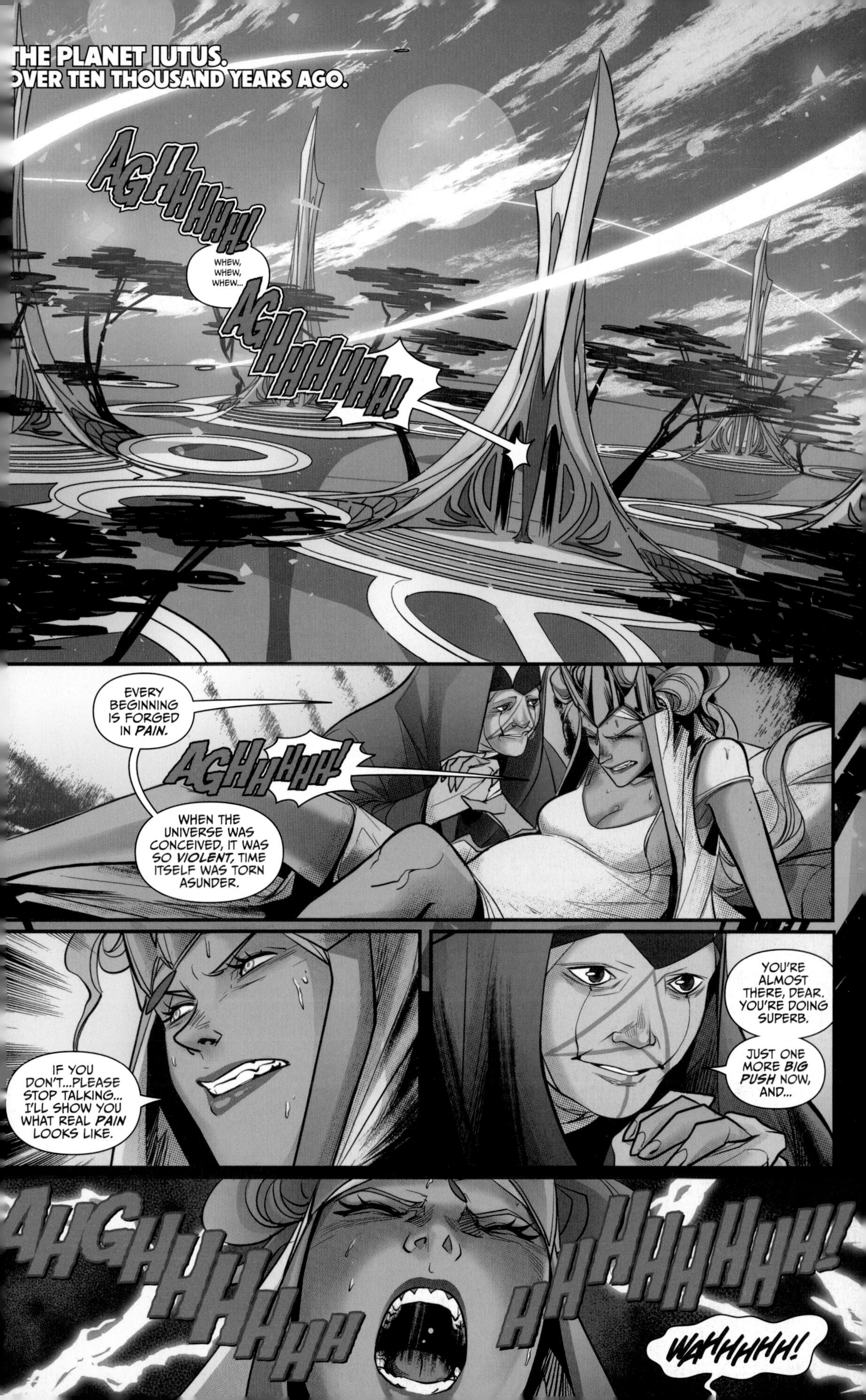

THE PLANET IUTUS.
OVER TEN THOUSAND YEARS AGO.
AGHHHHHH!
WHEW, WHEW, WHEW...
AGHHHHHHH!
EVERY BEGINNING IS FORGED IN PAIN.
AGHHHHH!
WHEN THE UNIVERSE WAS CONCEIVED, IT WAS SO VIOLENT, TIME ITSELF WAS TORN ASUNDER.
IF YOU DON'T...PLEASE STOP TALKING... I'LL SHOW YOU WHAT REAL PAIN LOOKS LIKE.
YOU'RE ALMOST THERE, DEAR. YOU'RE DOING SUPERB.
JUST ONE MORE BIG PUSH NOW, AND...
AHGHHHHHHHHHHHHHHHHHHHHHHH!
WAHHHHHH!

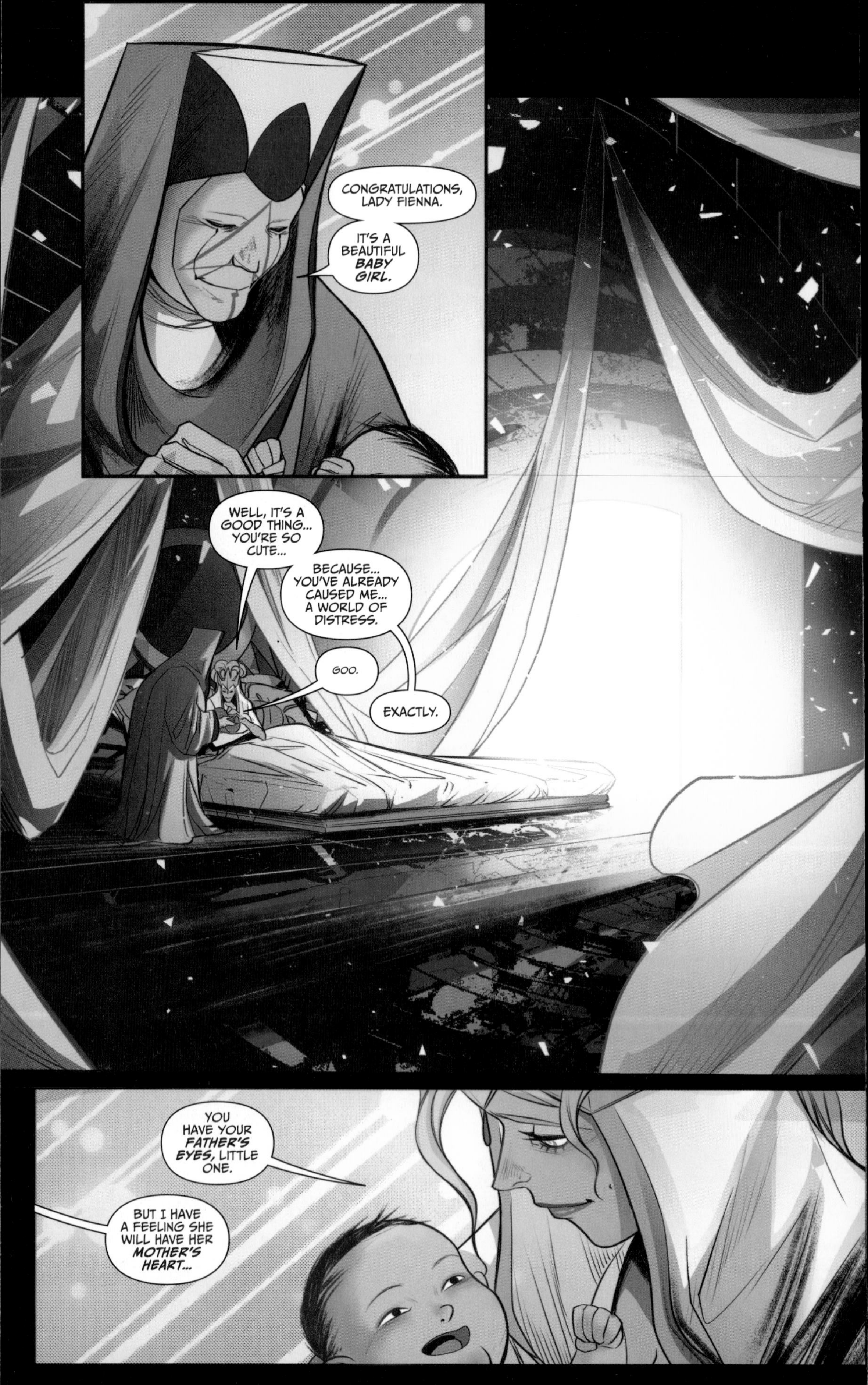
CONGRATULATIONS, LADY FIENNA.
IT'S A BEAUTIFUL BABY GIRL.
WELL, IT'S A GOOD THING... YOU'RE SO CUTE...
BECAUSE... YOU'VE ALREADY CAUSED ME... A WORLD OF DISTRESS.
GOO.
EXACTLY.
YOU HAVE YOUR FATHER'S EYES, LITTLE ONE.
BUT I HAVE A FEELING SHE WILL HAVE HER MOTHER'S HEART...

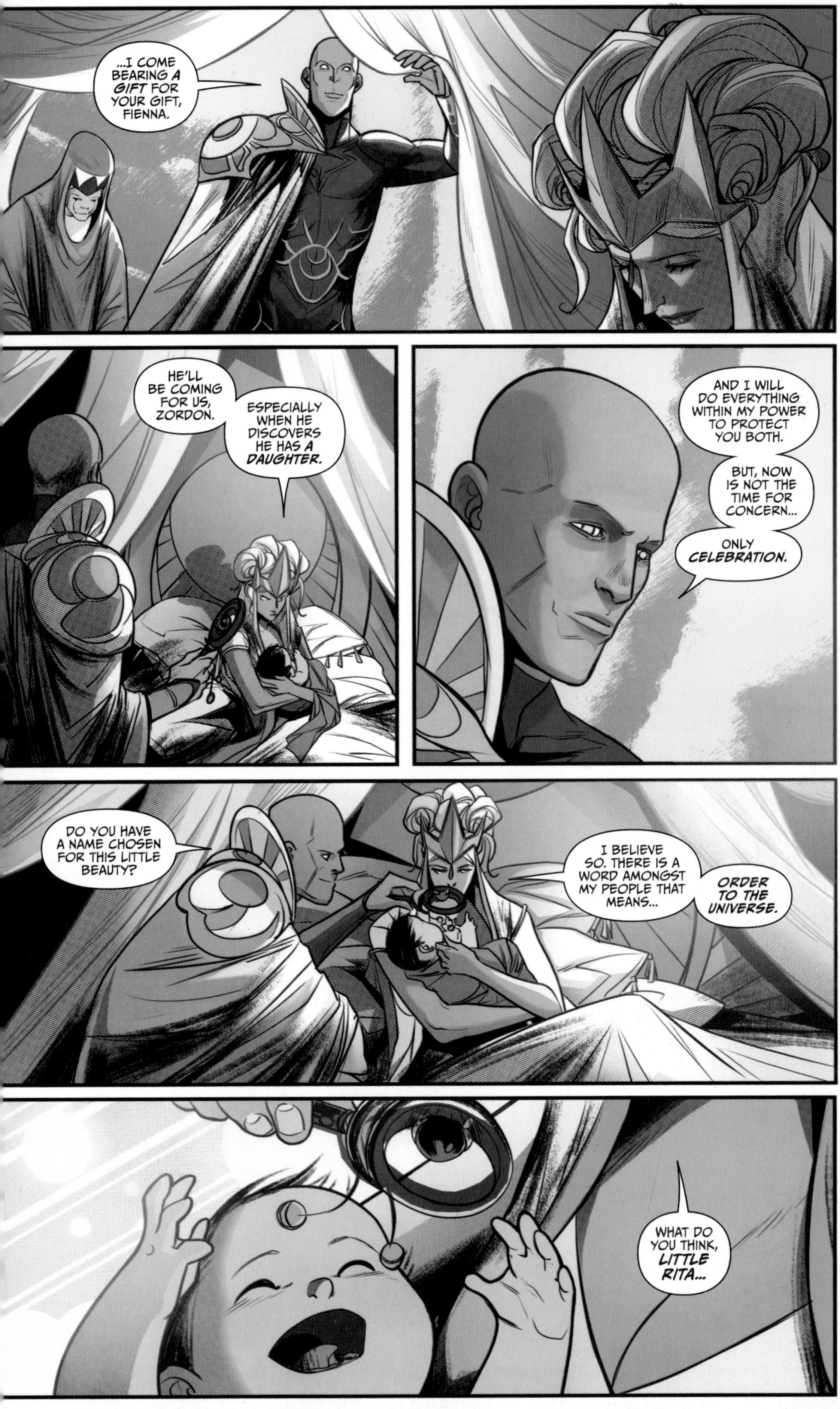

...I COME BEARING A GIFT FOR YOUR GIFT, FIENNA.
HE'LL BE COMING FOR US, ZORDON.
ESPECIALLY WHEN HE DISCOVERS HE HAS A DAUGHTER.
AND I WILL DO EVERYTHING WITHIN MY POWER TO PROTECT YOU BOTH.
BUT, NOW IS NOT THE TIME FOR CONCERN...
ONLY CELEBRATION.
DO YOU HAVE A NAME CHOSEN FOR THIS LITTLE BEAUTY?
I BELIEVE SO. THERE IS A WORD AMONGST MY PEOPLE THAT MEANS...
ORDER TO THE UNIVERSE.
WHAT DO YOU THINK, LITTLE RITA...

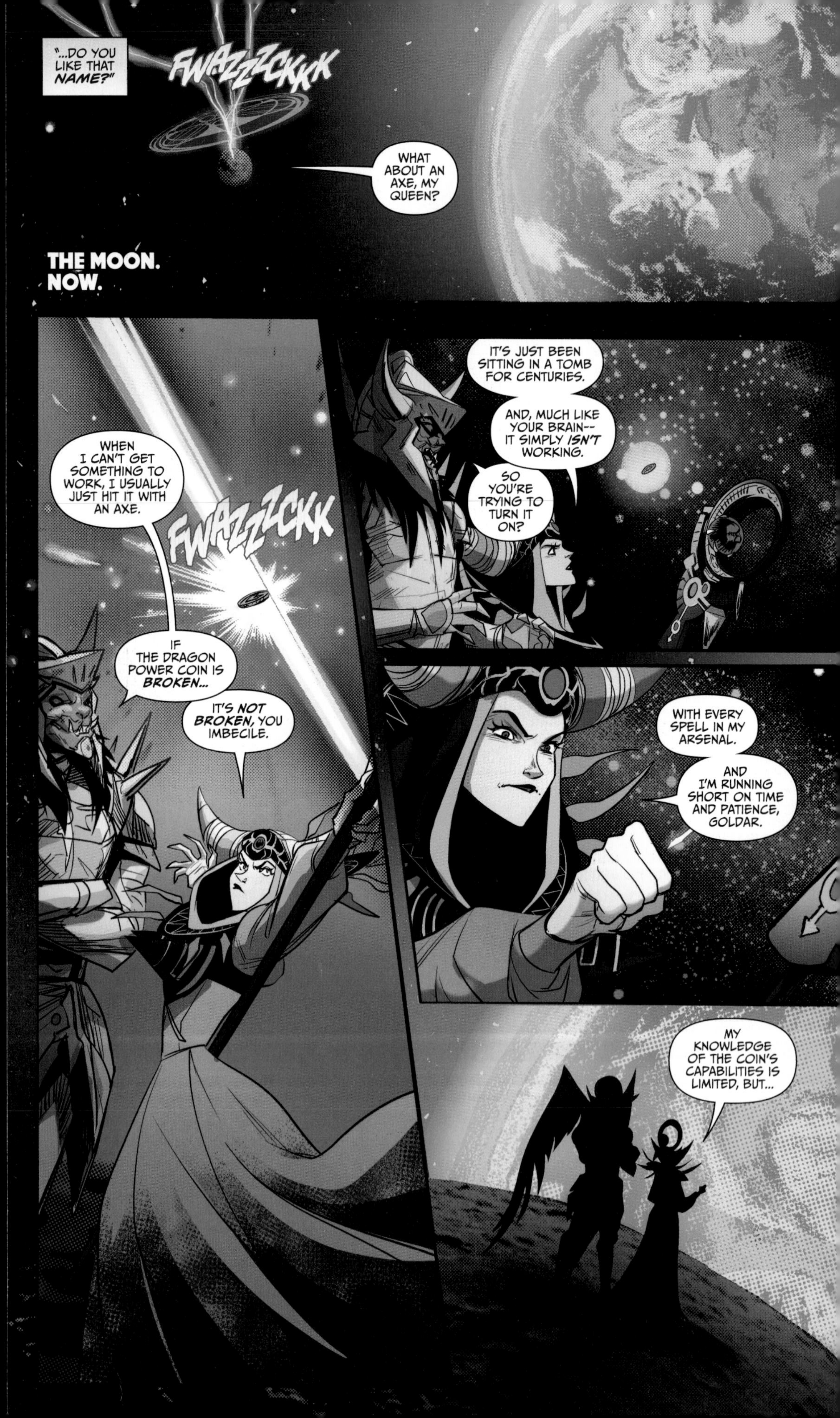
"...DO YOU LIKE THAT NAME?"
FWAZZZZCKKK
WHAT ABOUT AN AXE, MY QUEEN?
THE MOON. NOW.
WHEN I CAN'T GET SOMETHING TO WORK, I USUALLY JUST HIT IT WITH AN AXE.
FWAZZZZCKK
IF THE DRAGON POWER COIN IS BROKEN...
IT'S NOT BROKEN, YOU IMBECILE.
IT'S JUST BEEN SITTING IN A TOMB FOR CENTURIES.
AND, MUCH LIKE YOUR BRAIN-- IT SIMPLY ISN'T WORKING.
SO YOU'RE TRYING TO TURN IT ON?
WITH EVERY SPELL IN MY ARSENAL.
AND I'M RUNNING SHORT ON TIME AND PATIENCE, GOLDAR.
MY KNOWLEDGE OF THE COIN'S CAPABILITIES IS LIMITED, BUT...

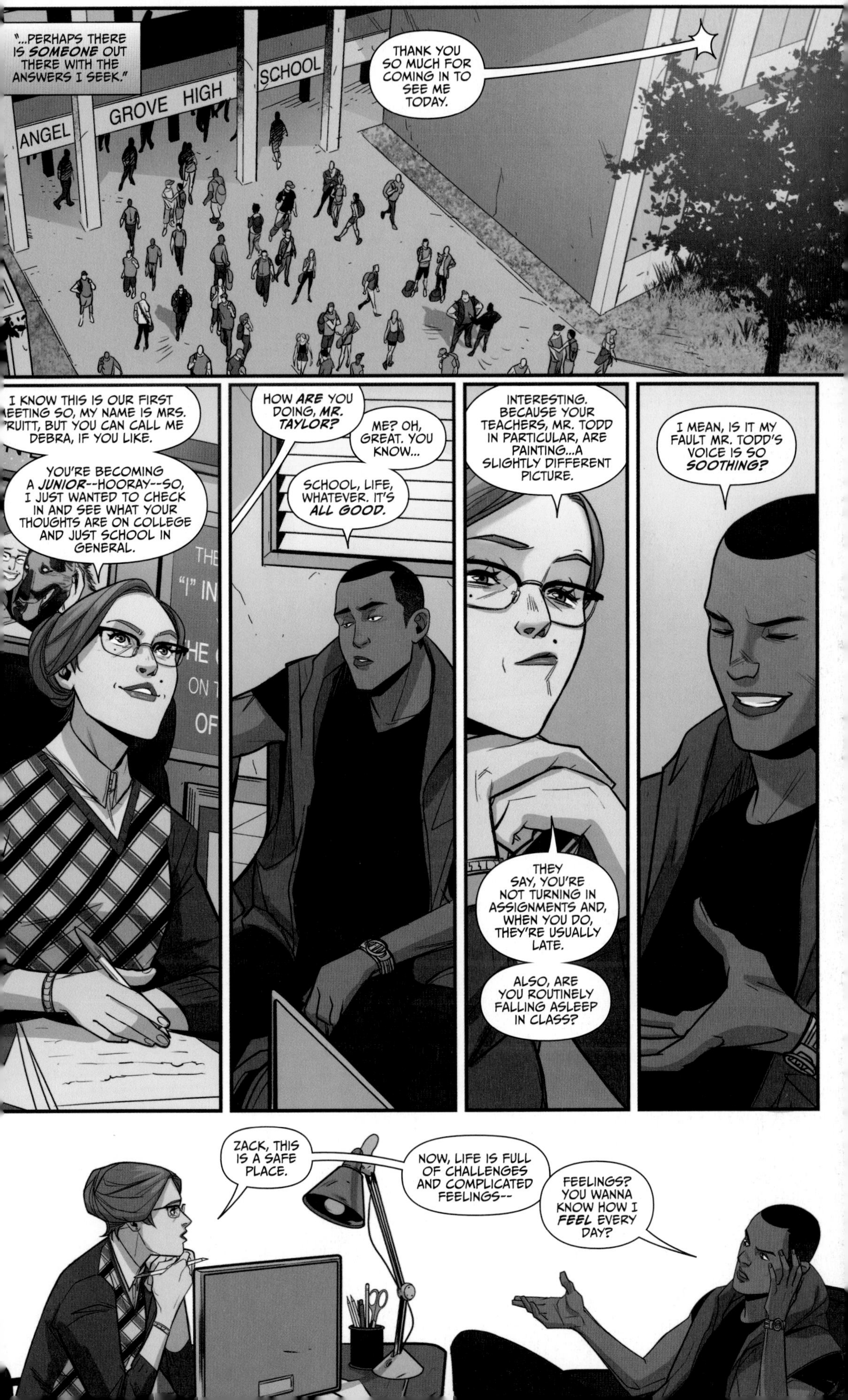
"...PERHAPS THERE IS *SOMEONE* OUT THERE WITH THE ANSWERS I SEEK."
ANGEL GROVE HIGH SCHOOL
THANK YOU SO MUCH FOR COMING IN TO SEE ME TODAY.
I KNOW THIS IS OUR FIRST MEETING SO, MY NAME IS MRS. PRUITT, BUT YOU CAN CALL ME DEBRA, IF YOU LIKE.
YOU'RE BECOMING A *JUNIOR*--HOORAY--SO, I JUST WANTED TO CHECK IN AND SEE WHAT YOUR THOUGHTS ARE ON COLLEGE AND JUST SCHOOL IN GENERAL.
HOW *ARE* YOU DOING, *MR. TAYLOR?*
ME? OH, GREAT. YOU KNOW...
SCHOOL, LIFE, WHATEVER. IT'S *ALL GOOD.*
INTERESTING. BECAUSE YOUR TEACHERS, MR. TODD IN PARTICULAR, ARE PAINTING...A SLIGHTLY DIFFERENT PICTURE.
THEY SAY, YOU'RE NOT TURNING IN ASSIGNMENTS AND, WHEN YOU DO, THEY'RE USUALLY LATE.
ALSO, ARE YOU ROUTINELY FALLING ASLEEP IN CLASS?
I MEAN, IS IT MY FAULT MR. TODD'S VOICE IS SO *SOOTHING?*
ZACK, THIS IS A SAFE PLACE.
NOW, LIFE IS FULL OF CHALLENGES AND COMPLICATED FEELINGS--
FEELINGS? YOU WANNA KNOW HOW I *FEEL* EVERY DAY?

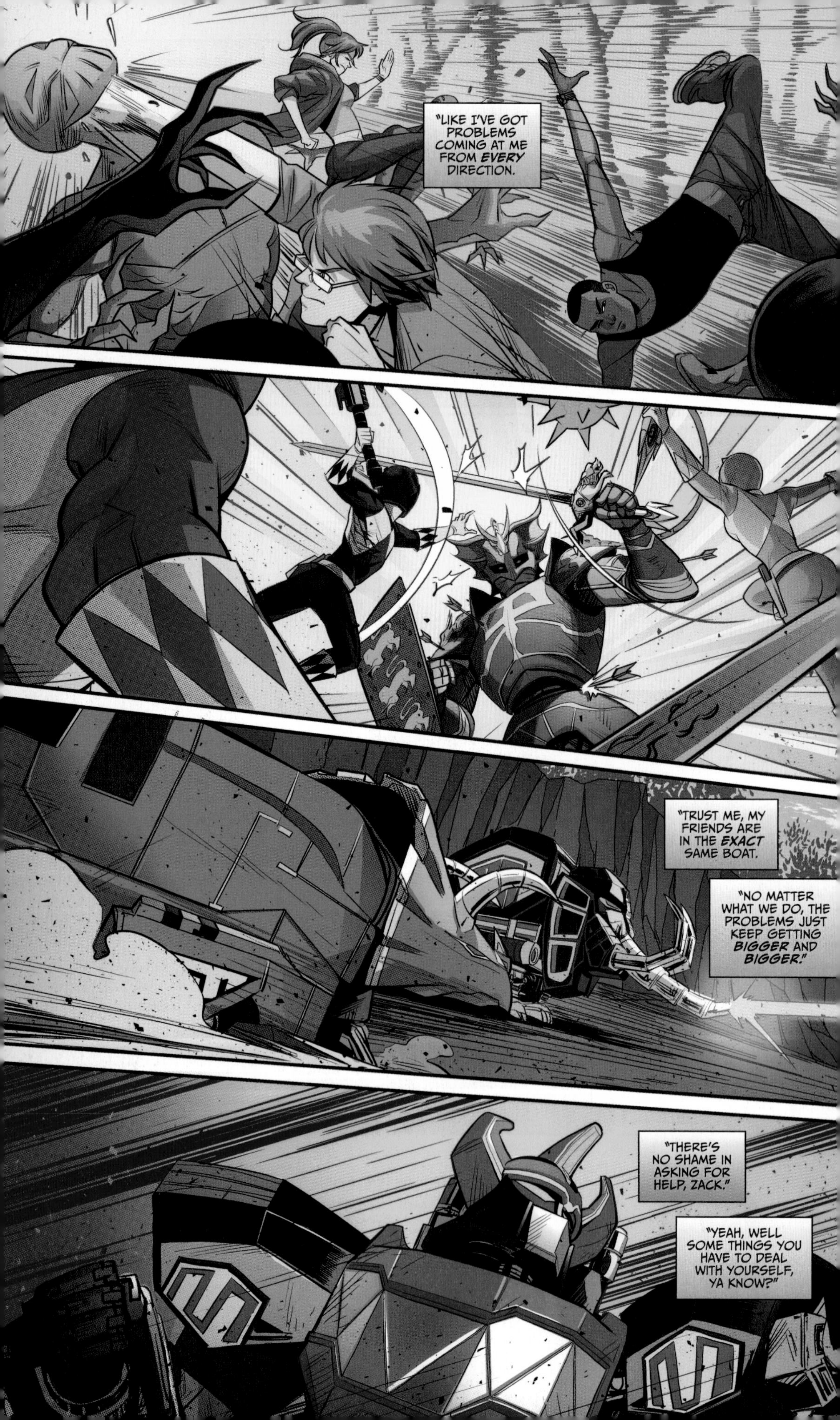
"LIKE I'VE GOT PROBLEMS COMING AT ME FROM *EVERY* DIRECTION.
"TRUST ME, MY FRIENDS ARE IN THE *EXACT* SAME BOAT.
"NO MATTER WHAT WE DO, THE PROBLEMS JUST KEEP GETTING *BIGGER* AND *BIGGER*."
"THERE'S NO SHAME IN ASKING FOR HELP, ZACK."
"YEAH, WELL SOME THINGS YOU HAVE TO DEAL WITH YOURSELF, YA KNOW?"

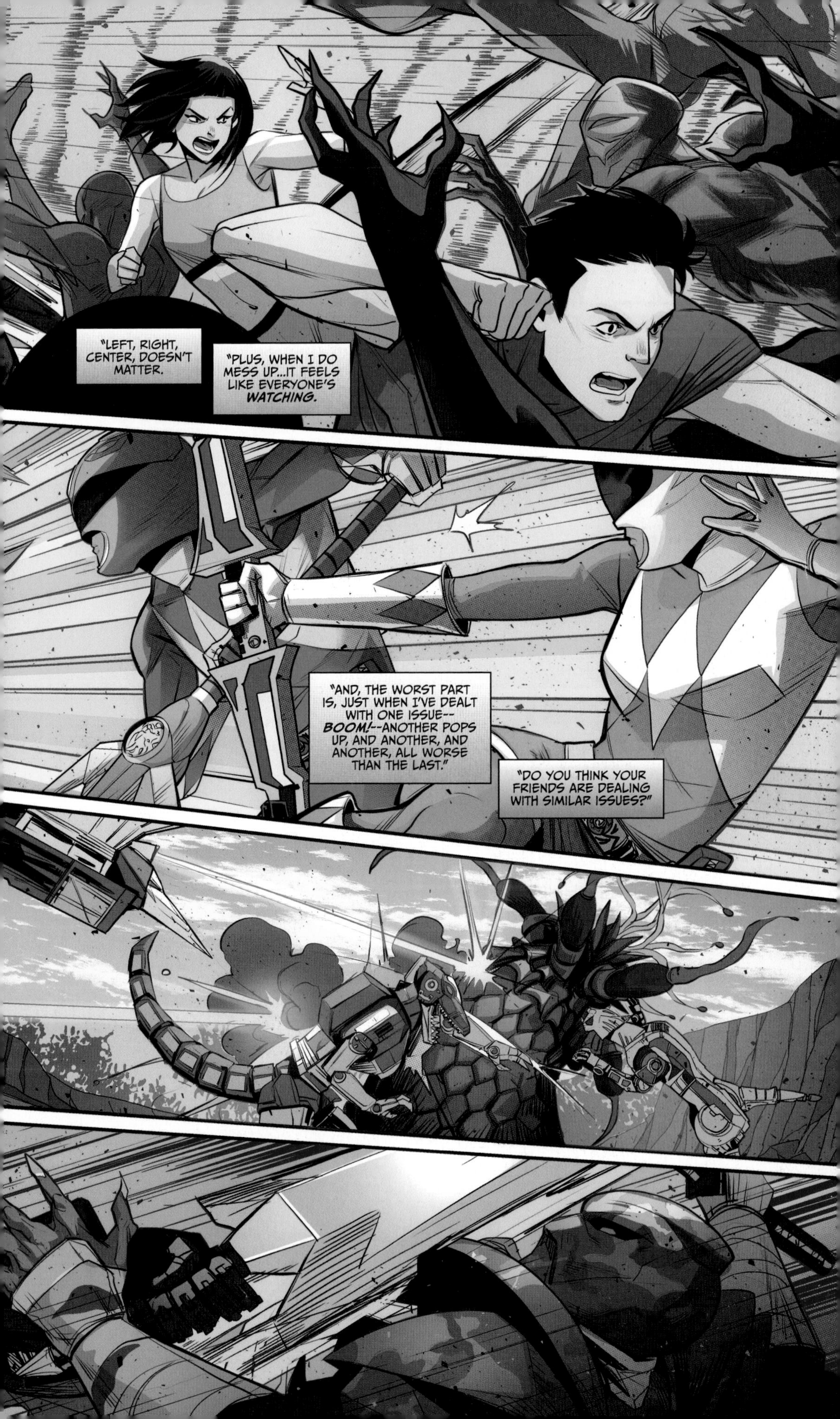
"LEFT, RIGHT, CENTER, DOESN'T MATTER.
"PLUS, WHEN I DO MESS UP...IT FEELS LIKE EVERYONE'S *WATCHING*.
"AND, THE WORST PART IS, JUST WHEN I'VE DEALT WITH ONE ISSUE-- *BOOM!*--ANOTHER POPS UP, AND ANOTHER, AND ANOTHER, ALL WORSE THAN THE LAST."
"DO YOU THINK YOUR FRIENDS ARE DEALING WITH SIMILAR ISSUES?"

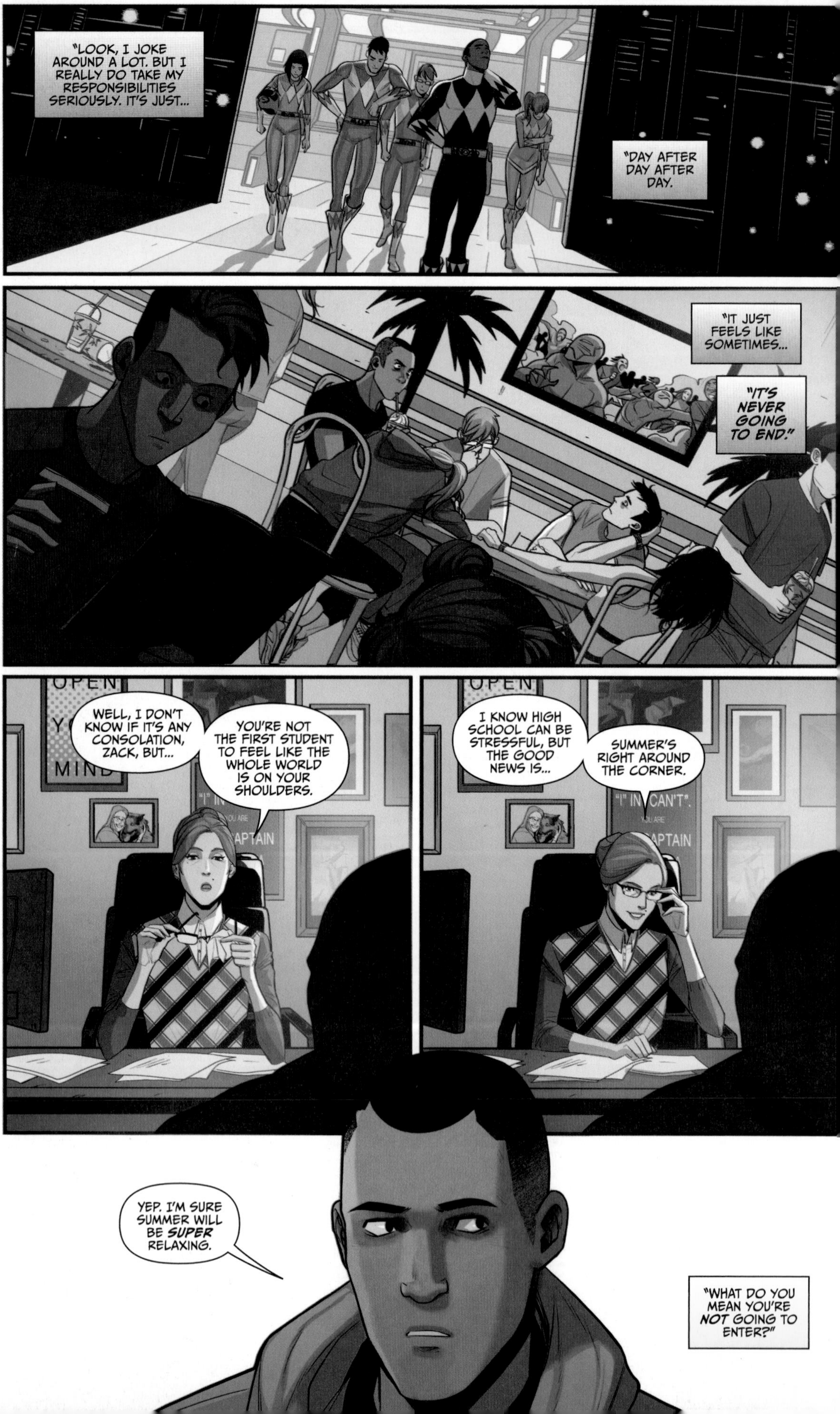
"LOOK, I JOKE AROUND A LOT. BUT I REALLY DO TAKE MY RESPONSIBILITIES SERIOUSLY. IT'S JUST...
"DAY AFTER DAY AFTER DAY.
"IT JUST FEELS LIKE SOMETIMES...
"IT'S NEVER GOING TO END."
WELL, I DON'T KNOW IF IT'S ANY CONSOLATION, ZACK, BUT...
YOU'RE NOT THE FIRST STUDENT TO FEEL LIKE THE WHOLE WORLD IS ON YOUR SHOULDERS.
I KNOW HIGH SCHOOL CAN BE STRESSFUL, BUT THE GOOD NEWS IS...
SUMMER'S RIGHT AROUND THE CORNER.
YEP. I'M SURE SUMMER WILL BE SUPER RELAXING.
"WHAT DO YOU MEAN YOU'RE NOT GOING TO ENTER?"

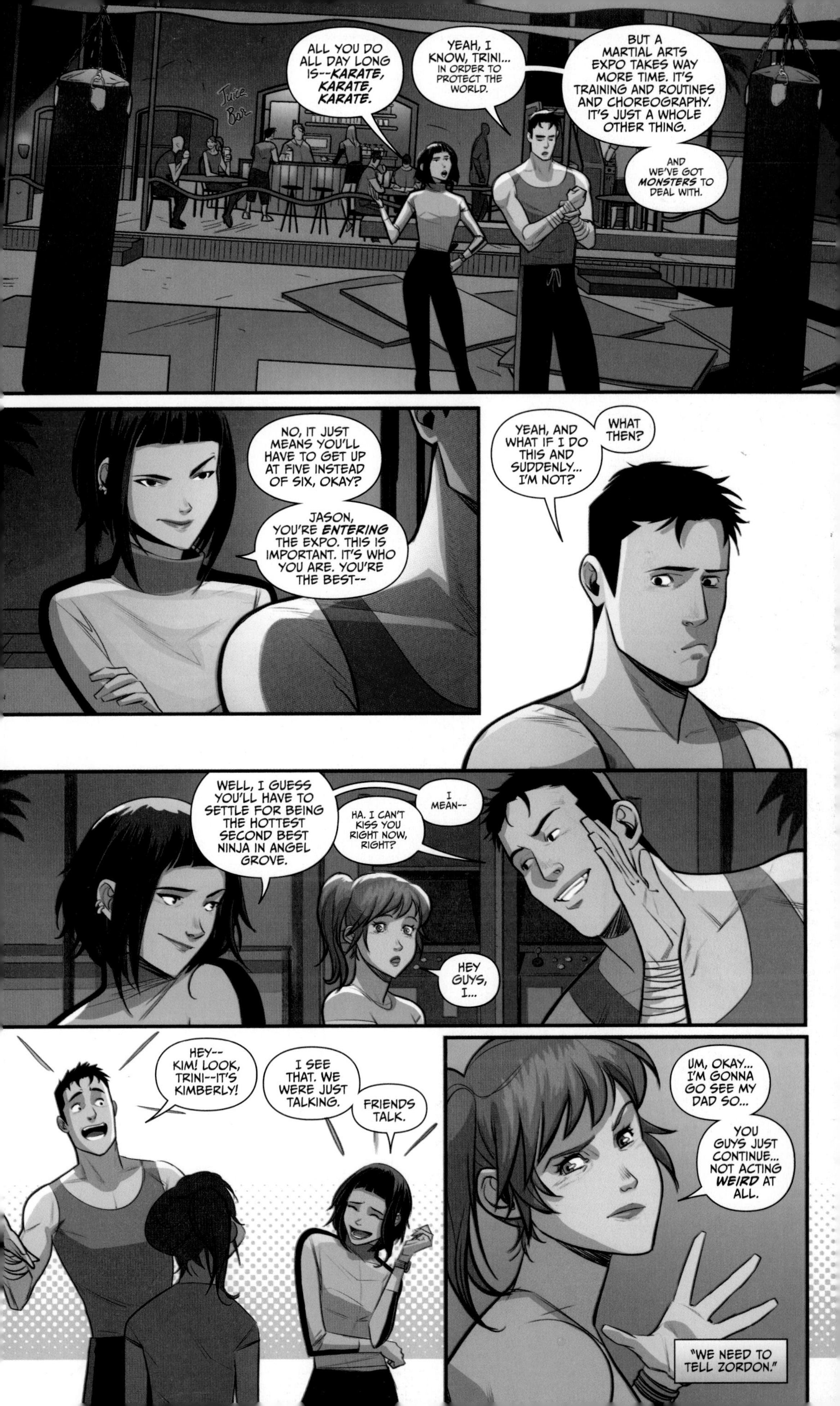

Juice Bar
ALL YOU DO ALL DAY LONG IS--KARATE, KARATE, KARATE.
YEAH, I KNOW, TRINI... IN ORDER TO PROTECT THE WORLD.
BUT A MARTIAL ARTS EXPO TAKES WAY MORE TIME. IT'S TRAINING AND ROUTINES AND CHOREOGRAPHY. IT'S JUST A WHOLE OTHER THING.
AND WE'VE GOT MONSTERS TO DEAL WITH.
NO, IT JUST MEANS YOU'LL HAVE TO GET UP AT FIVE INSTEAD OF SIX, OKAY?
JASON, YOU'RE ENTERING THE EXPO. THIS IS IMPORTANT. IT'S WHO YOU ARE. YOU'RE THE BEST--
YEAH, AND WHAT IF I DO THIS AND SUDDENLY... I'M NOT?
WHAT THEN?
WELL, I GUESS YOU'LL HAVE TO SETTLE FOR BEING THE HOTTEST SECOND BEST NINJA IN ANGEL GROVE.
HA. I CAN'T KISS YOU RIGHT NOW, RIGHT?
I MEAN--
HEY GUYS, I...
HEY-- KIM! LOOK, TRINI--IT'S KIMBERLY!
I SEE THAT. WE WERE JUST TALKING.
FRIENDS TALK.
UM, OKAY... I'M GONNA GO SEE MY DAD SO...
YOU GUYS JUST CONTINUE... NOT ACTING WEIRD AT ALL.
"WE NEED TO TELL ZORDON."

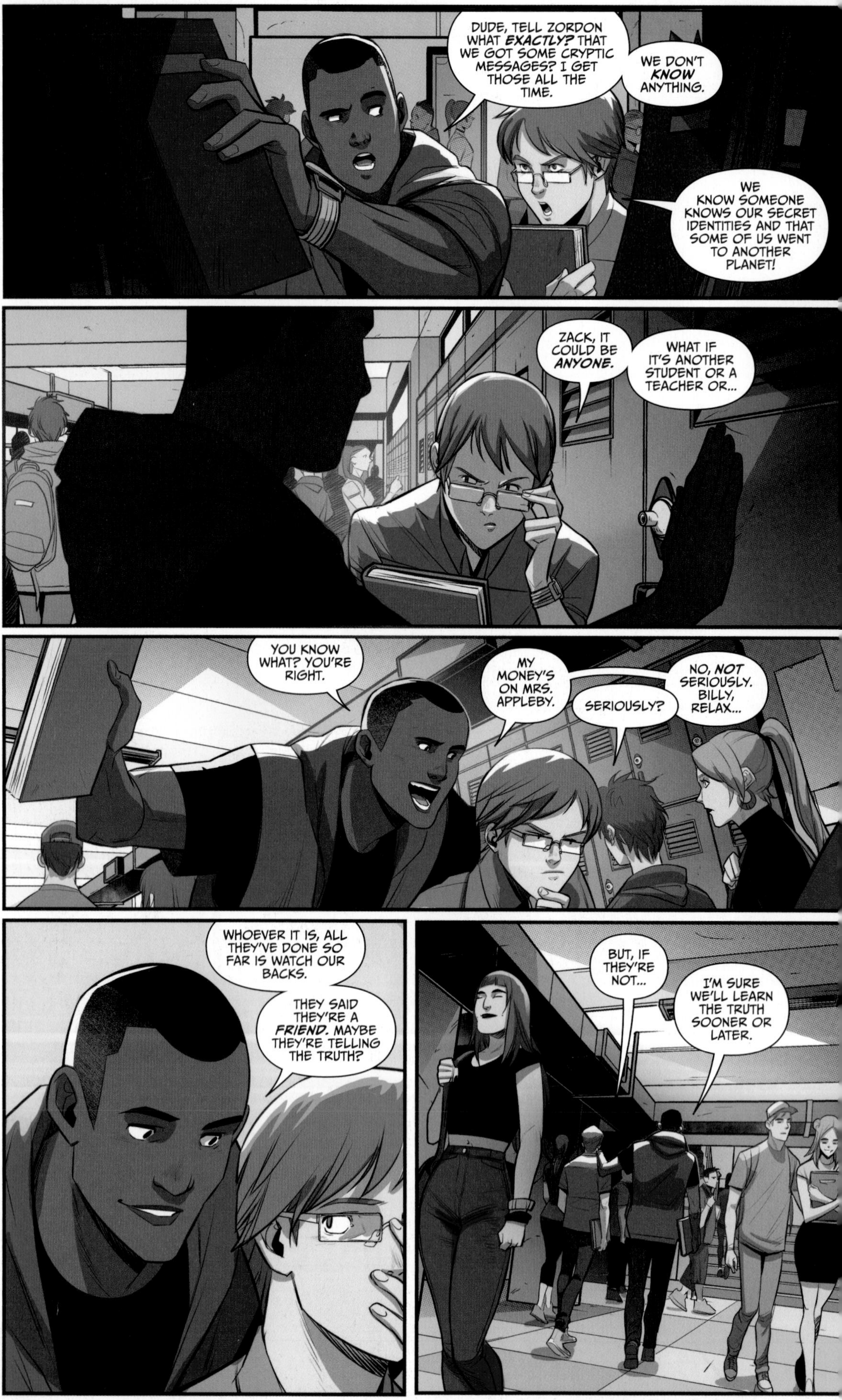
DUDE, TELL ZORDON WHAT EXACTLY? THAT WE GOT SOME CRYPTIC MESSAGES? I GET THOSE ALL THE TIME.
WE DON'T KNOW ANYTHING.
WE KNOW SOMEONE KNOWS OUR SECRET IDENTITIES AND THAT SOME OF US WENT TO ANOTHER PLANET!
ZACK, IT COULD BE ANYONE.
WHAT IF IT'S ANOTHER STUDENT OR A TEACHER OR...
YOU KNOW WHAT? YOU'RE RIGHT.
MY MONEY'S ON MRS. APPLEBY.
SERIOUSLY?
NO, NOT SERIOUSLY. BILLY, RELAX...
WHOEVER IT IS, ALL THEY'VE DONE SO FAR IS WATCH OUR BACKS.
THEY SAID THEY'RE A FRIEND. MAYBE THEY'RE TELLING THE TRUTH?
BUT, IF THEY'RE NOT...
I'M SURE WE'LL LEARN THE TRUTH SOONER OR LATER.

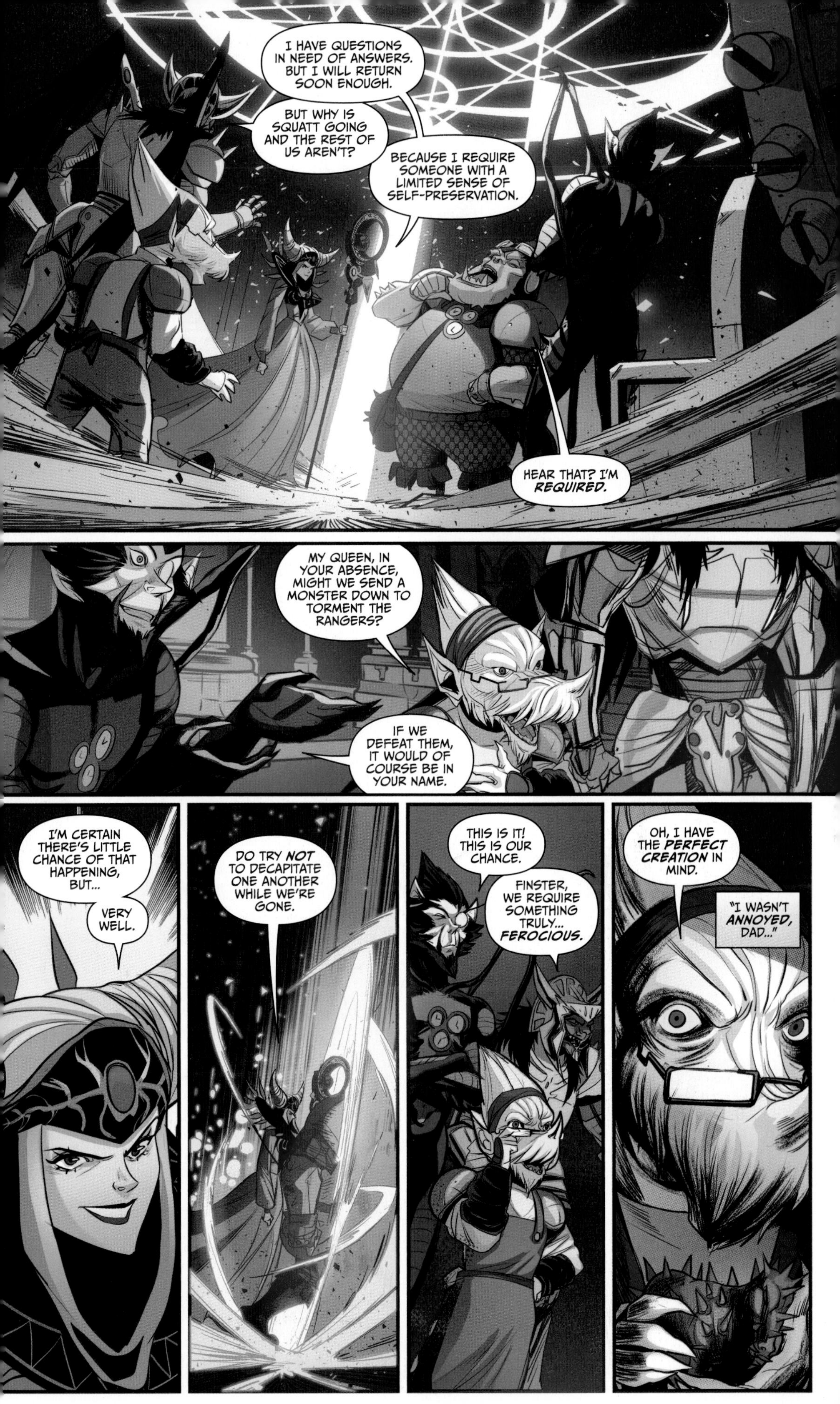
I HAVE QUESTIONS IN NEED OF ANSWERS. BUT I WILL RETURN SOON ENOUGH.
BUT WHY IS SQUATT GOING AND THE REST OF US AREN'T?
BECAUSE I REQUIRE SOMEONE WITH A LIMITED SENSE OF SELF-PRESERVATION.
HEAR THAT? I'M ***REQUIRED.***
MY QUEEN, IN YOUR ABSENCE, MIGHT WE SEND A MONSTER DOWN TO TORMENT THE RANGERS?
IF WE DEFEAT THEM, IT WOULD OF COURSE BE IN YOUR NAME.
I'M CERTAIN THERE'S LITTLE CHANCE OF THAT HAPPENING, BUT...
VERY WELL.
DO TRY ***NOT*** TO DECAPITATE ONE ANOTHER WHILE WE'RE GONE.
THIS IS IT! THIS IS OUR CHANCE.
FINSTER, WE REQUIRE SOMETHING TRULY... ***FEROCIOUS.***
OH, I HAVE THE ***PERFECT CREATION*** IN MIND.
"I WASN'T ***ANNOYED,*** DAD..."

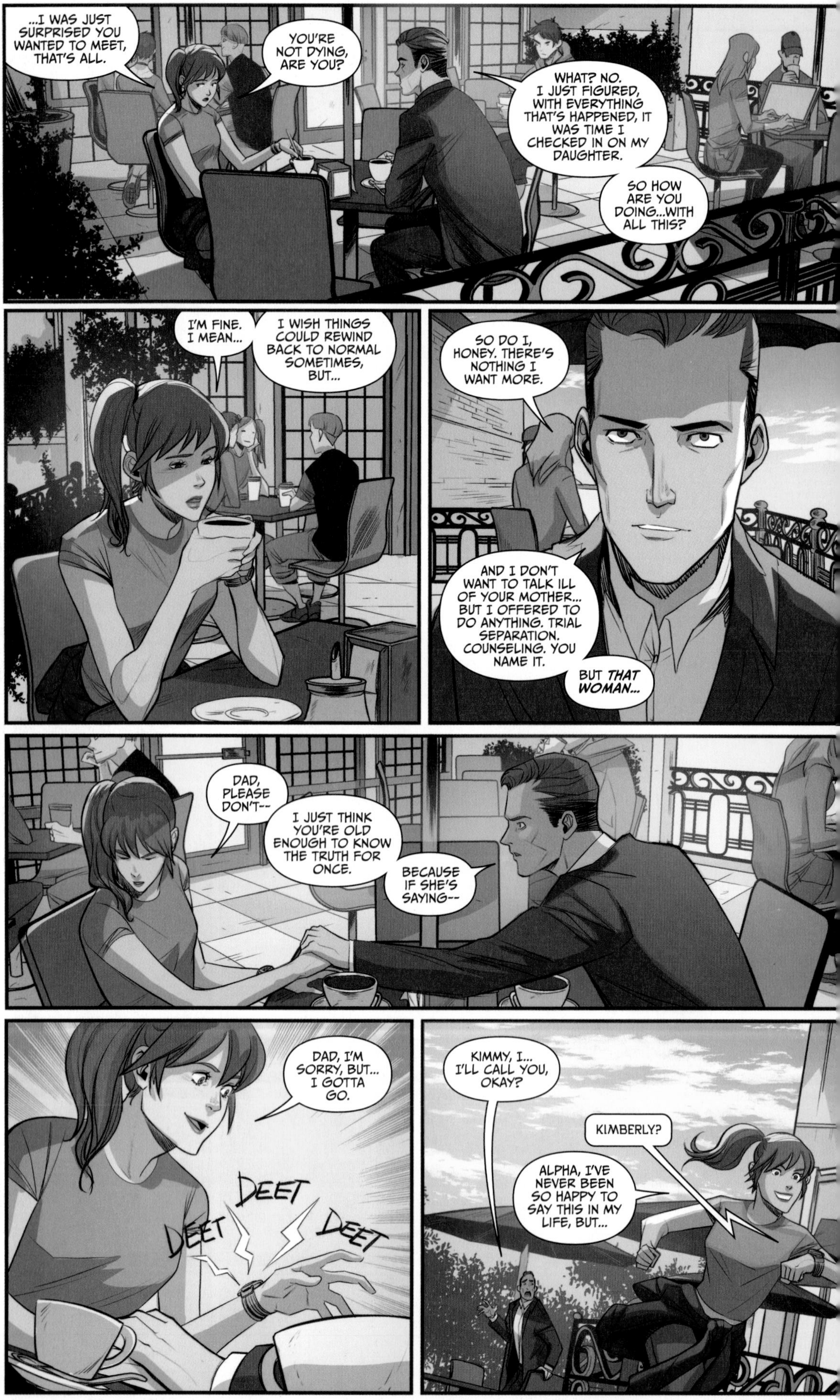
...I WAS JUST SURPRISED YOU WANTED TO MEET, THAT'S ALL.
YOU'RE NOT DYING, ARE YOU?
WHAT? NO. I JUST FIGURED, WITH EVERYTHING THAT'S HAPPENED, IT WAS TIME I CHECKED IN ON MY DAUGHTER.
SO HOW ARE YOU DOING...WITH ALL THIS?
I'M FINE. I MEAN...
I WISH THINGS COULD REWIND BACK TO NORMAL SOMETIMES, BUT...
SO DO I, HONEY. THERE'S NOTHING I WANT MORE.
AND I DON'T WANT TO TALK ILL OF YOUR MOTHER... BUT I OFFERED TO DO ANYTHING. TRIAL SEPARATION. COUNSELING. YOU NAME IT.
BUT *THAT WOMAN...*
DAD, PLEASE DON'T--
I JUST THINK YOU'RE OLD ENOUGH TO KNOW THE TRUTH FOR ONCE.
BECAUSE IF SHE'S SAYING--
DAD, I'M SORRY, BUT... I GOTTA GO.
DEET
DEET
DEET
KIMMY, I... I'LL CALL YOU, OKAY?
KIMBERLY?
ALPHA, I'VE NEVER BEEN SO HAPPY TO SAY THIS IN MY LIFE, BUT...

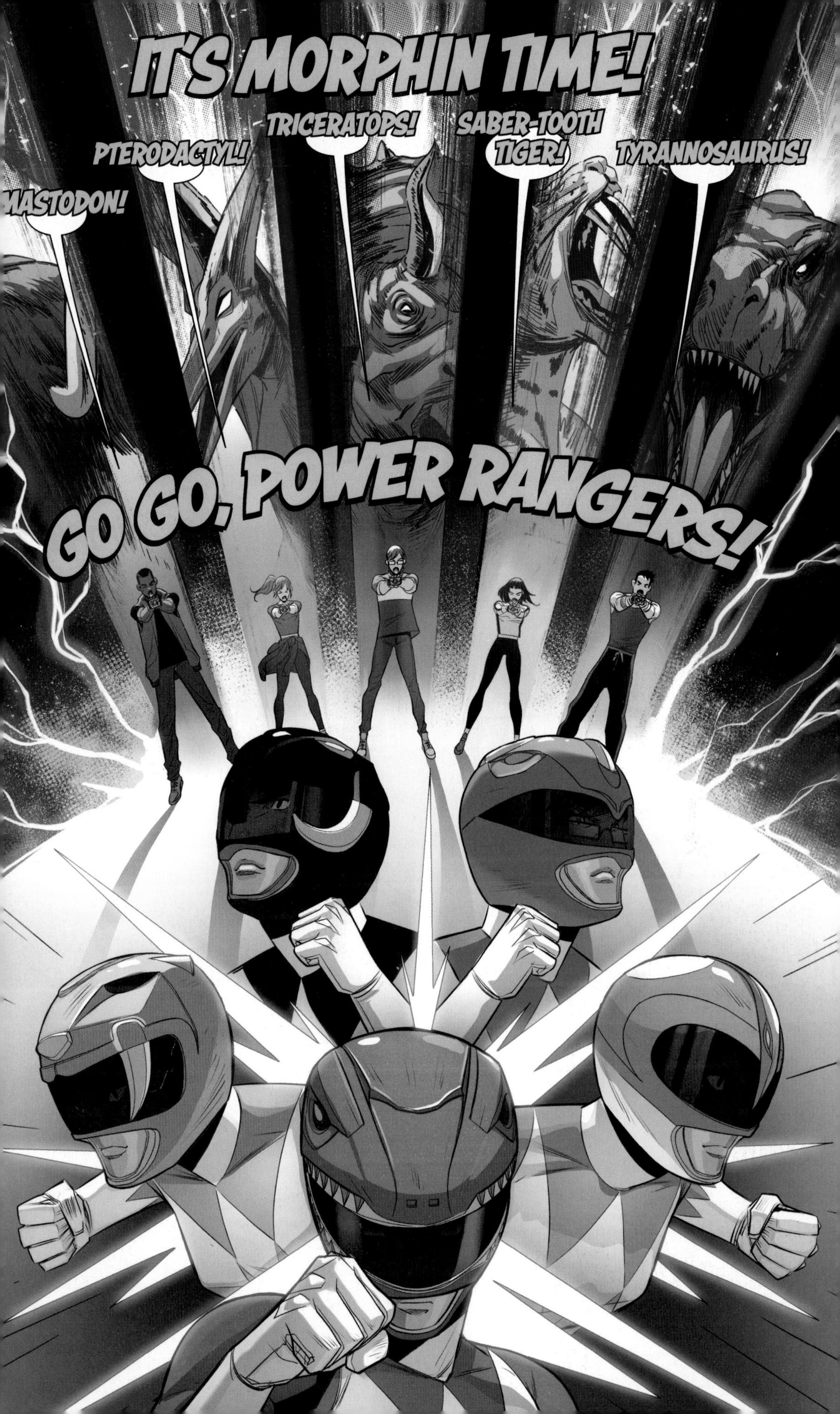

IT'S MORPHIN TIME!
MASTODON!
PTERODACTYL!
TRICERATOPS!
SABER-TOOTH TIGER!
TYRANNOSAURUS!
GO GO, POWER RANGERS!

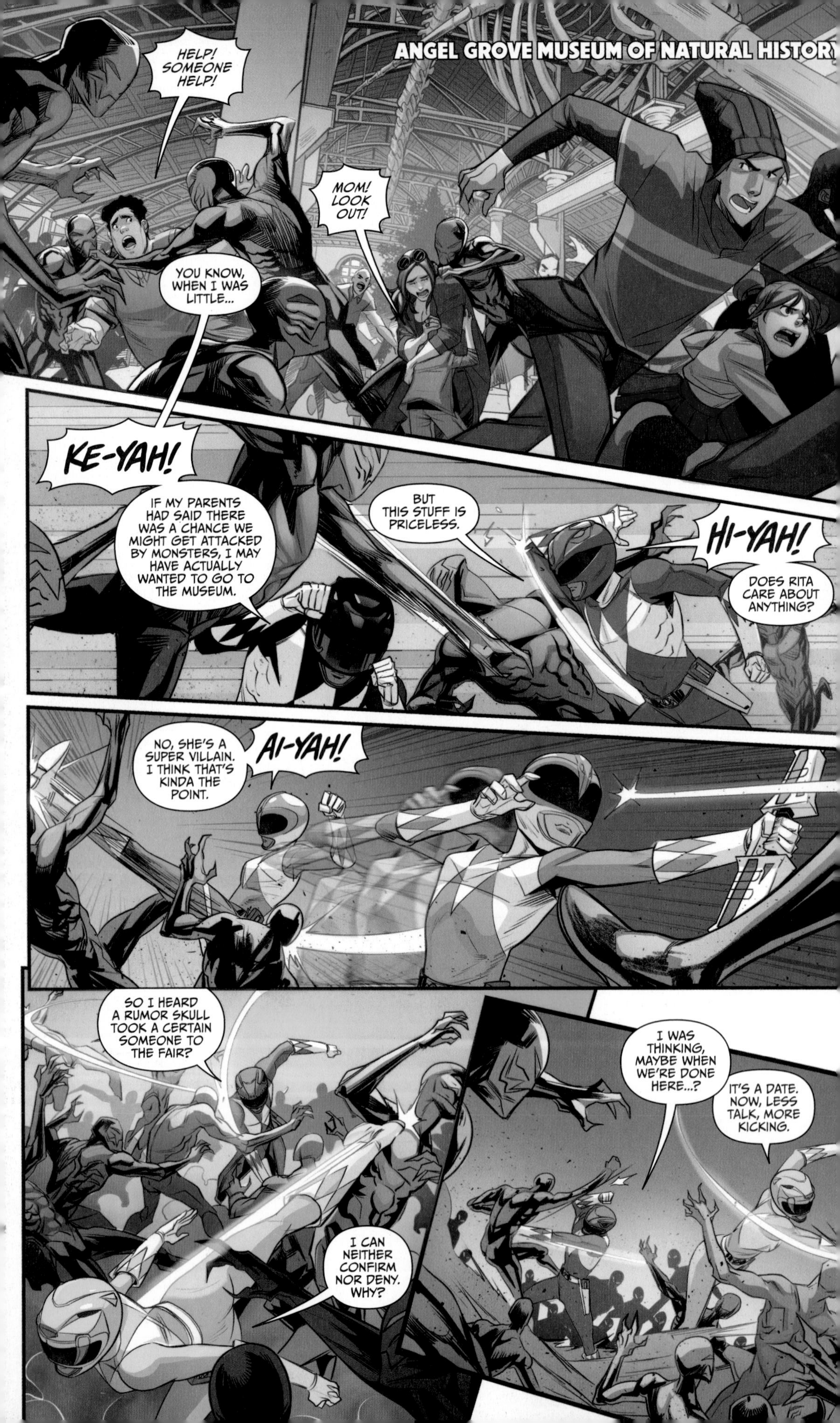
ANGEL GROVE MUSEUM OF NATURAL HISTORY
HELP! SOMEONE HELP!
MOM! LOOK OUT!
YOU KNOW, WHEN I WAS LITTLE...
KE-YAH!
IF MY PARENTS HAD SAID THERE WAS A CHANCE WE MIGHT GET ATTACKED BY MONSTERS, I MAY HAVE ACTUALLY WANTED TO GO TO THE MUSEUM.
BUT THIS STUFF IS PRICELESS.
HI-YAH!
DOES RITA CARE ABOUT ANYTHING?
NO, SHE'S A SUPER VILLAIN. I THINK THAT'S KINDA THE POINT.
AI-YAH!
SO I HEARD A RUMOR SKULL TOOK A CERTAIN SOMEONE TO THE FAIR?
I CAN NEITHER CONFIRM NOR DENY. WHY?
I WAS THINKING, MAYBE WHEN WE'RE DONE HERE...?
IT'S A DATE. NOW, LESS TALK, MORE KICKING.

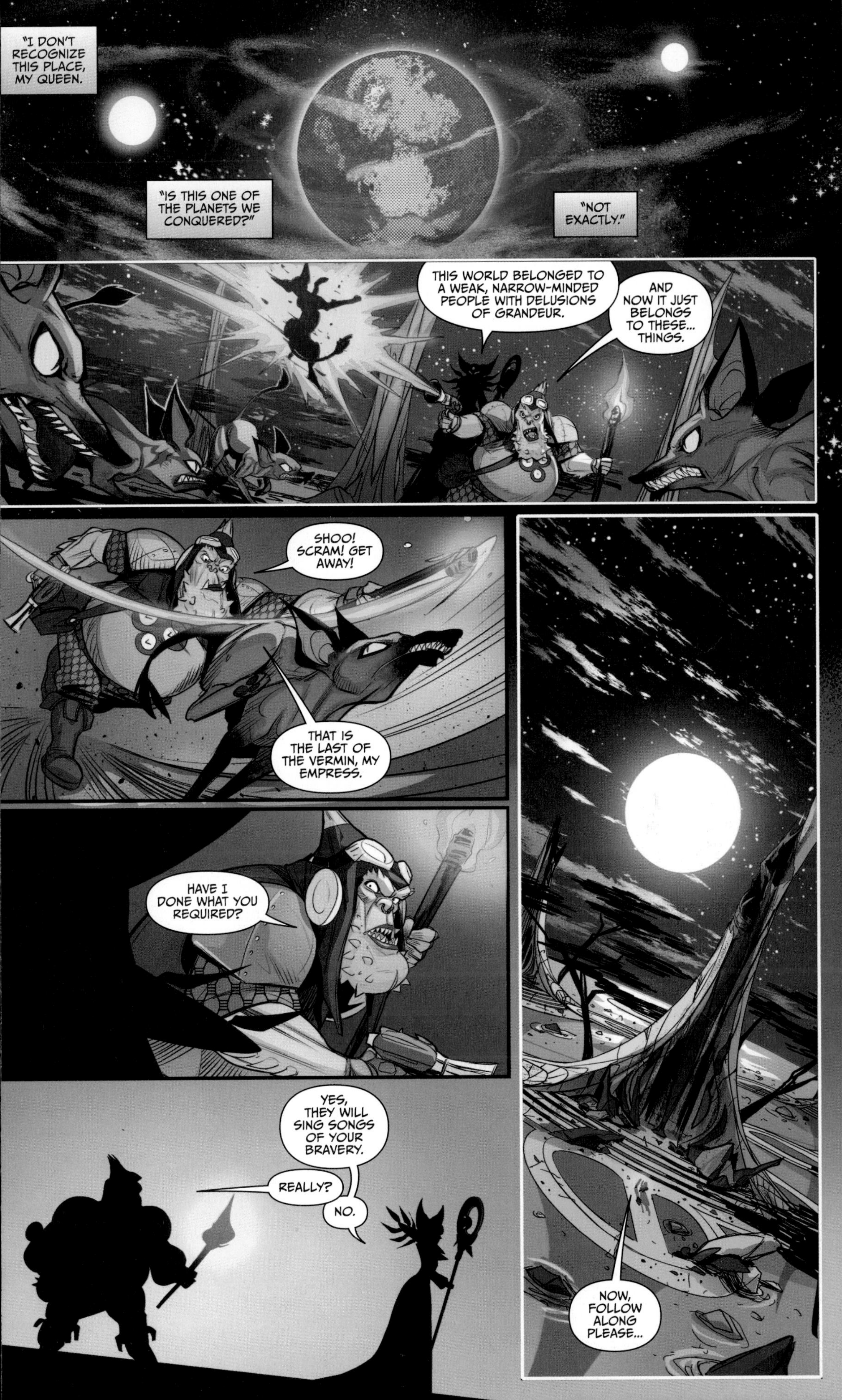
"I DON'T RECOGNIZE THIS PLACE, MY QUEEN.
"IS THIS ONE OF THE PLANETS WE CONQUERED?"
"NOT EXACTLY."
THIS WORLD BELONGED TO A WEAK, NARROW-MINDED PEOPLE WITH DELUSIONS OF GRANDEUR.
AND NOW IT JUST BELONGS TO THESE... THINGS.
SHOO! SCRAM! GET AWAY!
THAT IS THE LAST OF THE VERMIN, MY EMPRESS.
HAVE I DONE WHAT YOU REQUIRED?
YES, THEY WILL SING SONGS OF YOUR BRAVERY.
REALLY?
NO.
NOW, FOLLOW ALONG PLEASE...

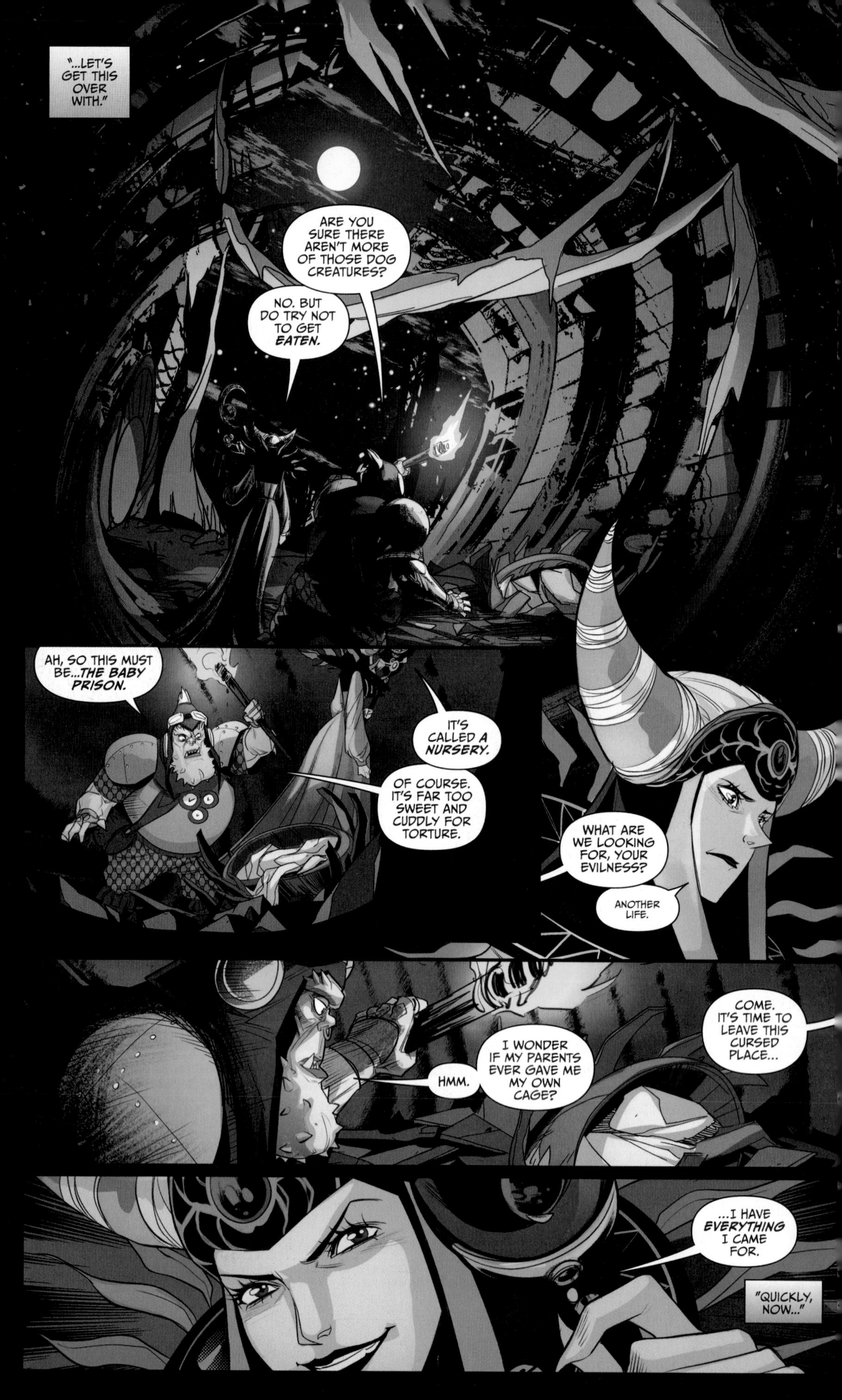

"...LET'S GET THIS OVER WITH."
ARE YOU SURE THERE AREN'T MORE OF THOSE DOG CREATURES?
NO. BUT DO TRY NOT TO GET *EATEN.*
AH, SO THIS MUST BE...*THE BABY PRISON.*
IT'S CALLED A *NURSERY.*
OF COURSE. IT'S FAR TOO SWEET AND CUDDLY FOR TORTURE.
WHAT ARE WE LOOKING FOR, YOUR EVILNESS?
ANOTHER LIFE.
HMM.
I WONDER IF MY PARENTS EVER GAVE ME MY OWN CAGE?
COME. IT'S TIME TO LEAVE THIS CURSED PLACE...
...I HAVE *EVERYTHING* I CAME FOR.
"QUICKLY, NOW..."

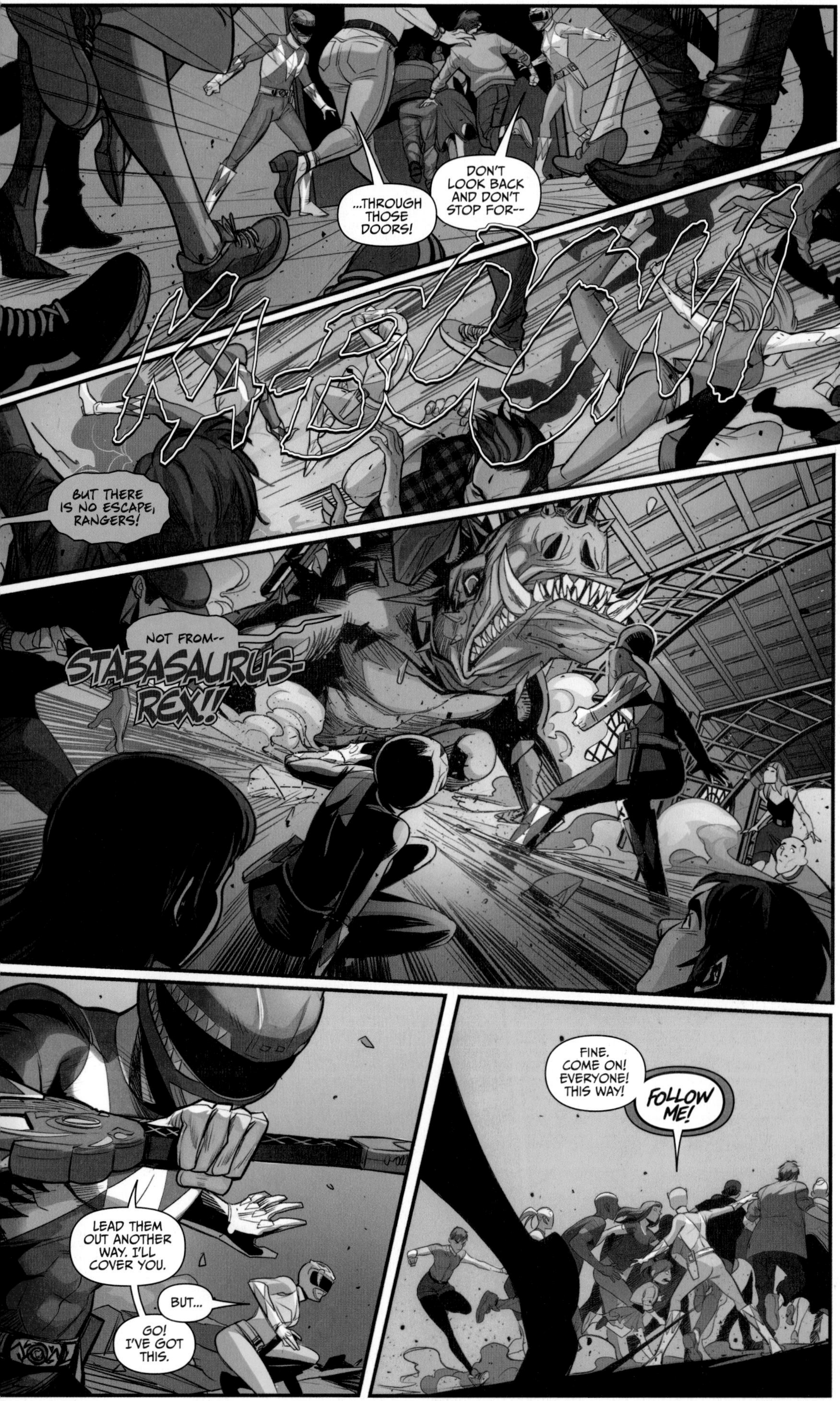
...THROUGH THOSE DOORS!
DON'T LOOK BACK AND DON'T STOP FOR--
KA-BOOM
BUT THERE IS NO ESCAPE, RANGERS!
NOT FROM--
STABASAURUS-REX!!
LEAD THEM OUT ANOTHER WAY. I'LL COVER YOU.
BUT...
GO! I'VE GOT THIS.
FINE. COME ON! EVERYONE! THIS WAY!
FOLLOW ME!

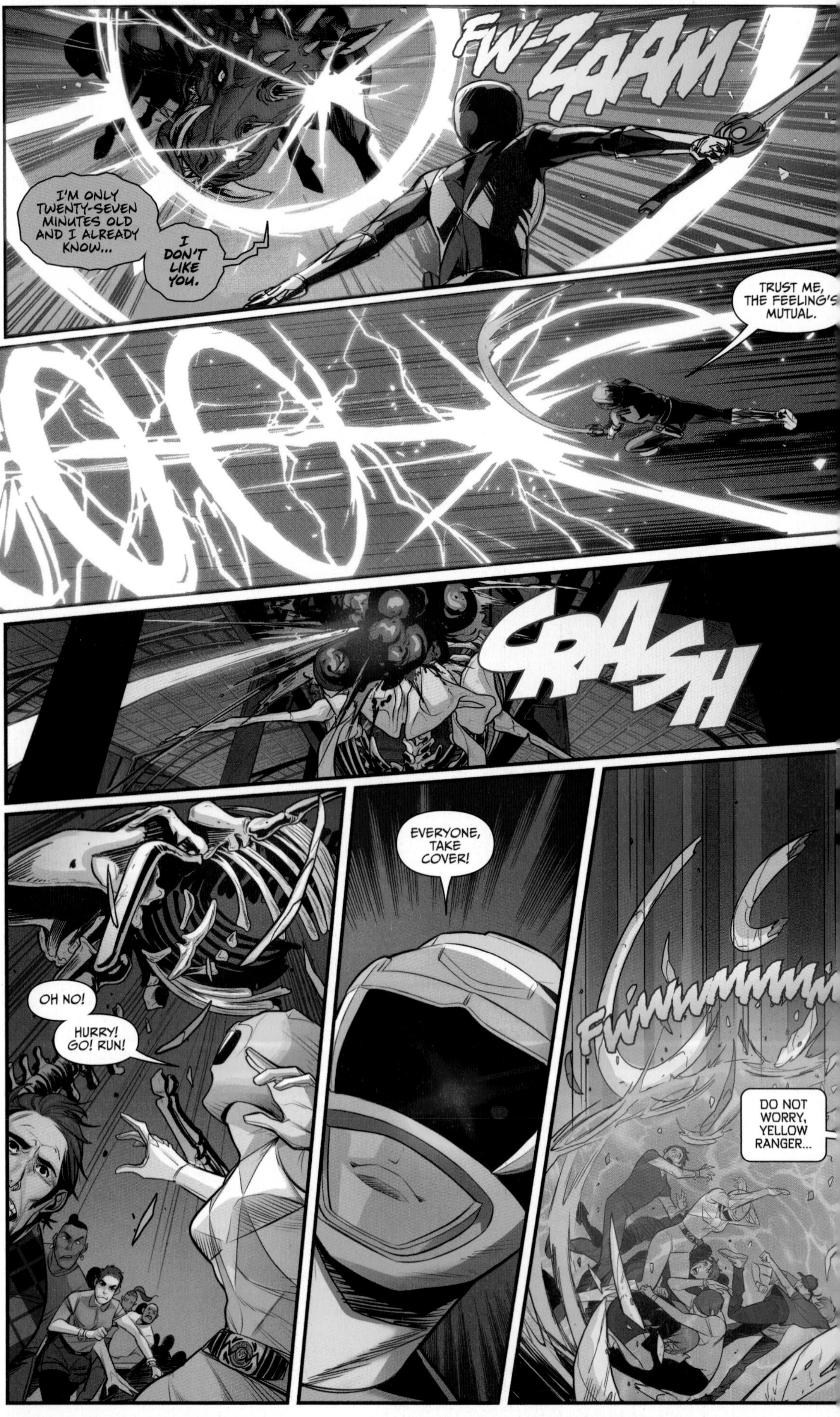
FW-ZAAM
I'M ONLY TWENTY-SEVEN MINUTES OLD AND I ALREADY KNOW...
I DON'T LIKE YOU.
TRUST ME, THE FEELING'S MUTUAL.
CRASH
OH NO!
HURRY! GO! RUN!
EVERYONE, TAKE COVER!
DO NOT WORRY, YELLOW RANGER...

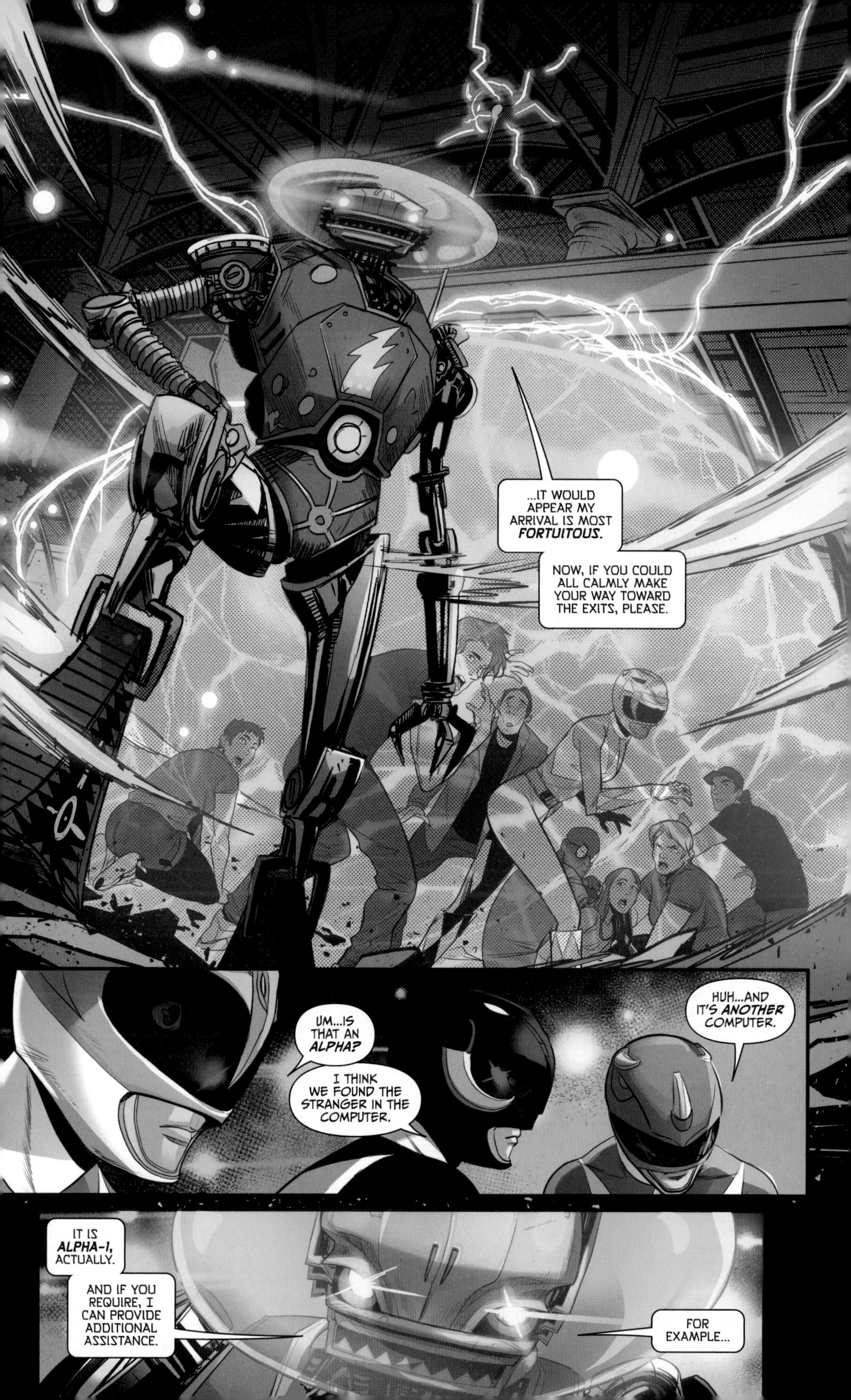
...IT WOULD APPEAR MY ARRIVAL IS MOST FORTUITOUS.
NOW, IF YOU COULD ALL CALMLY MAKE YOUR WAY TOWARD THE EXITS, PLEASE.
UM...IS THAT AN ALPHA?
I THINK WE FOUND THE STRANGER IN THE COMPUTER.
HUH...AND IT'S ANOTHER COMPUTER.
IT IS ALPHA-1, ACTUALLY.
AND IF YOU REQUIRE, I CAN PROVIDE ADDITIONAL ASSISTANCE.
FOR EXAMPLE...

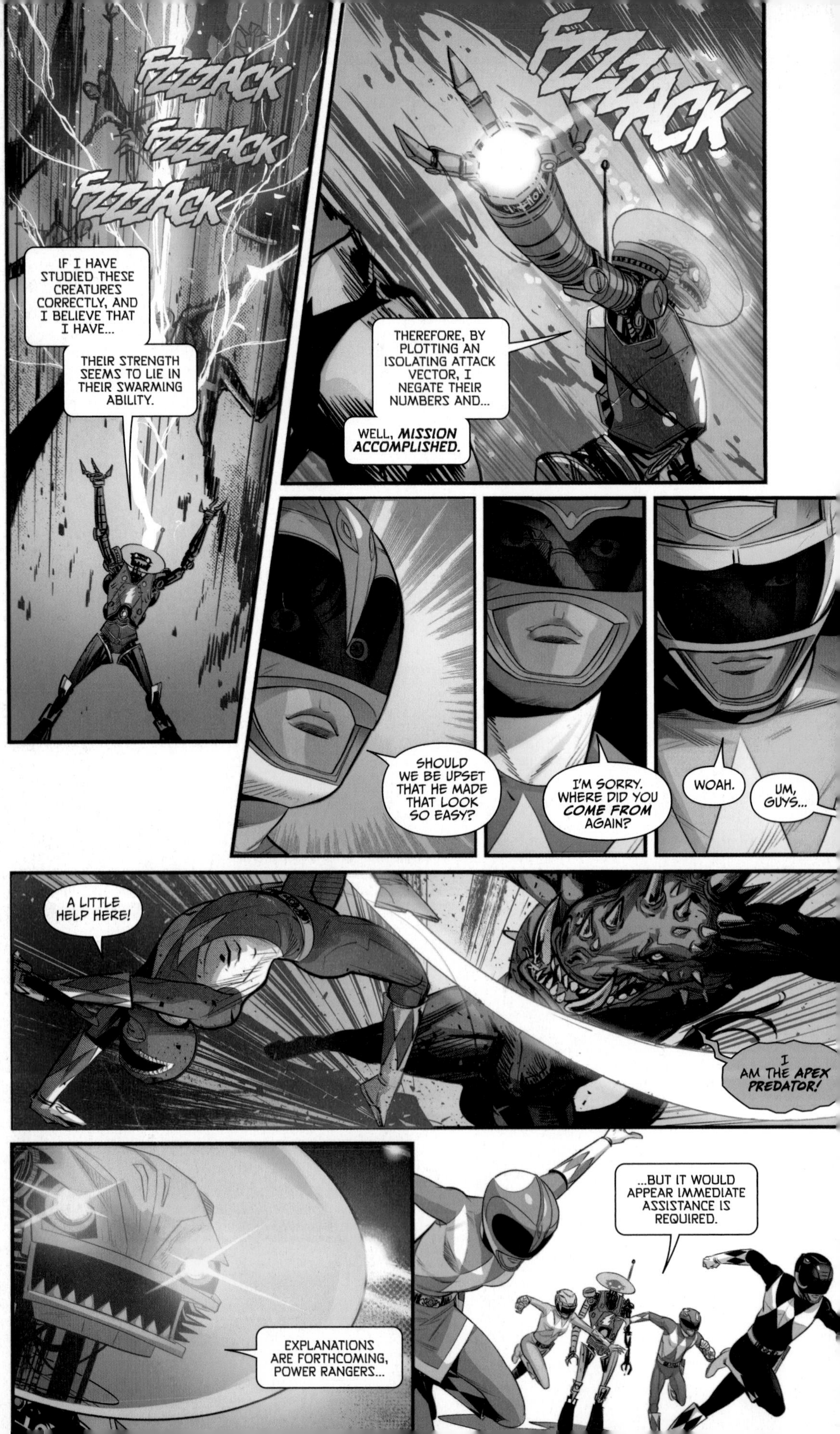
FZZZACK
FZZZACK
FZZZACK
FZZZACK
IF I HAVE STUDIED THESE CREATURES CORRECTLY, AND I BELIEVE THAT I HAVE...
THEIR STRENGTH SEEMS TO LIE IN THEIR SWARMING ABILITY.
THEREFORE, BY PLOTTING AN ISOLATING ATTACK VECTOR, I NEGATE THEIR NUMBERS AND...
WELL, MISSION ACCOMPLISHED.
SHOULD WE BE UPSET THAT HE MADE THAT LOOK SO EASY?
I'M SORRY. WHERE DID YOU COME FROM AGAIN?
WOAH.
UM, GUYS...
A LITTLE HELP HERE!
I AM THE APEX PREDATOR!
EXPLANATIONS ARE FORTHCOMING, POWER RANGERS...
...BUT IT WOULD APPEAR IMMEDIATE ASSISTANCE IS REQUIRED.

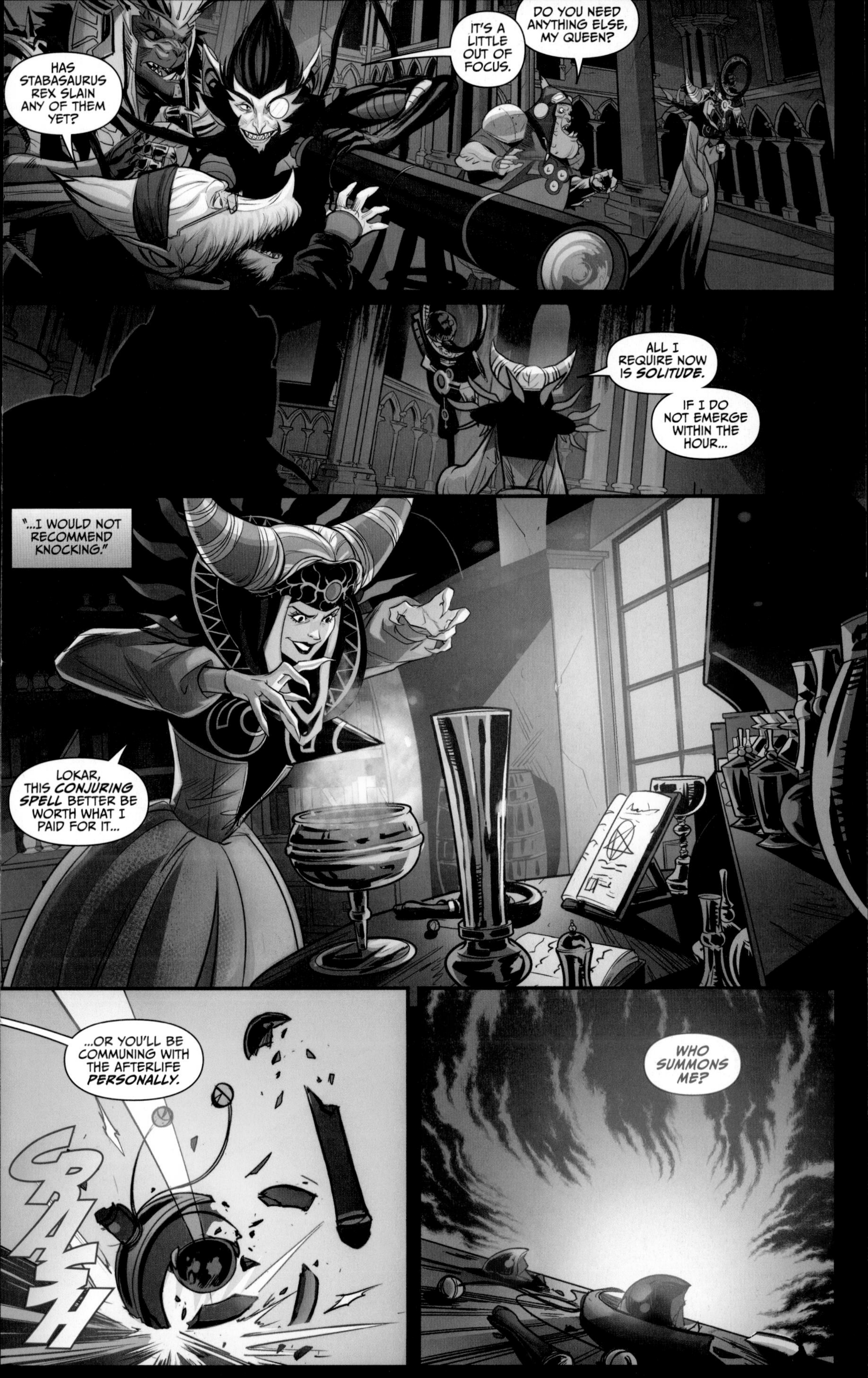
HAS STABASAURUS REX SLAIN ANY OF THEM YET?
IT'S A LITTLE OUT OF FOCUS.
DO YOU NEED ANYTHING ELSE, MY QUEEN?
ALL I REQUIRE NOW IS SOLITUDE.
IF I DO NOT EMERGE WITHIN THE HOUR...
"...I WOULD NOT RECOMMEND KNOCKING."
LOKAR, THIS CONJURING SPELL BETTER BE WORTH WHAT I PAID FOR IT...
...OR YOU'LL BE COMMUNING WITH THE AFTERLIFE PERSONALLY.
CRASH
WHO SUMMONS ME?

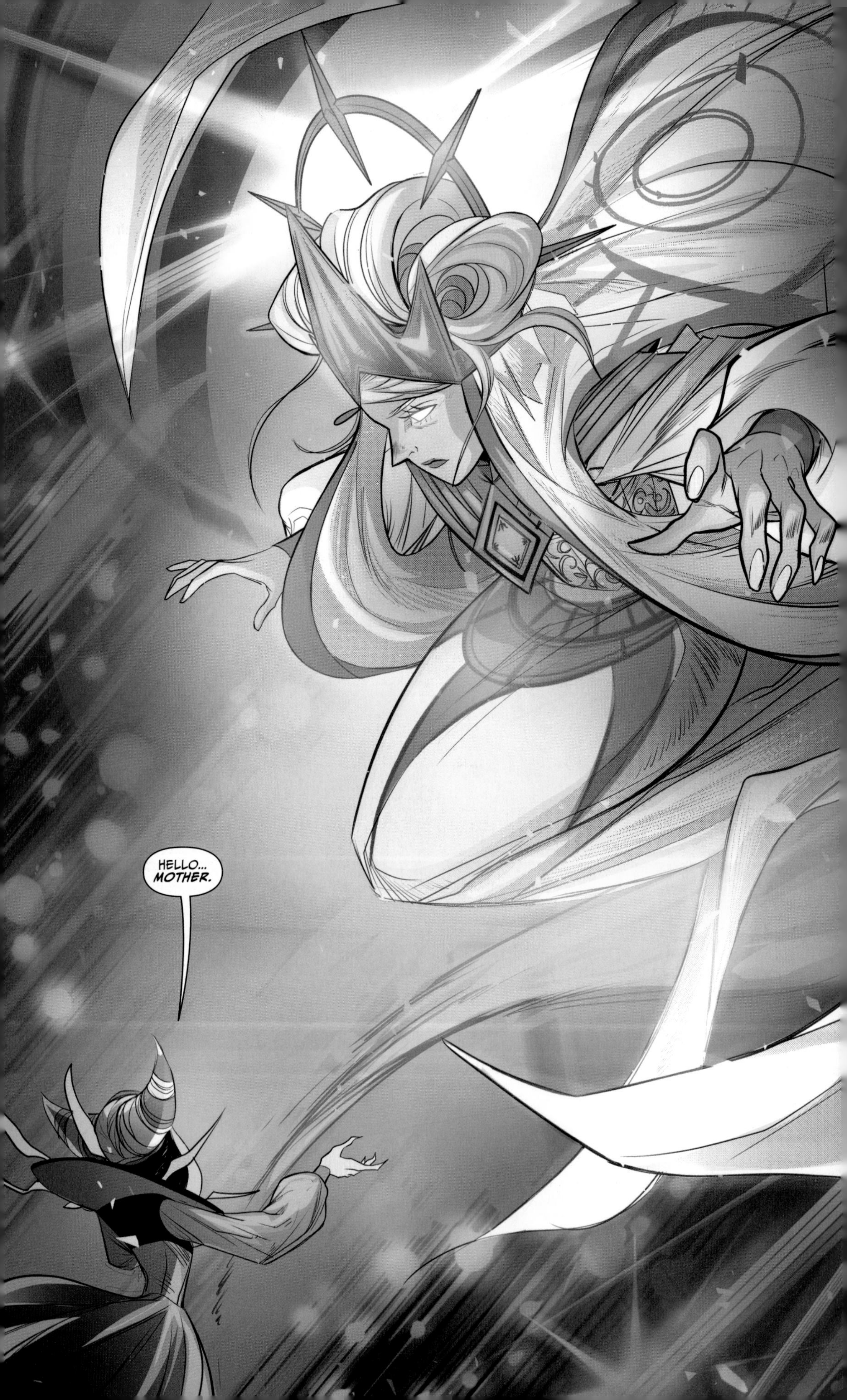
HELLO... MOTHER.

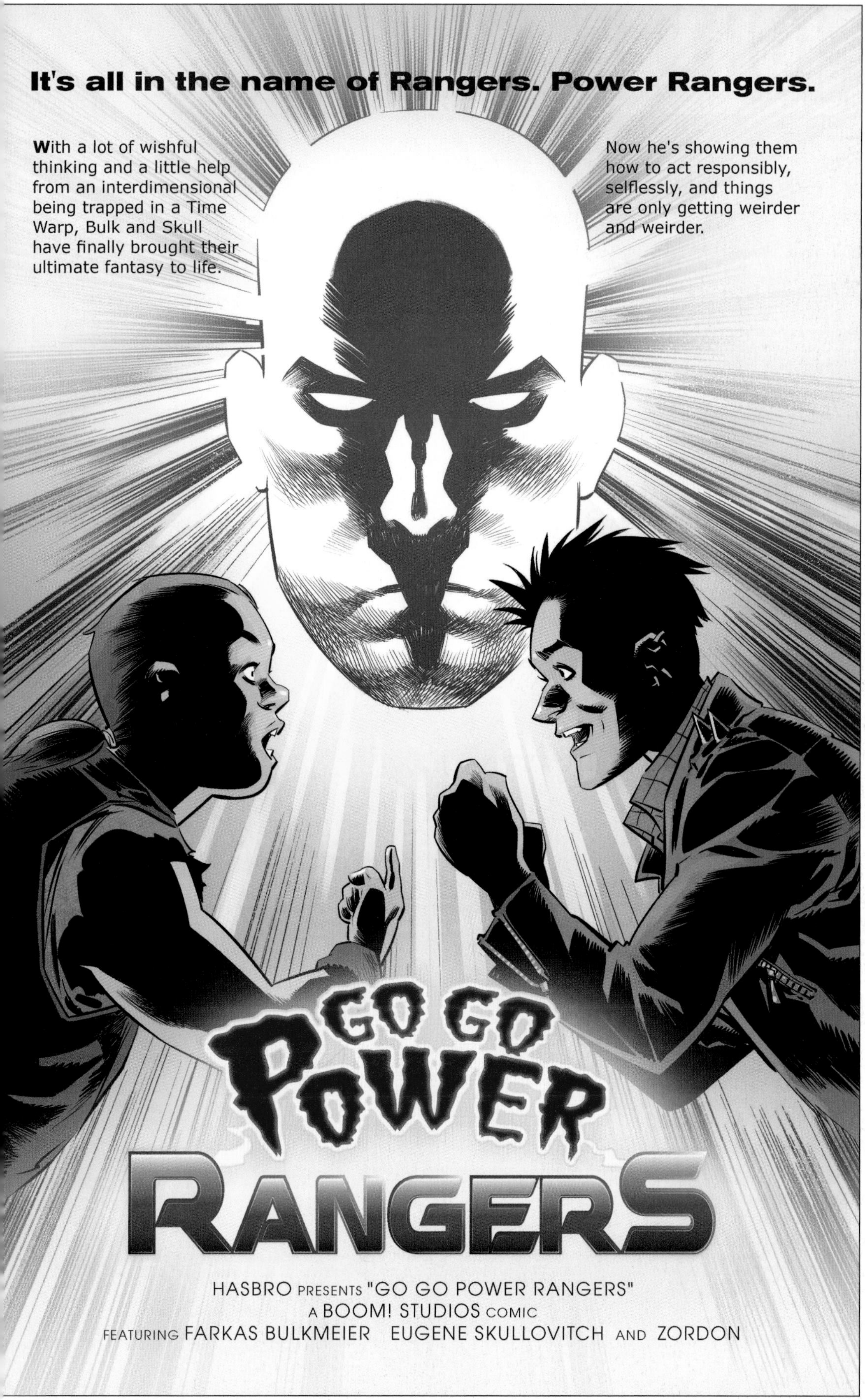

It's all in the name of Rangers. Power Rangers.
With a lot of wishful thinking and a little help from an interdimensional being trapped in a Time Warp, Bulk and Skull have finally brought their ultimate fantasy to life.
Now he's showing them how to act responsibly, selflessly, and things are only getting weirder and weirder.
GO GO POWER RANGERS
HASBRO PRESENTS "GO GO POWER RANGERS"
A BOOM! STUDIOS COMIC
FEATURING FARKAS BULKMEIER EUGENE SKULLOVITCH AND ZORDON

GLEB MELNIKOV WITH DESIGN BY **DYLAN TODD** ISSUE SEVENTEEN MOVIE HOMAGE VARIANT

EIGHTEEN

MARCUS TO WITH COLORS BY **RAÚL ANGULO** | ISSUE EIGHTEEN MAIN COVER

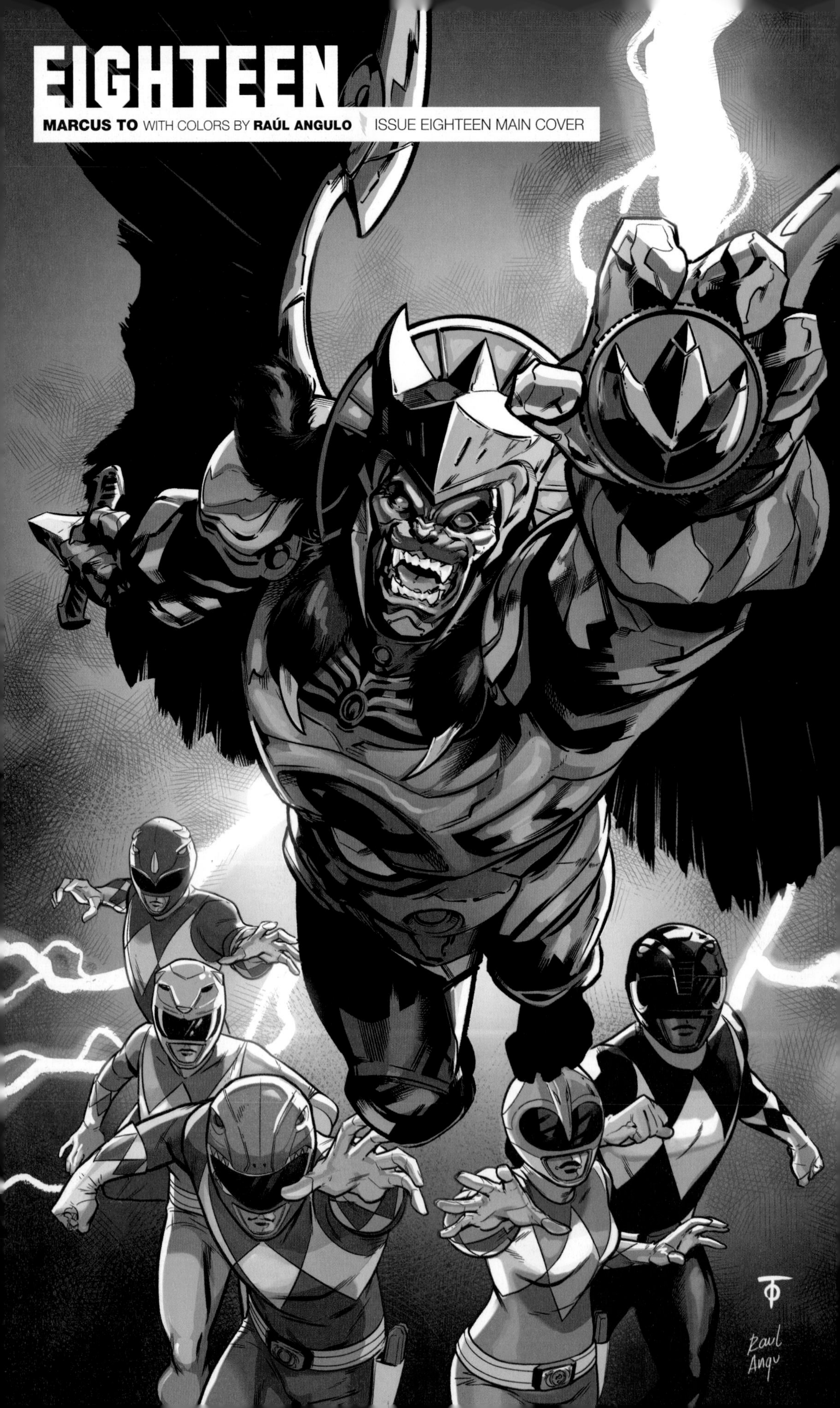

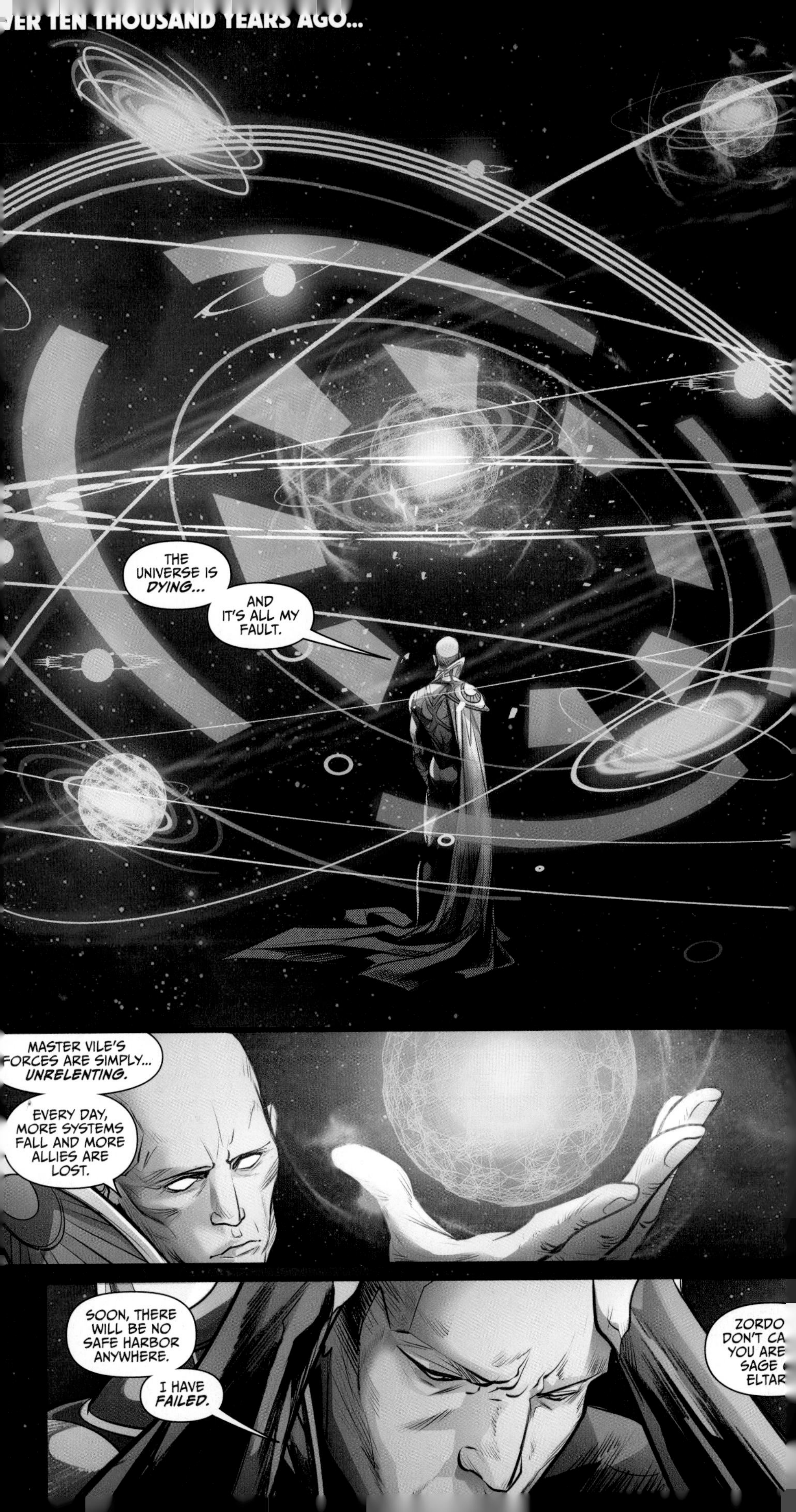
VER TEN THOUSAND YEARS AGO...
THE UNIVERSE IS *DYING...*
AND IT'S ALL MY FAULT.
MASTER VILE'S FORCES ARE SIMPLY... *UNRELENTING.*
EVERY DAY, MORE SYSTEMS FALL AND MORE ALLIES ARE LOST.
SOON, THERE WILL BE NO SAFE HARBOR ANYWHERE.
I HAVE *FAILED.*

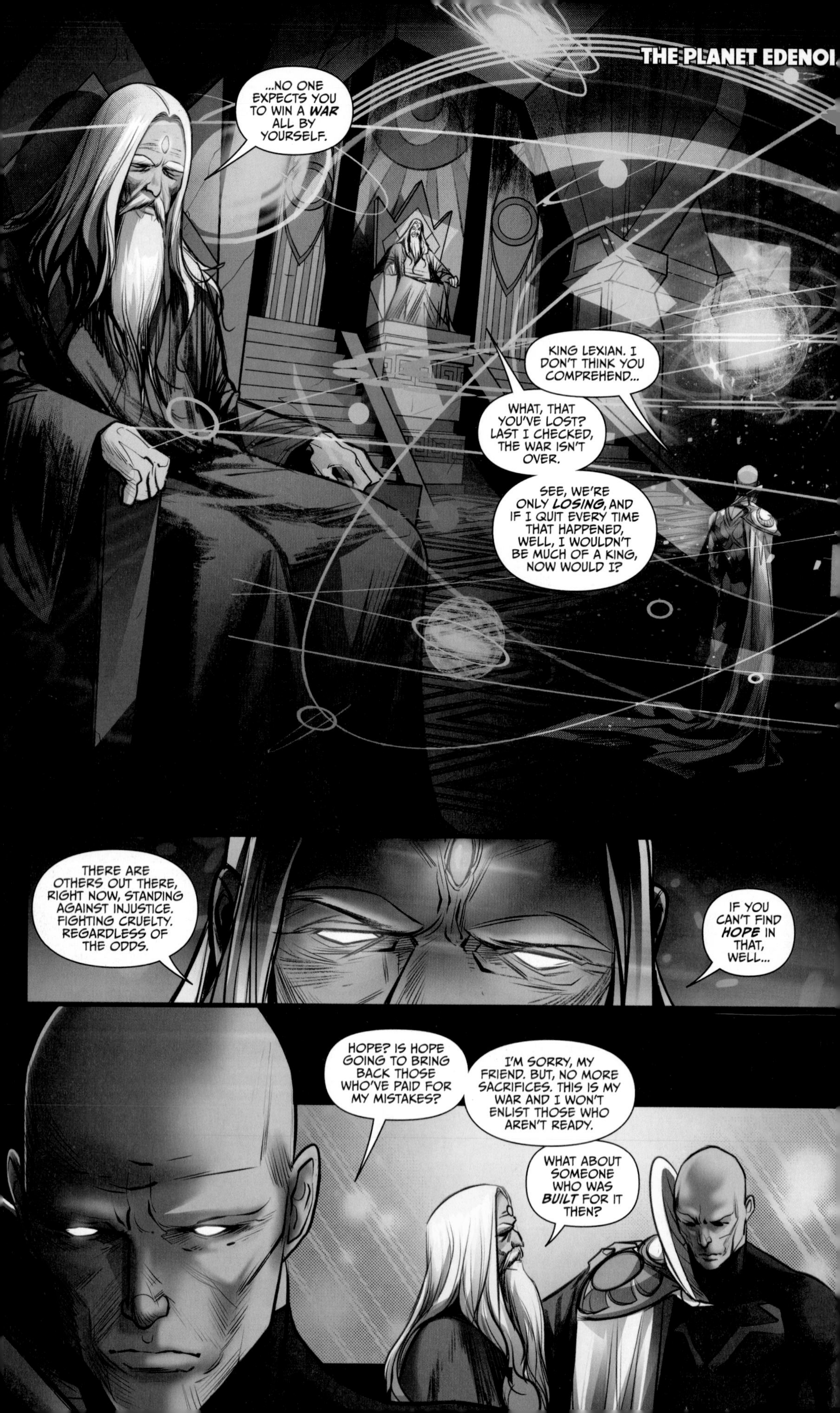
THE PLANET EDENOI
...NO ONE EXPECTS YOU TO WIN A WAR ALL BY YOURSELF.
KING LEXIAN. I DON'T THINK YOU COMPREHEND...
WHAT, THAT YOU'VE LOST? LAST I CHECKED, THE WAR ISN'T OVER.
SEE, WE'RE ONLY LOSING, AND IF I QUIT EVERY TIME THAT HAPPENED, WELL, I WOULDN'T BE MUCH OF A KING, NOW WOULD I?
THERE ARE OTHERS OUT THERE, RIGHT NOW, STANDING AGAINST INJUSTICE. FIGHTING CRUELTY. REGARDLESS OF THE ODDS.
IF YOU CAN'T FIND HOPE IN THAT, WELL...
HOPE? IS HOPE GOING TO BRING BACK THOSE WHO'VE PAID FOR MY MISTAKES?
I'M SORRY, MY FRIEND. BUT, NO MORE SACRIFICES. THIS IS MY WAR AND I WON'T ENLIST THOSE WHO AREN'T READY.
WHAT ABOUT SOMEONE WHO WAS BUILT FOR IT THEN?

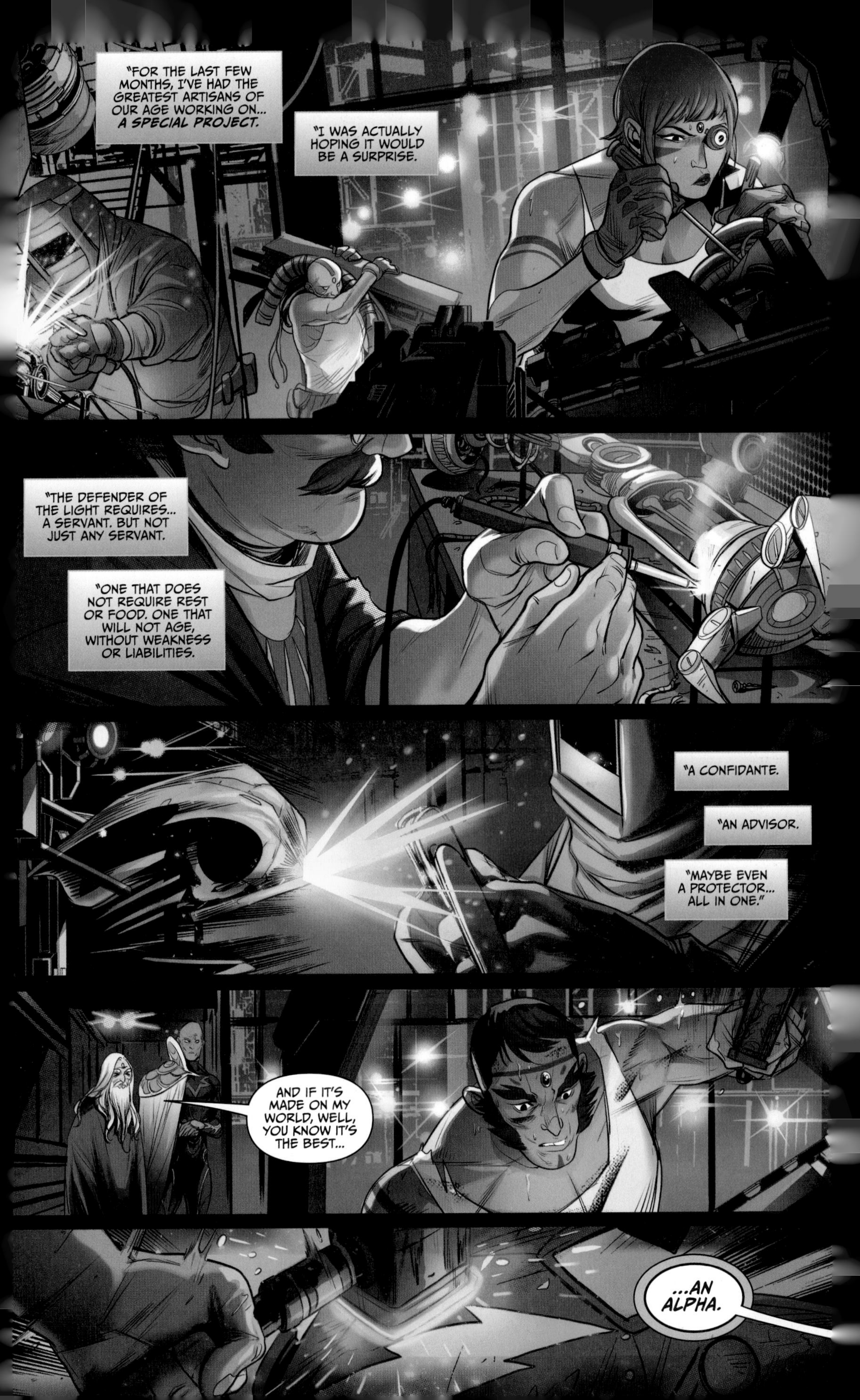
"FOR THE LAST FEW MONTHS, I'VE HAD THE GREATEST ARTISANS OF OUR AGE WORKING ON... A SPECIAL PROJECT.
"I WAS ACTUALLY HOPING IT WOULD BE A SURPRISE.
"THE DEFENDER OF THE LIGHT REQUIRES... A SERVANT. BUT NOT JUST ANY SERVANT.
"ONE THAT DOES NOT REQUIRE REST OR FOOD. ONE THAT WILL NOT AGE, WITHOUT WEAKNESS OR LIABILITIES.
"A CONFIDANTE.
"AN ADVISOR.
"MAYBE EVEN A PROTECTOR... ALL IN ONE."
AND IF IT'S MADE ON MY WORLD, WELL, YOU KNOW IT'S THE BEST...
...AN ALPHA.

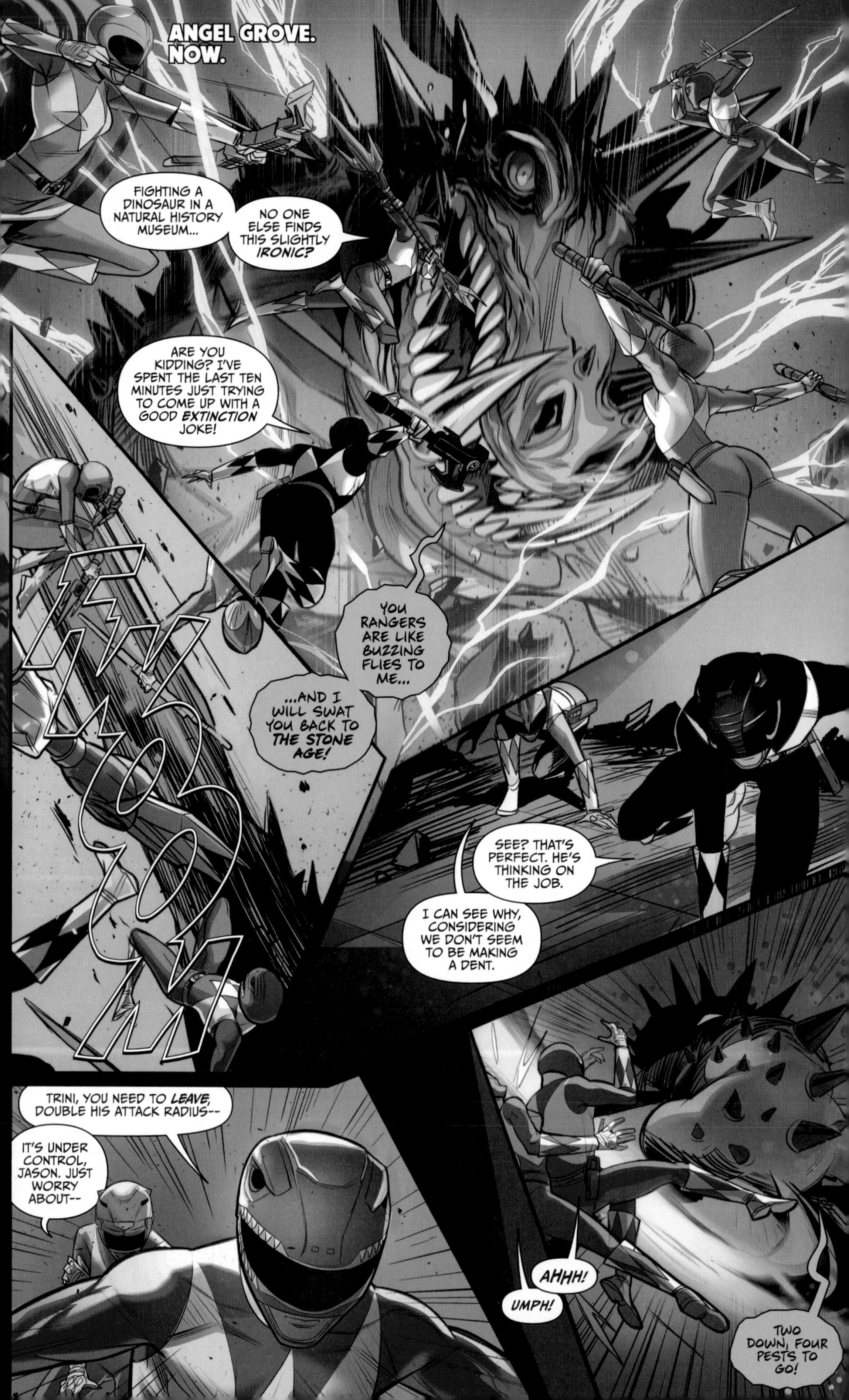
ANGEL GROVE. NOW.
FIGHTING A DINOSAUR IN A NATURAL HISTORY MUSEUM...
NO ONE ELSE FINDS THIS SLIGHTLY *IRONIC?*
ARE YOU KIDDING? I'VE SPENT THE LAST TEN MINUTES JUST TRYING TO COME UP WITH A GOOD *EXTINCTION* JOKE!
YOU RANGERS ARE LIKE BUZZING FLIES TO ME...
...AND I WILL SWAT YOU BACK TO **THE STONE AGE!**
SEE? THAT'S PERFECT. HE'S THINKING ON THE JOB.
I CAN SEE WHY, CONSIDERING WE DON'T SEEM TO BE MAKING A DENT.
TRINI, YOU NEED TO *LEAVE*, DOUBLE HIS ATTACK RADIUS--
IT'S UNDER CONTROL, JASON. JUST WORRY ABOUT--
AHHH!
UMPH!
TWO DOWN, FOUR PESTS TO GO!

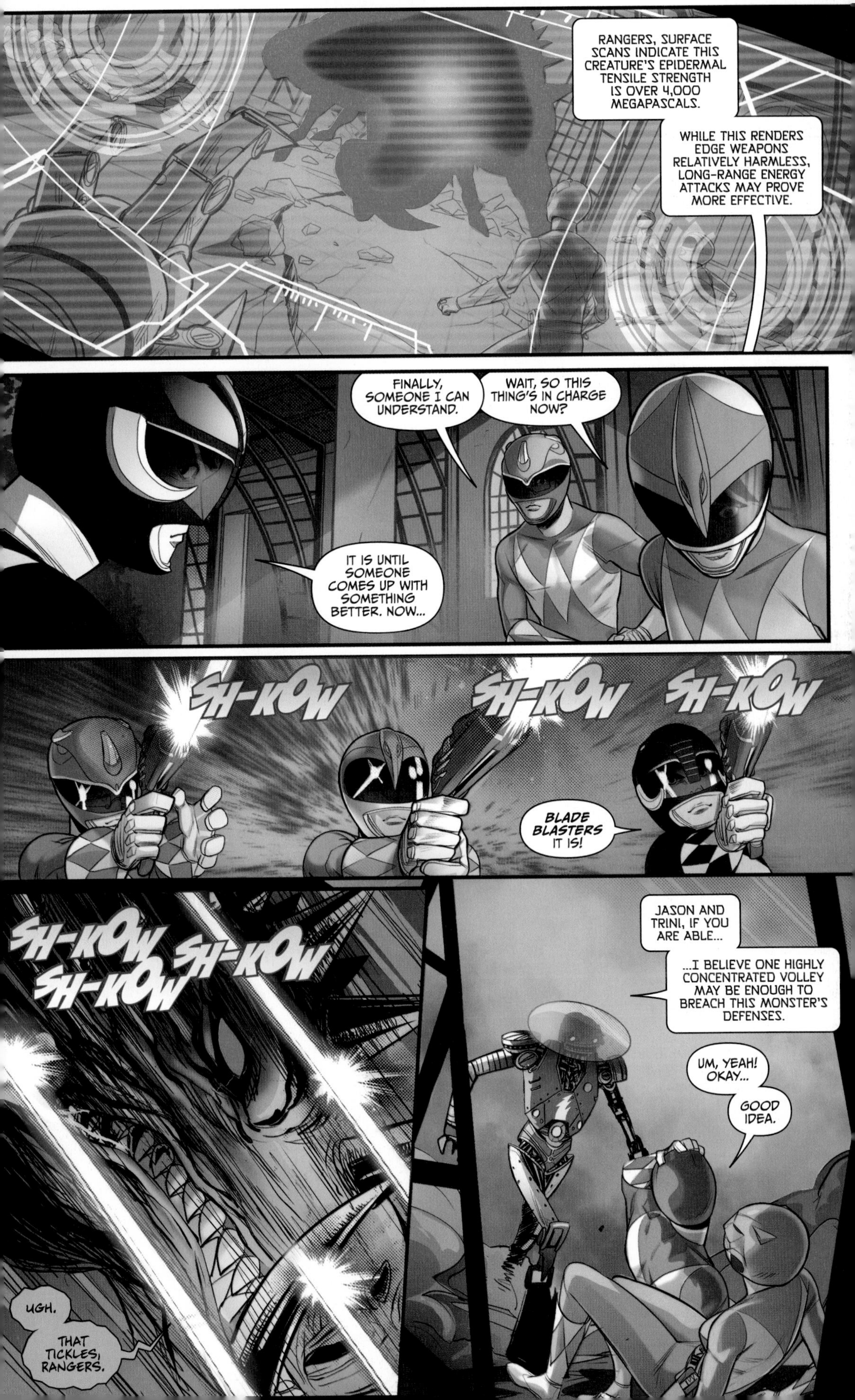
RANGERS, SURFACE SCANS INDICATE THIS CREATURE'S EPIDERMAL TENSILE STRENGTH IS OVER 4,000 MEGAPASCALS.
WHILE THIS RENDERS EDGE WEAPONS RELATIVELY HARMLESS, LONG-RANGE ENERGY ATTACKS MAY PROVE MORE EFFECTIVE.
FINALLY, SOMEONE I CAN UNDERSTAND.
WAIT, SO THIS THING'S IN CHARGE NOW?
IT IS UNTIL SOMEONE COMES UP WITH SOMETHING BETTER. NOW...
SH-KOW
SH-KOW
SH-KOW
BLADE BLASTERS IT IS!
SH-KOW
SH-KOW
SH-KOW
SH-KOW
UGH.
THAT TICKLES, RANGERS.
JASON AND TRINI, IF YOU ARE ABLE...
...I BELIEVE ONE HIGHLY CONCENTRATED VOLLEY MAY BE ENOUGH TO BREACH THIS MONSTER'S DEFENSES.
UM, YEAH! OKAY...
GOOD IDEA.

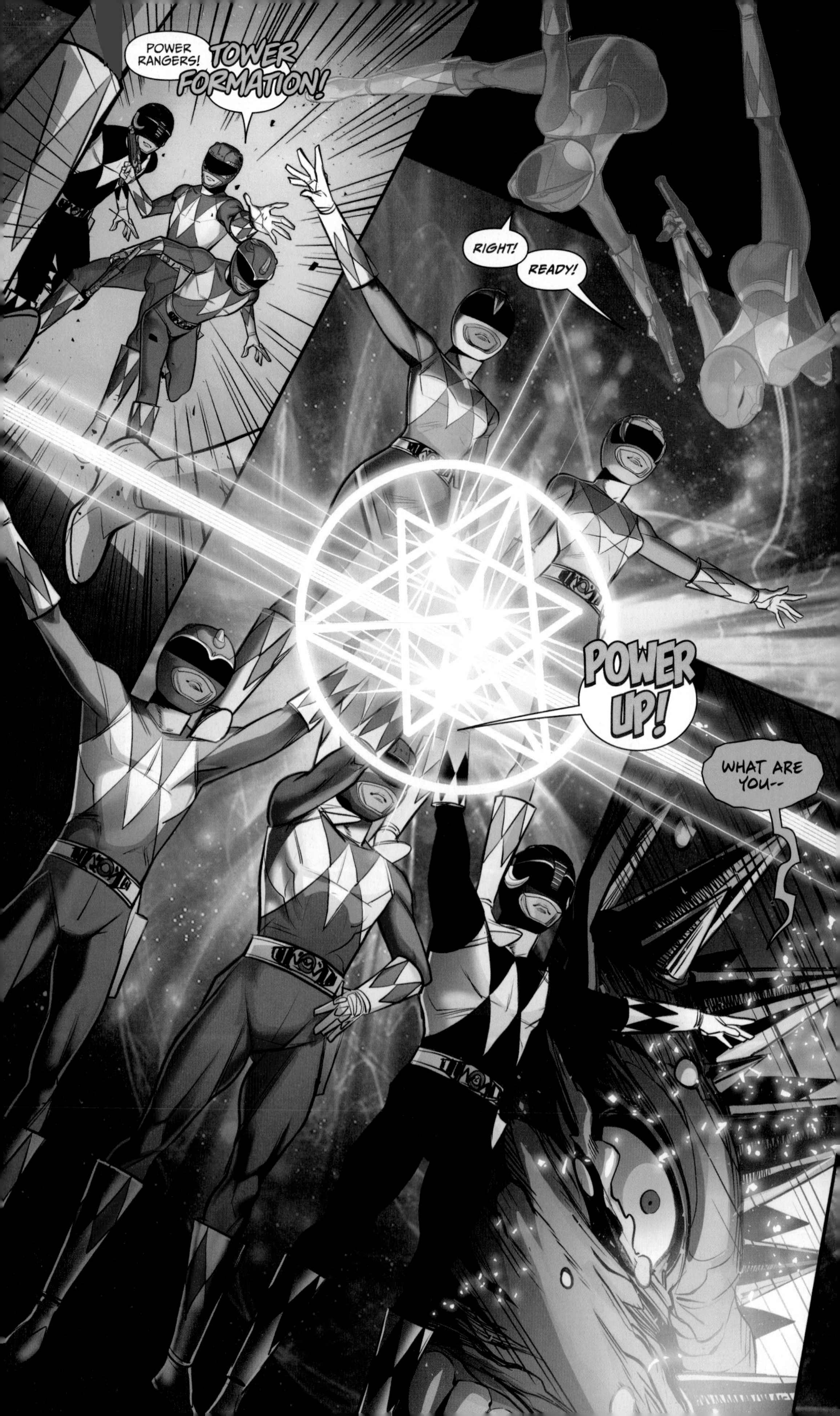
POWER RANGERS!
TOWER FORMATION!
RIGHT!
READY!
POWER UP!
WHAT ARE YOU--

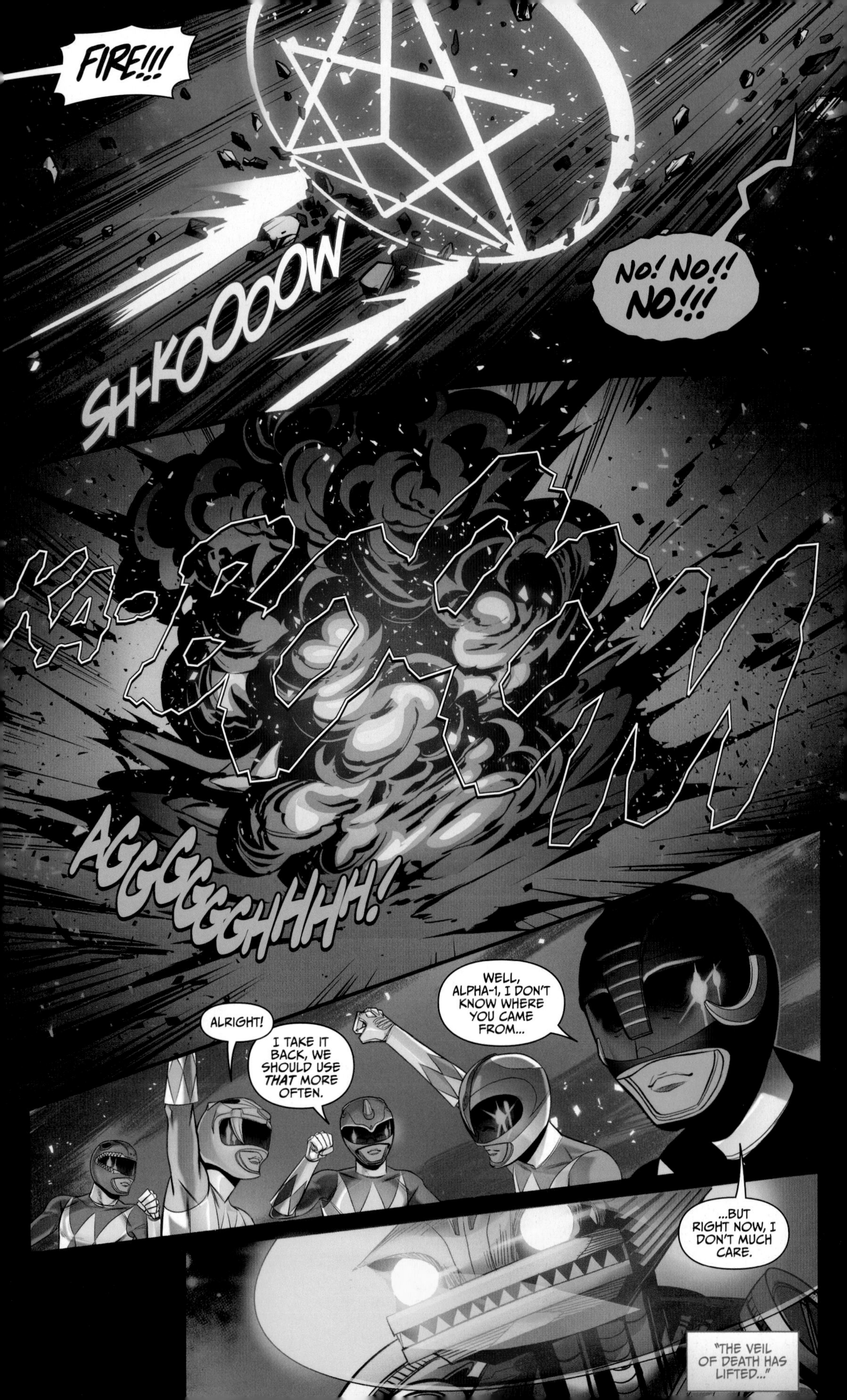
FIRE!!!
SHKOOOOOW
NO! NO!!
NO!!!
KA-BOOOM
AGGGGGHHHH!
ALRIGHT!
I TAKE IT BACK, WE SHOULD USE *THAT* MORE OFTEN.
WELL, ALPHA-1, I DON'T KNOW WHERE YOU CAME FROM...
...BUT RIGHT NOW, I DON'T MUCH CARE.
"THE VEIL OF DEATH HAS LIFTED..."

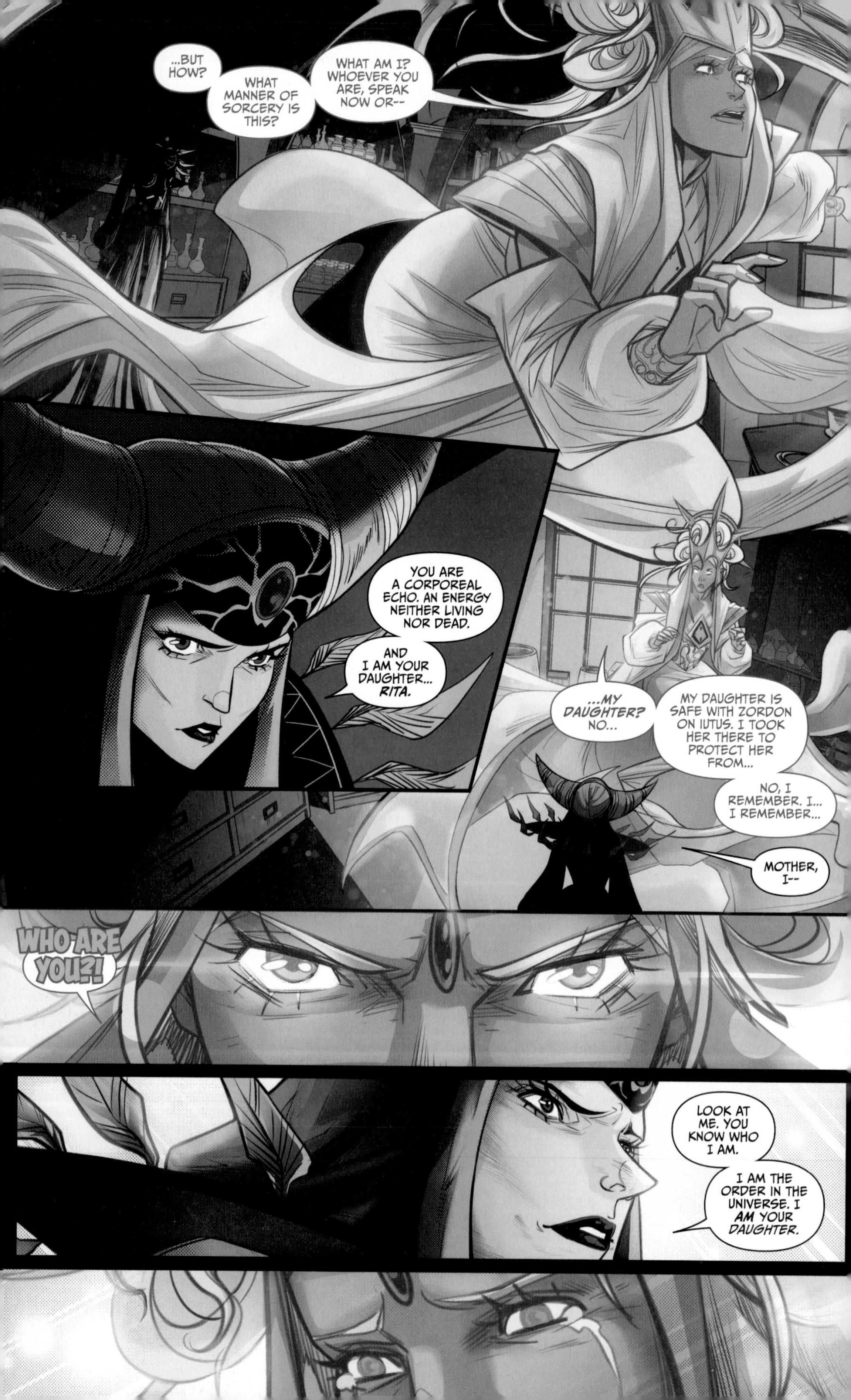

...BUT HOW?
WHAT MANNER OF SORCERY IS THIS?
WHAT AM I? WHOEVER YOU ARE, SPEAK NOW OR--
YOU ARE A CORPOREAL ECHO. AN ENERGY NEITHER LIVING NOR DEAD.
AND I AM YOUR DAUGHTER... RITA.
...MY DAUGHTER? NO...
MY DAUGHTER IS SAFE WITH ZORDON ON IUTUS. I TOOK HER THERE TO PROTECT HER FROM...
NO, I REMEMBER. I... I REMEMBER...
MOTHER, I--
WHO ARE YOU?!
LOOK AT ME. YOU KNOW WHO I AM.
I AM THE ORDER IN THE UNIVERSE. I AM YOUR DAUGHTER.

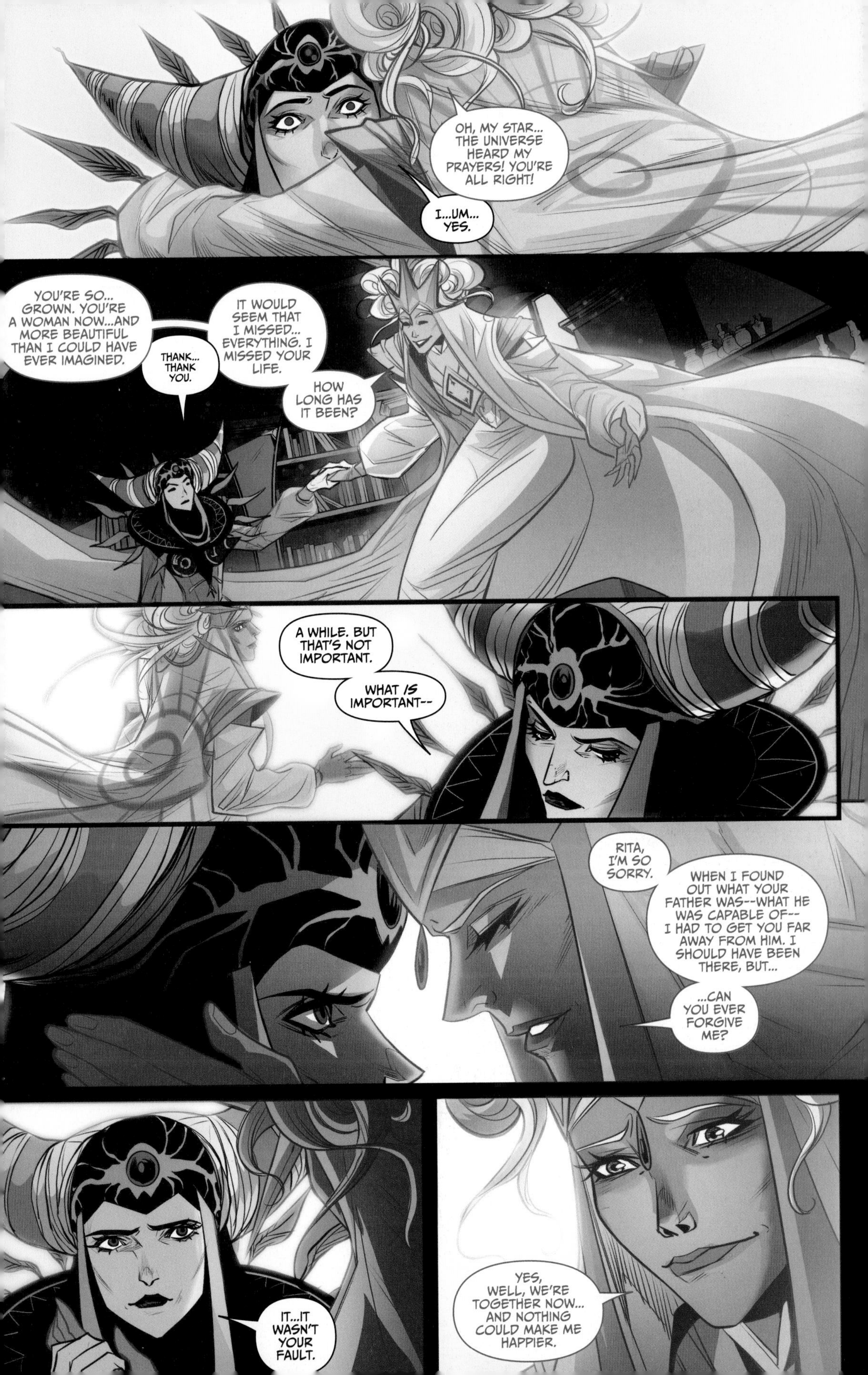
OH, MY STAR... THE UNIVERSE HEARD MY PRAYERS! YOU'RE ALL RIGHT!
I...UM... YES.
YOU'RE SO... GROWN. YOU'RE A WOMAN NOW...AND MORE BEAUTIFUL THAN I COULD HAVE EVER IMAGINED.
THANK... THANK YOU.
IT WOULD SEEM THAT I MISSED... EVERYTHING. I MISSED YOUR LIFE.
HOW LONG HAS IT BEEN?
A WHILE. BUT THAT'S NOT IMPORTANT.
WHAT *IS* IMPORTANT--
RITA, I'M SO SORRY.
WHEN I FOUND OUT WHAT YOUR FATHER WAS--WHAT HE WAS CAPABLE OF-- I HAD TO GET YOU FAR AWAY FROM HIM. I SHOULD HAVE BEEN THERE, BUT...
...CAN YOU EVER FORGIVE ME?
IT...IT WASN'T YOUR FAULT.
YES, WELL, WE'RE TOGETHER NOW... AND NOTHING COULD MAKE ME HAPPIER.

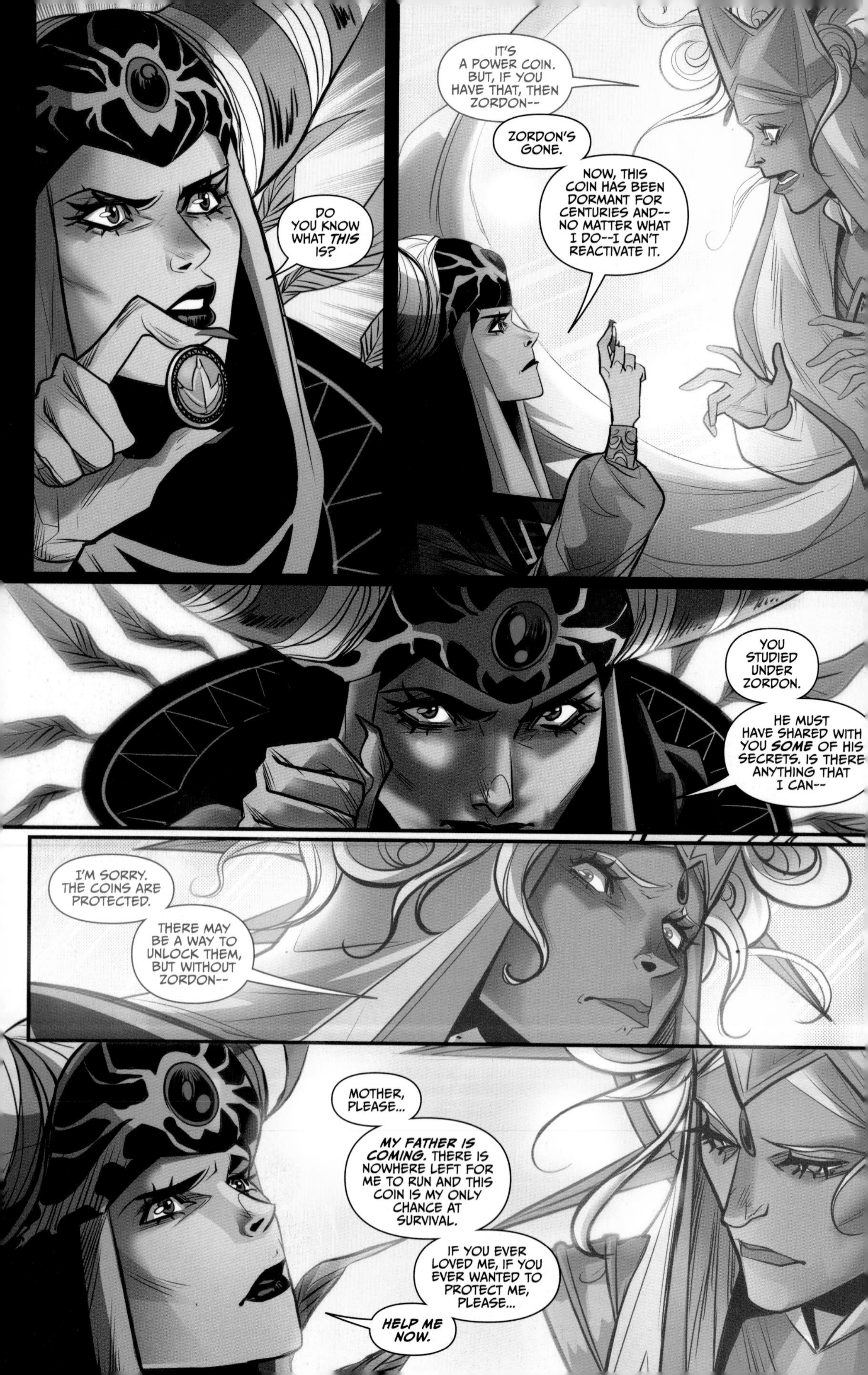
DO YOU KNOW WHAT *THIS* IS?
IT'S A POWER COIN. BUT, IF YOU HAVE THAT, THEN ZORDON--
ZORDON'S GONE.
NOW, THIS COIN HAS BEEN DORMANT FOR CENTURIES AND-- NO MATTER WHAT I DO--I CAN'T REACTIVATE IT.
YOU STUDIED UNDER ZORDON.
HE MUST HAVE SHARED WITH YOU ***SOME*** OF HIS SECRETS. IS THERE ANYTHING THAT I CAN--
I'M SORRY. THE COINS ARE PROTECTED.
THERE MAY BE A WAY TO UNLOCK THEM, BUT WITHOUT ZORDON--
MOTHER, PLEASE...
MY FATHER IS COMING. THERE IS NOWHERE LEFT FOR ME TO RUN AND THIS COIN IS MY ONLY CHANCE AT SURVIVAL.
IF YOU EVER LOVED ME, IF YOU EVER WANTED TO PROTECT ME, PLEASE...
HELP ME NOW.

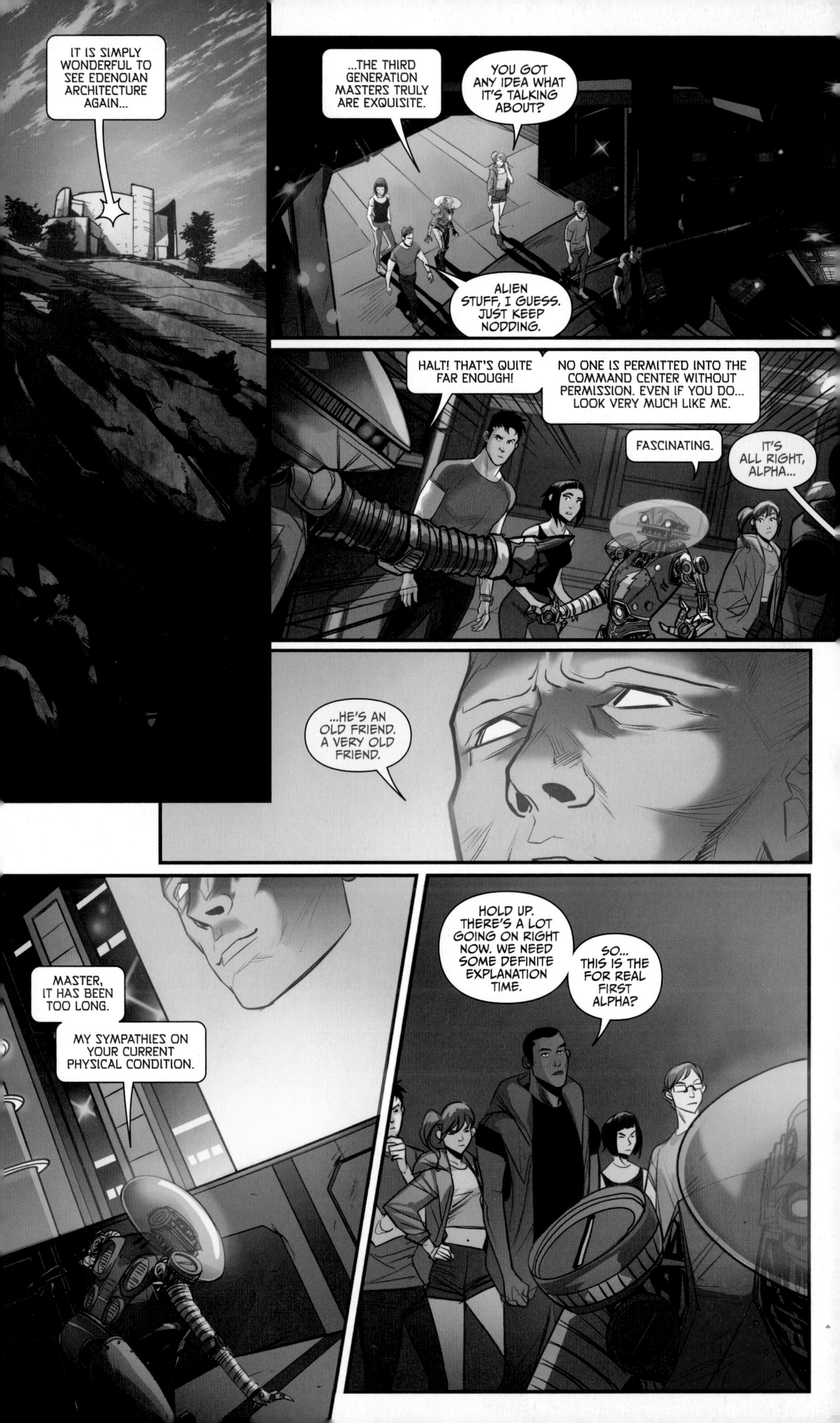
IT IS SIMPLY WONDERFUL TO SEE EDENOIAN ARCHITECTURE AGAIN...
...THE THIRD GENERATION MASTERS TRULY ARE EXQUISITE.
YOU GOT ANY IDEA WHAT IT'S TALKING ABOUT?
ALIEN STUFF, I GUESS. JUST KEEP NODDING.
HALT! THAT'S QUITE FAR ENOUGH!
NO ONE IS PERMITTED INTO THE COMMAND CENTER WITHOUT PERMISSION. EVEN IF YOU DO... LOOK VERY MUCH LIKE ME.
FASCINATING.
IT'S ALL RIGHT, ALPHA...
...HE'S AN OLD FRIEND. A VERY OLD FRIEND.
MASTER, IT HAS BEEN TOO LONG.
MY SYMPATHIES ON YOUR CURRENT PHYSICAL CONDITION.
HOLD UP. THERE'S A LOT GOING ON RIGHT NOW. WE NEED SOME DEFINITE EXPLANATION TIME.
SO... THIS IS THE FOR REAL FIRST ALPHA?

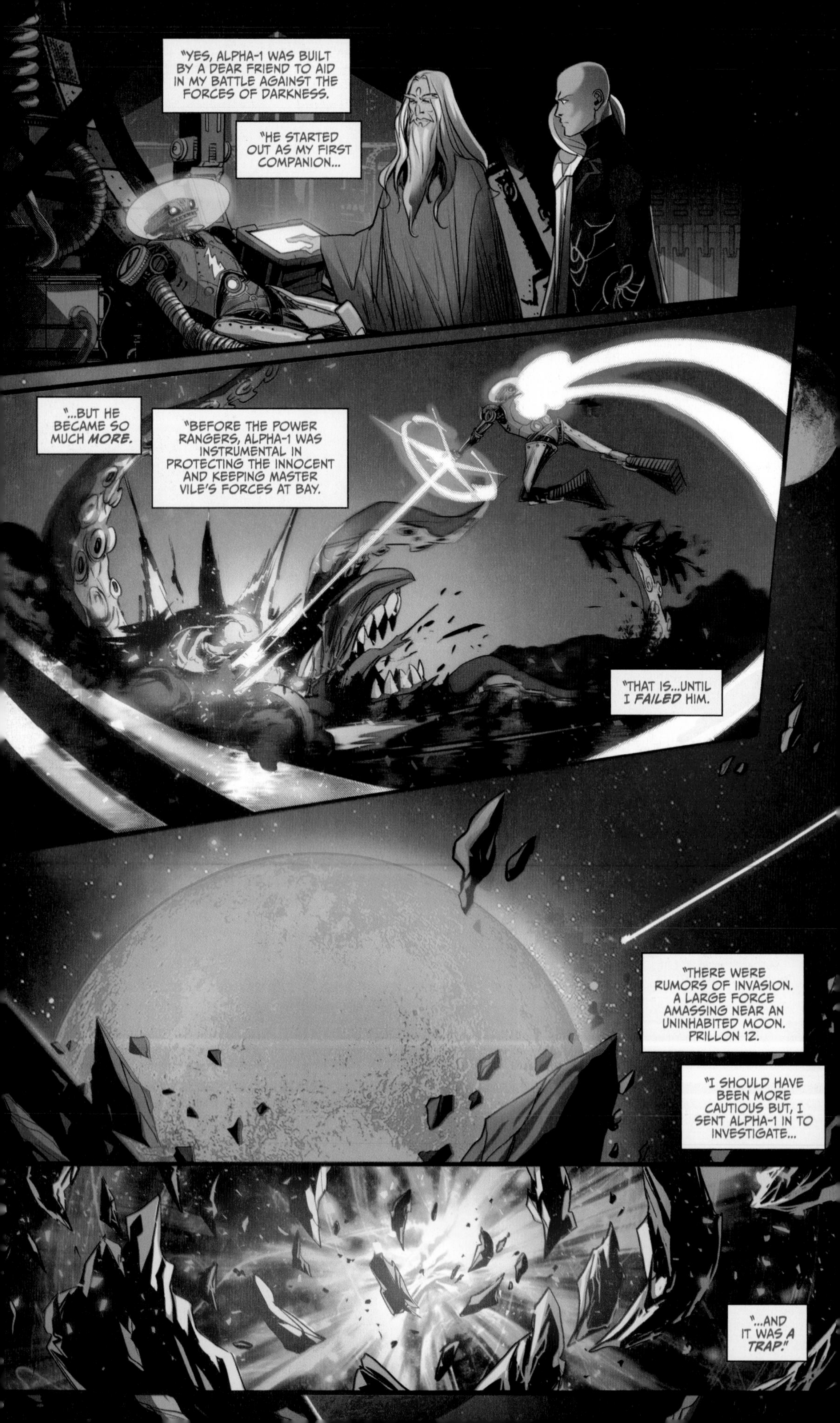

"YES, ALPHA-1 WAS BUILT BY A DEAR FRIEND TO AID IN MY BATTLE AGAINST THE FORCES OF DARKNESS.
"HE STARTED OUT AS MY FIRST COMPANION...
"...BUT HE BECAME SO MUCH *MORE*.
"BEFORE THE POWER RANGERS, ALPHA-1 WAS INSTRUMENTAL IN PROTECTING THE INNOCENT AND KEEPING MASTER VILE'S FORCES AT BAY.
"THAT IS...UNTIL I *FAILED* HIM.
"THERE WERE RUMORS OF INVASION. A LARGE FORCE AMASSING NEAR AN UNINHABITED MOON. PRILLON 12.
"I SHOULD HAVE BEEN MORE CAUTIOUS BUT, I SENT ALPHA-1 IN TO INVESTIGATE...
"...AND IT WAS A *TRAP*."

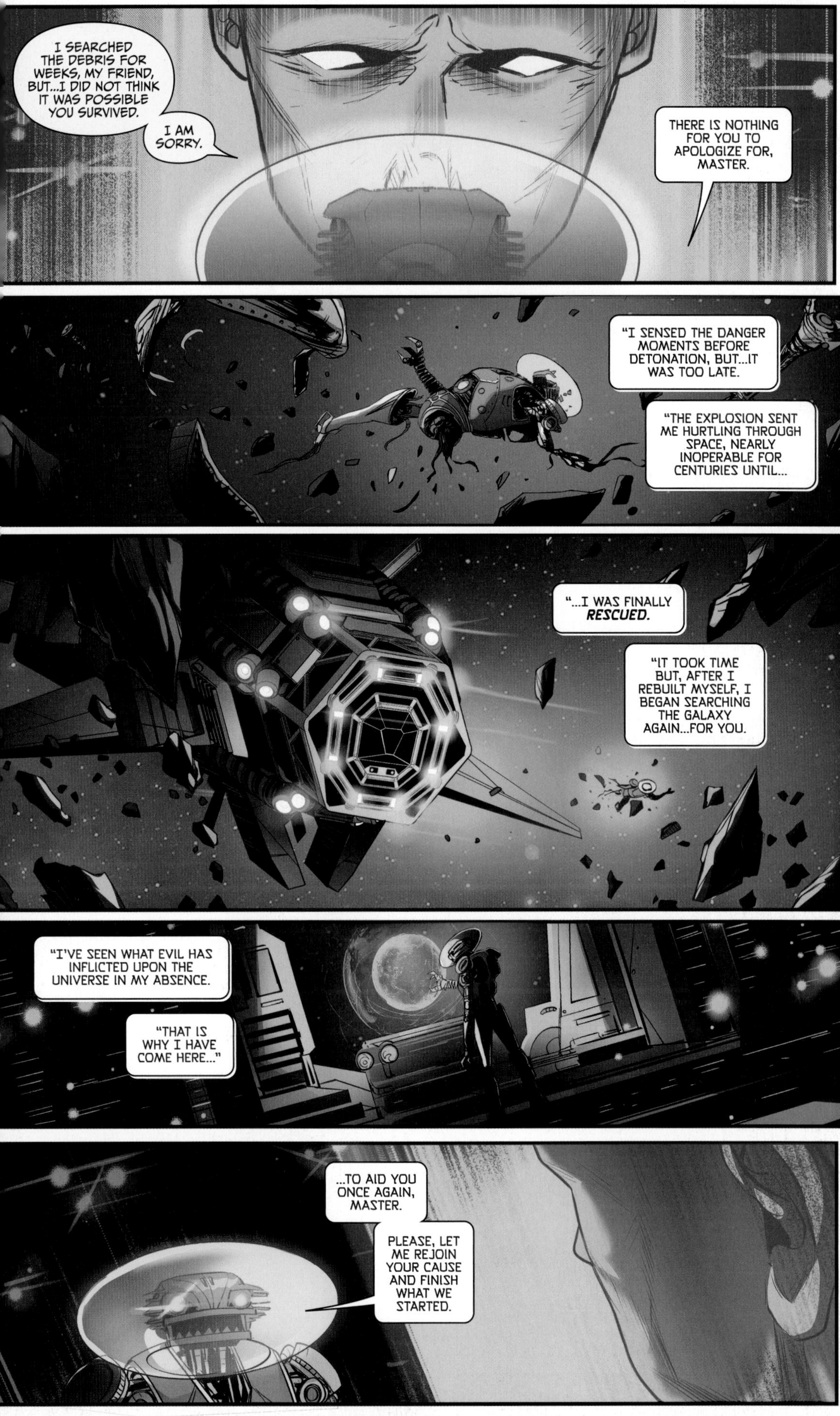

I SEARCHED THE DEBRIS FOR WEEKS, MY FRIEND, BUT...I DID NOT THINK IT WAS POSSIBLE YOU SURVIVED.
I AM SORRY.
THERE IS NOTHING FOR YOU TO APOLOGIZE FOR, MASTER.
"I SENSED THE DANGER MOMENTS BEFORE DETONATION, BUT...IT WAS TOO LATE.
"THE EXPLOSION SENT ME HURTLING THROUGH SPACE, NEARLY INOPERABLE FOR CENTURIES UNTIL...
"...I WAS FINALLY ***RESCUED.***
"IT TOOK TIME BUT, AFTER I REBUILT MYSELF, I BEGAN SEARCHING THE GALAXY AGAIN...FOR YOU.
"I'VE SEEN WHAT EVIL HAS INFLICTED UPON THE UNIVERSE IN MY ABSENCE.
"THAT IS WHY I HAVE COME HERE..."
...TO AID YOU ONCE AGAIN, MASTER.
PLEASE, LET ME REJOIN YOUR CAUSE AND FINISH WHAT WE STARTED.

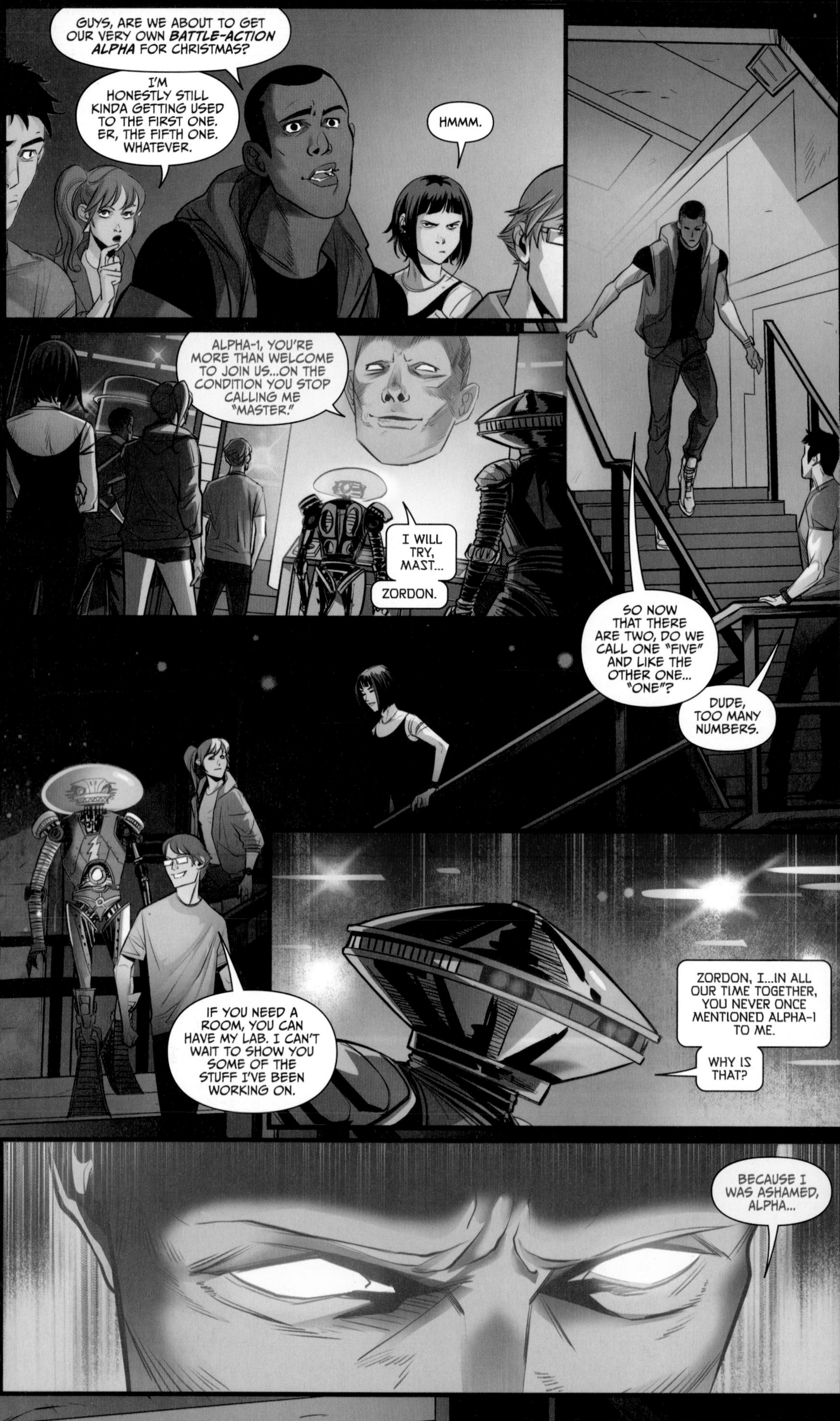
GUYS, ARE WE ABOUT TO GET OUR VERY OWN BATTLE-ACTION ALPHA FOR CHRISTMAS?
I'M HONESTLY STILL KINDA GETTING USED TO THE FIRST ONE. ER, THE FIFTH ONE. WHATEVER.
HMMM.
ALPHA-1, YOU'RE MORE THAN WELCOME TO JOIN US...ON THE CONDITION YOU STOP CALLING ME "MASTER."
I WILL TRY, MAST...
ZORDON.
SO NOW THAT THERE ARE TWO, DO WE CALL ONE "FIVE" AND LIKE THE OTHER ONE... "ONE"?
DUDE, TOO MANY NUMBERS.
IF YOU NEED A ROOM, YOU CAN HAVE MY LAB. I CAN'T WAIT TO SHOW YOU SOME OF THE STUFF I'VE BEEN WORKING ON.
ZORDON, I...IN ALL OUR TIME TOGETHER, YOU NEVER ONCE MENTIONED ALPHA-1 TO ME.
WHY IS THAT?
BECAUSE I WAS ASHAMED, ALPHA...

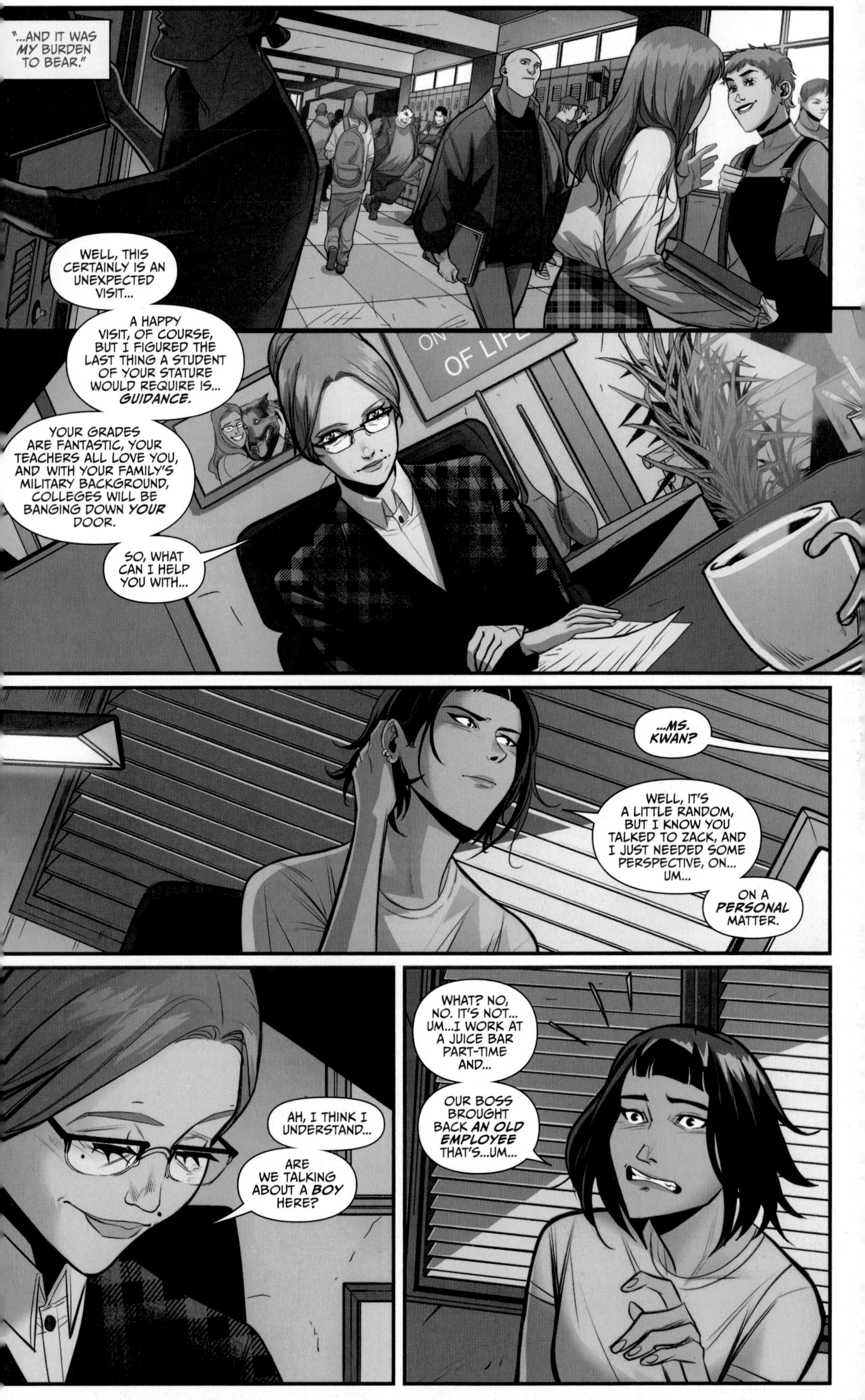
"...AND IT WAS MY BURDEN TO BEAR."
WELL, THIS CERTAINLY IS AN UNEXPECTED VISIT...
A HAPPY VISIT, OF COURSE, BUT I FIGURED THE LAST THING A STUDENT OF YOUR STATURE WOULD REQUIRE IS... GUIDANCE.
YOUR GRADES ARE FANTASTIC, YOUR TEACHERS ALL LOVE YOU, AND WITH YOUR FAMILY'S MILITARY BACKGROUND, COLLEGES WILL BE BANGING DOWN YOUR DOOR.
SO, WHAT CAN I HELP YOU WITH...
...MS. KWAN?
WELL, IT'S A LITTLE RANDOM, BUT I KNOW YOU TALKED TO ZACK, AND I JUST NEEDED SOME PERSPECTIVE, ON... UM...
ON A PERSONAL MATTER.
AH, I THINK I UNDERSTAND...
ARE WE TALKING ABOUT A BOY HERE?
WHAT? NO, NO. IT'S NOT... UM...I WORK AT A JUICE BAR PART-TIME AND...
OUR BOSS BROUGHT BACK AN OLD EMPLOYEE THAT'S...UM...

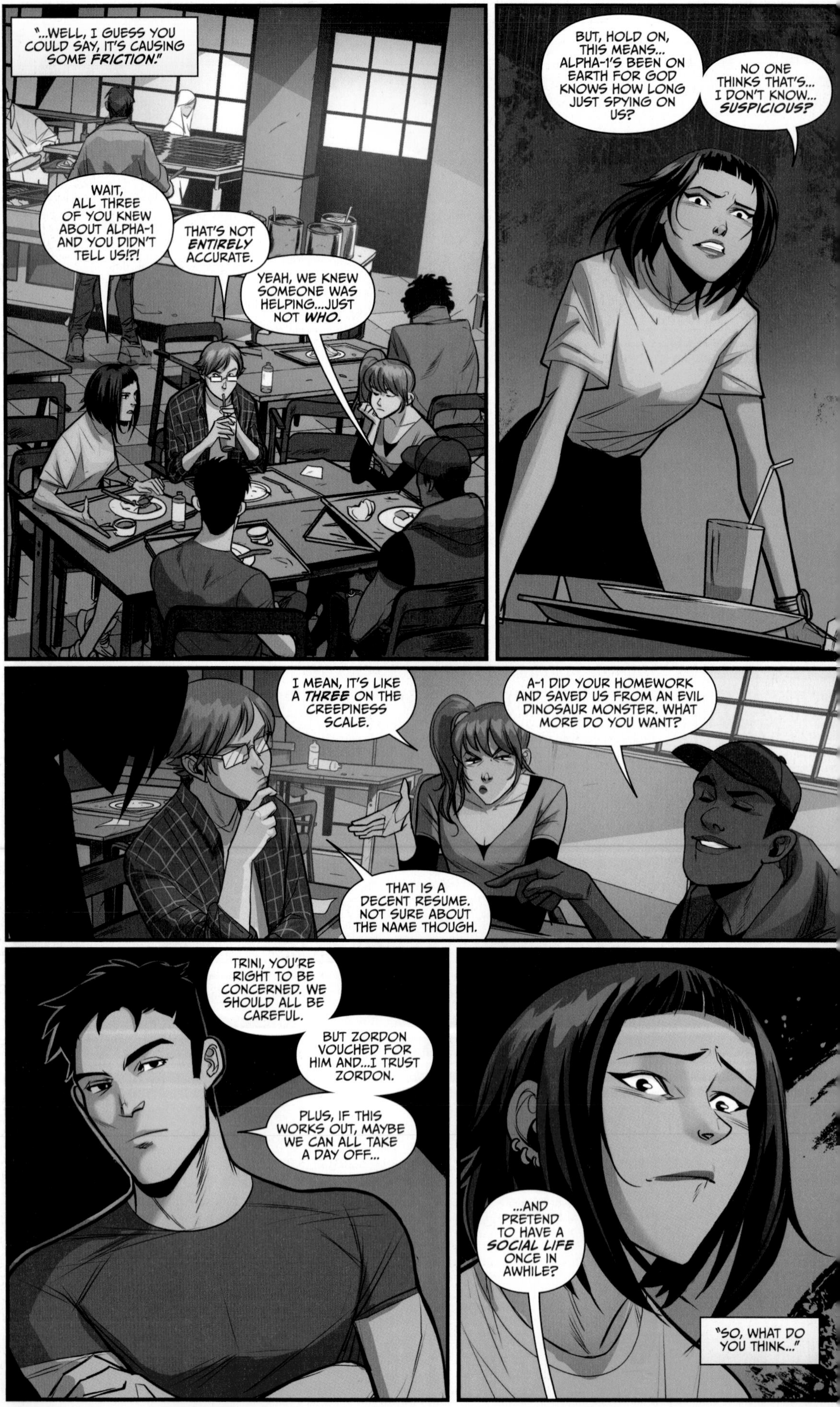
"...WELL, I GUESS YOU COULD SAY, IT'S CAUSING SOME FRICTION."
WAIT, ALL THREE OF YOU KNEW ABOUT ALPHA-1 AND YOU DIDN'T TELL US!?!
THAT'S NOT ENTIRELY ACCURATE.
YEAH, WE KNEW SOMEONE WAS HELPING...JUST NOT WHO.
BUT, HOLD ON, THIS MEANS... ALPHA-1'S BEEN ON EARTH FOR GOD KNOWS HOW LONG JUST SPYING ON US?
NO ONE THINKS THAT'S... I DON'T KNOW... SUSPICIOUS?
I MEAN, IT'S LIKE A THREE ON THE CREEPINESS SCALE.
A-1 DID YOUR HOMEWORK AND SAVED US FROM AN EVIL DINOSAUR MONSTER. WHAT MORE DO YOU WANT?
THAT IS A DECENT RESUME. NOT SURE ABOUT THE NAME THOUGH.
TRINI, YOU'RE RIGHT TO BE CONCERNED. WE SHOULD ALL BE CAREFUL.
BUT ZORDON VOUCHED FOR HIM AND...I TRUST ZORDON.
PLUS, IF THIS WORKS OUT, MAYBE WE CAN ALL TAKE A DAY OFF...
...AND PRETEND TO HAVE A SOCIAL LIFE ONCE IN AWHILE?
"SO, WHAT DO YOU THINK..."

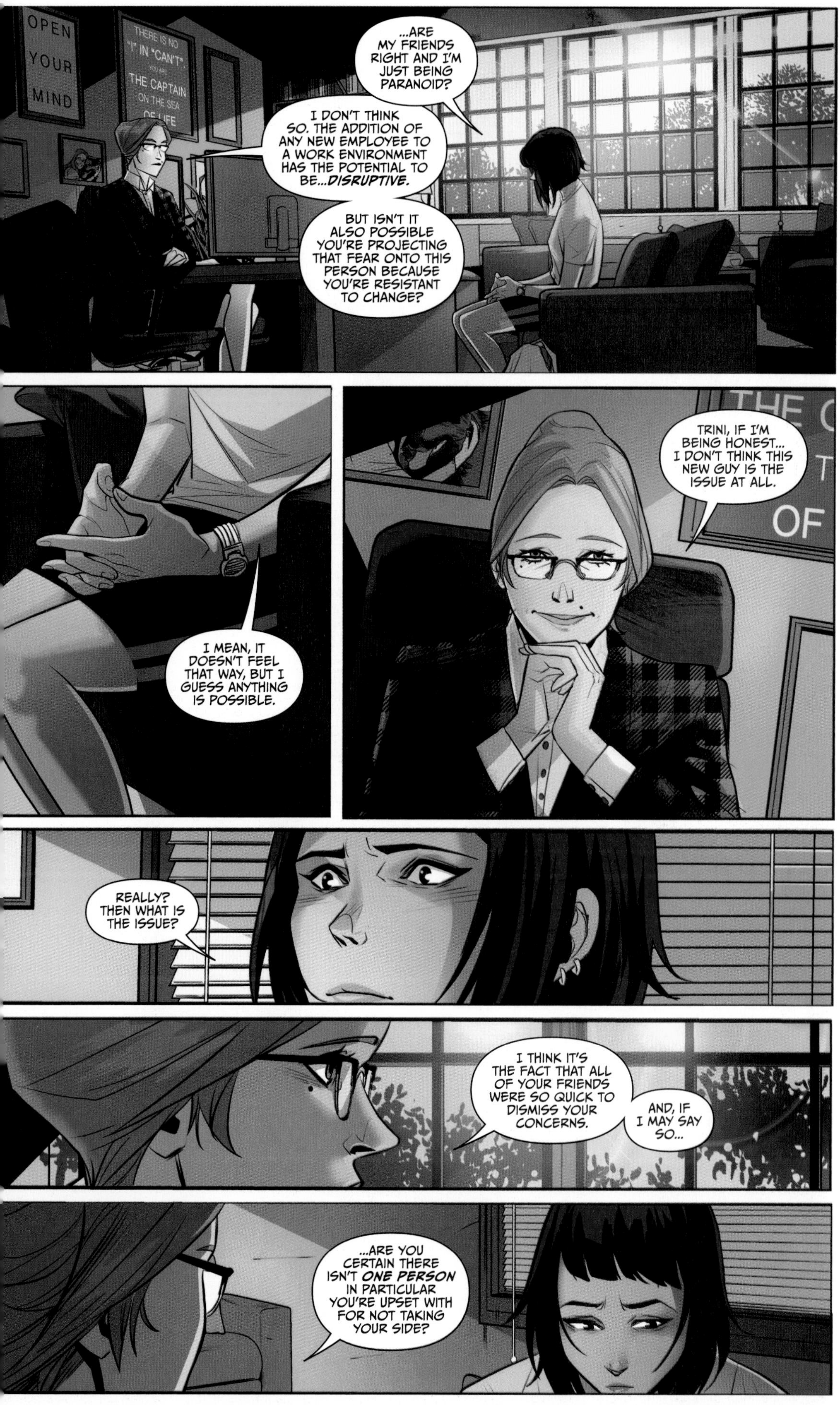
OPEN YOUR MIND
THERE IS NO "I" IN "CAN'T". YOU ARE THE CAPTAIN ON THE SEA OF LIFE
...ARE MY FRIENDS RIGHT AND I'M JUST BEING PARANOID?
I DON'T THINK SO. THE ADDITION OF ANY NEW EMPLOYEE TO A WORK ENVIRONMENT HAS THE POTENTIAL TO BE...*DISRUPTIVE.*
BUT ISN'T IT ALSO POSSIBLE YOU'RE PROJECTING THAT FEAR ONTO THIS PERSON BECAUSE YOU'RE RESISTANT TO CHANGE?
I MEAN, IT DOESN'T FEEL THAT WAY, BUT I GUESS ANYTHING IS POSSIBLE.
TRINI, IF I'M BEING HONEST... I DON'T THINK THIS NEW GUY IS THE ISSUE AT ALL.
REALLY? THEN WHAT IS THE ISSUE?
I THINK IT'S THE FACT THAT ALL OF YOUR FRIENDS WERE SO QUICK TO DISMISS YOUR CONCERNS.
AND, IF I MAY SAY SO...
...ARE YOU CERTAIN THERE ISN'T *ONE PERSON* IN PARTICULAR YOU'RE UPSET WITH FOR NOT TAKING YOUR SIDE?

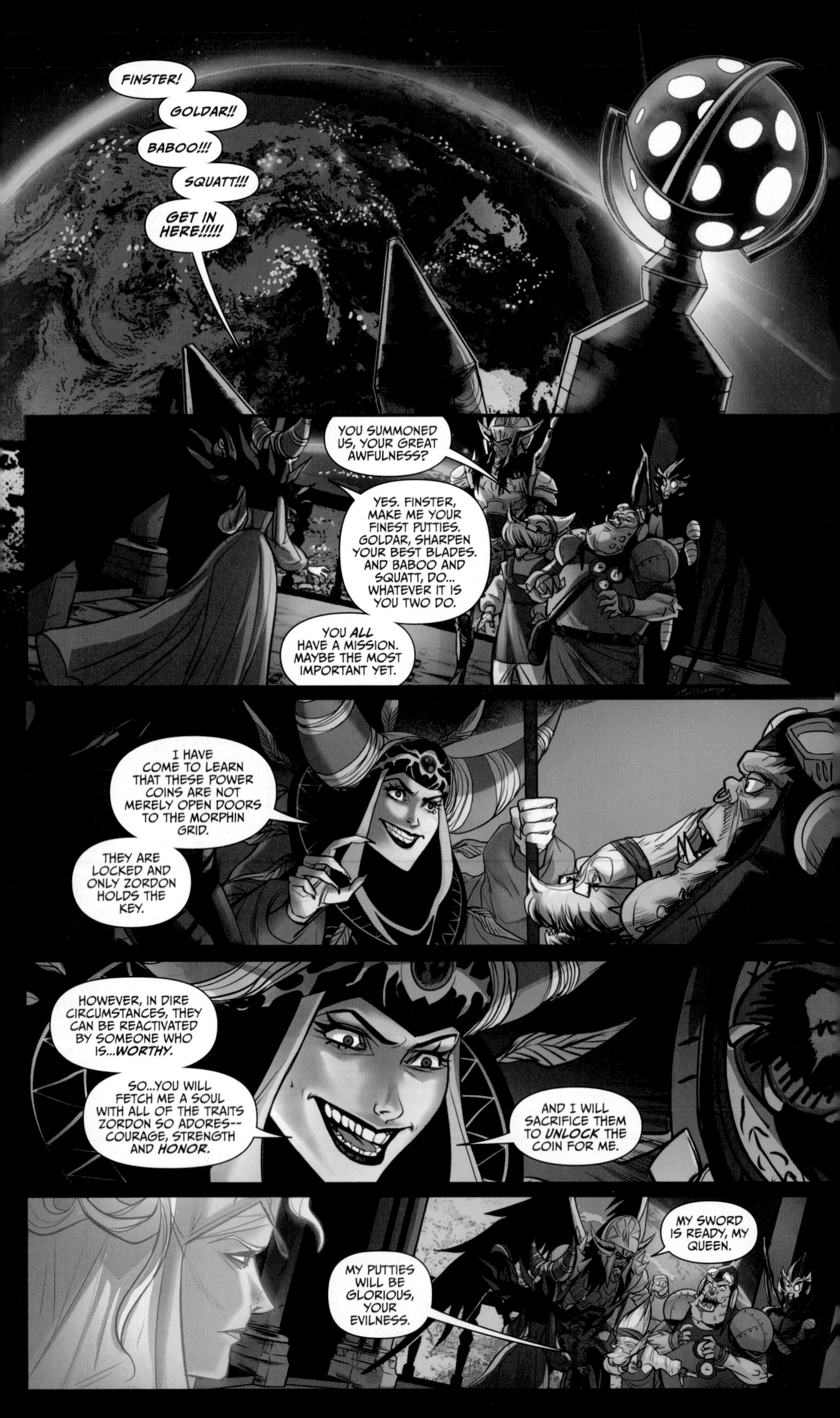
FINSTER!
GOLDAR!!
BABOO!!!
SQUATT!!!
GET IN HERE!!!!!
YOU SUMMONED US, YOUR GREAT AWFULNESS?
YES. FINSTER, MAKE ME YOUR FINEST PUTTIES. GOLDAR, SHARPEN YOUR BEST BLADES. AND BABOO AND SQUATT, DO... WHATEVER IT IS YOU TWO DO.
YOU ALL HAVE A MISSION. MAYBE THE MOST IMPORTANT YET.
I HAVE COME TO LEARN THAT THESE POWER COINS ARE NOT MERELY OPEN DOORS TO THE MORPHIN GRID.
THEY ARE LOCKED AND ONLY ZORDON HOLDS THE KEY.
HOWEVER, IN DIRE CIRCUMSTANCES, THEY CAN BE REACTIVATED BY SOMEONE WHO IS...WORTHY.
SO...YOU WILL FETCH ME A SOUL WITH ALL OF THE TRAITS ZORDON SO ADORES-- COURAGE, STRENGTH AND HONOR.
AND I WILL SACRIFICE THEM TO UNLOCK THE COIN FOR ME.
MY SWORD IS READY, MY QUEEN.
MY PUTTIES WILL BE GLORIOUS, YOUR EVILNESS.

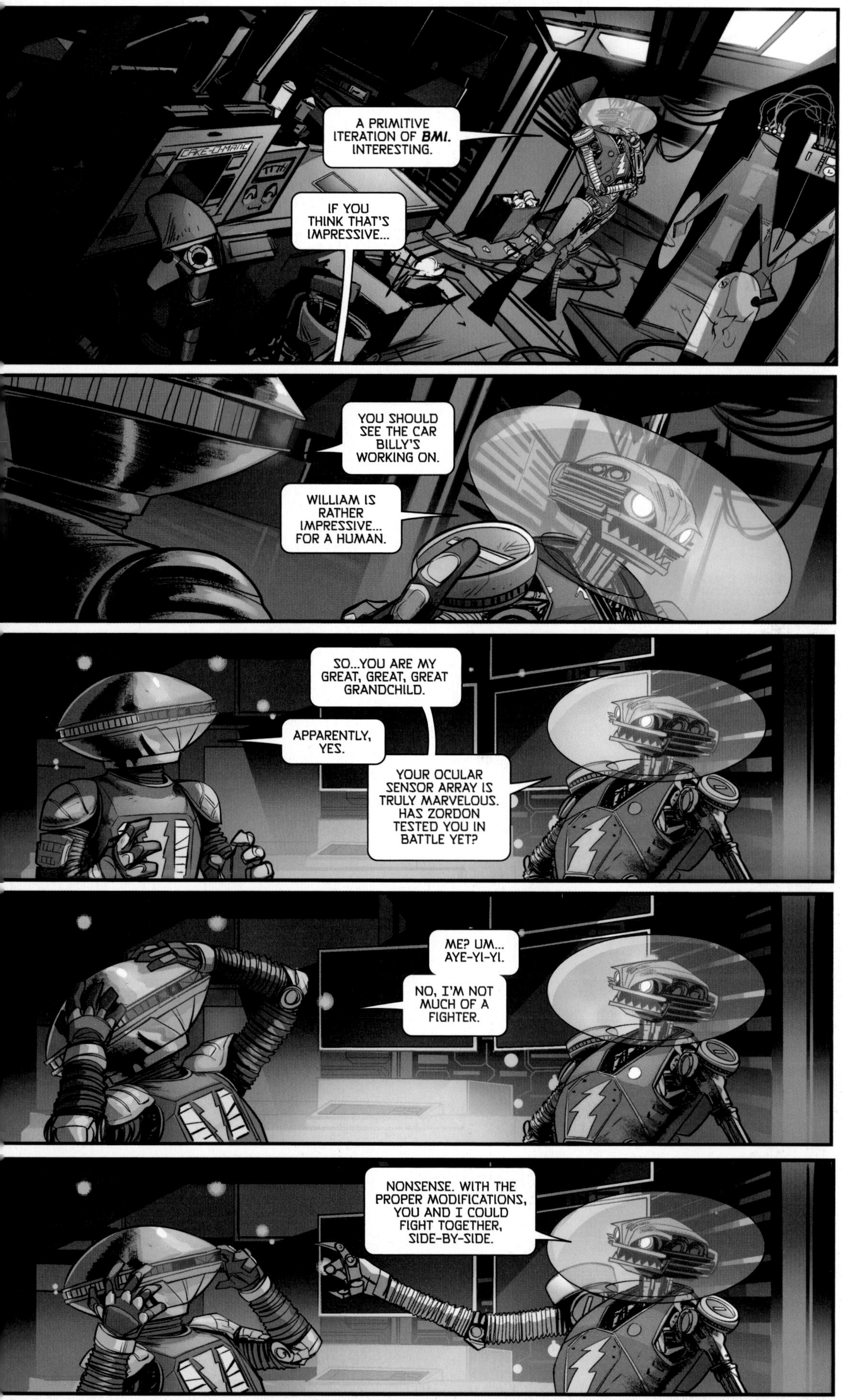

A PRIMITIVE ITERATION OF **BMI.** INTERESTING.
IF YOU THINK THAT'S IMPRESSIVE...
YOU SHOULD SEE THE CAR BILLY'S WORKING ON.
WILLIAM IS RATHER IMPRESSIVE... FOR A HUMAN.
CAKE-O-MATIC
SO...YOU ARE MY GREAT, GREAT, GREAT GRANDCHILD.
APPARENTLY, YES.
YOUR OCULAR SENSOR ARRAY IS TRULY MARVELOUS. HAS ZORDON TESTED YOU IN BATTLE YET?
ME? UM... AYE-YI-YI.
NO, I'M NOT MUCH OF A FIGHTER.
NONSENSE. WITH THE PROPER MODIFICATIONS, YOU AND I COULD FIGHT TOGETHER, SIDE-BY-SIDE.

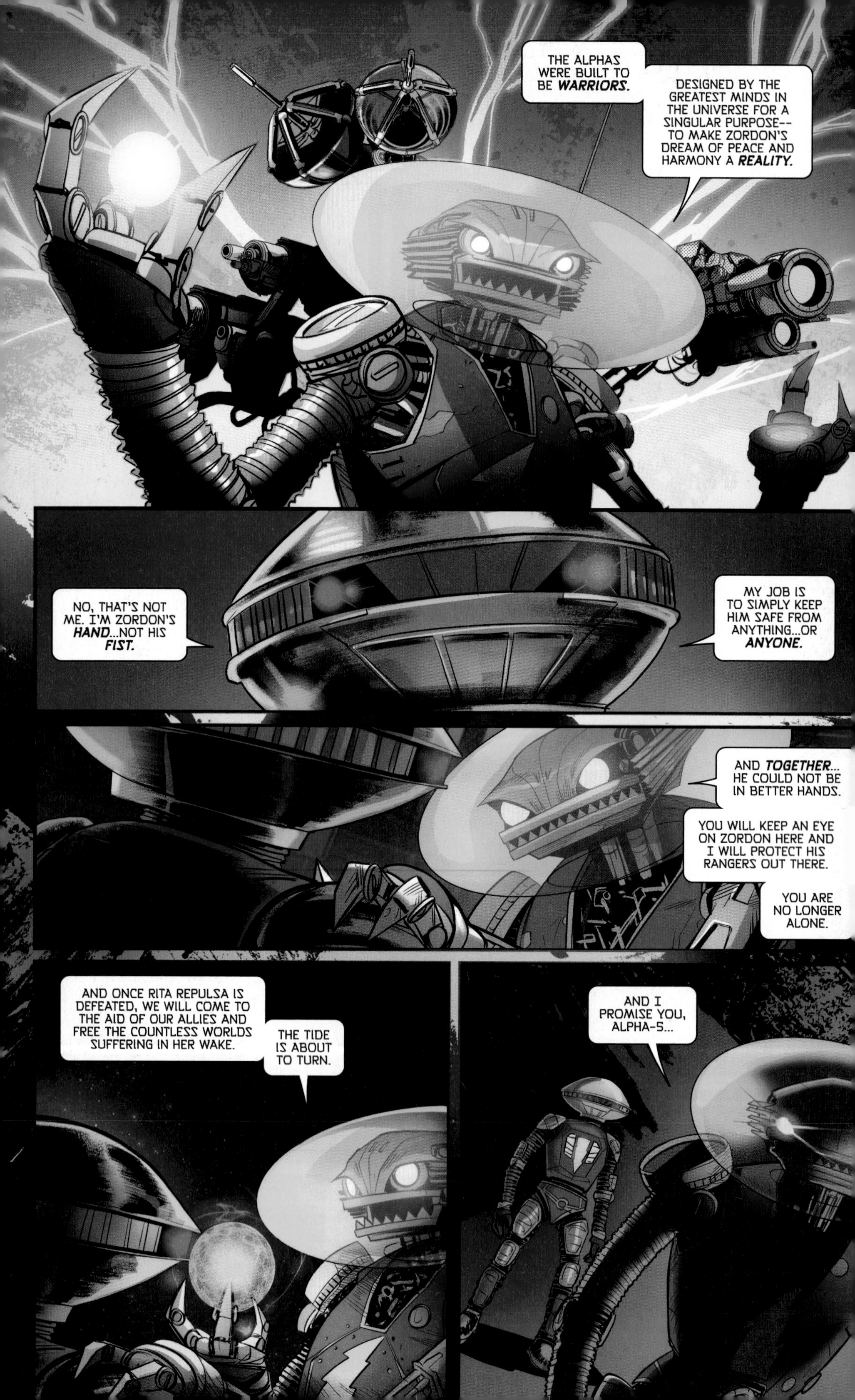

THE ALPHAS WERE BUILT TO BE **WARRIORS.**
DESIGNED BY THE GREATEST MINDS IN THE UNIVERSE FOR A SINGULAR PURPOSE-- TO MAKE ZORDON'S DREAM OF PEACE AND HARMONY A **REALITY.**
NO, THAT'S NOT ME. I'M ZORDON'S **HAND**...NOT HIS **FIST.**
MY JOB IS TO SIMPLY KEEP HIM SAFE FROM ANYTHING...OR **ANYONE.**
AND **TOGETHER**... HE COULD NOT BE IN BETTER HANDS.
YOU WILL KEEP AN EYE ON ZORDON HERE AND I WILL PROTECT HIS RANGERS OUT THERE.
YOU ARE NO LONGER ALONE.
AND ONCE RITA REPULSA IS DEFEATED, WE WILL COME TO THE AID OF OUR ALLIES AND FREE THE COUNTLESS WORLDS SUFFERING IN HER WAKE.
THE TIDE IS ABOUT TO TURN.
AND I PROMISE YOU, ALPHA-5...

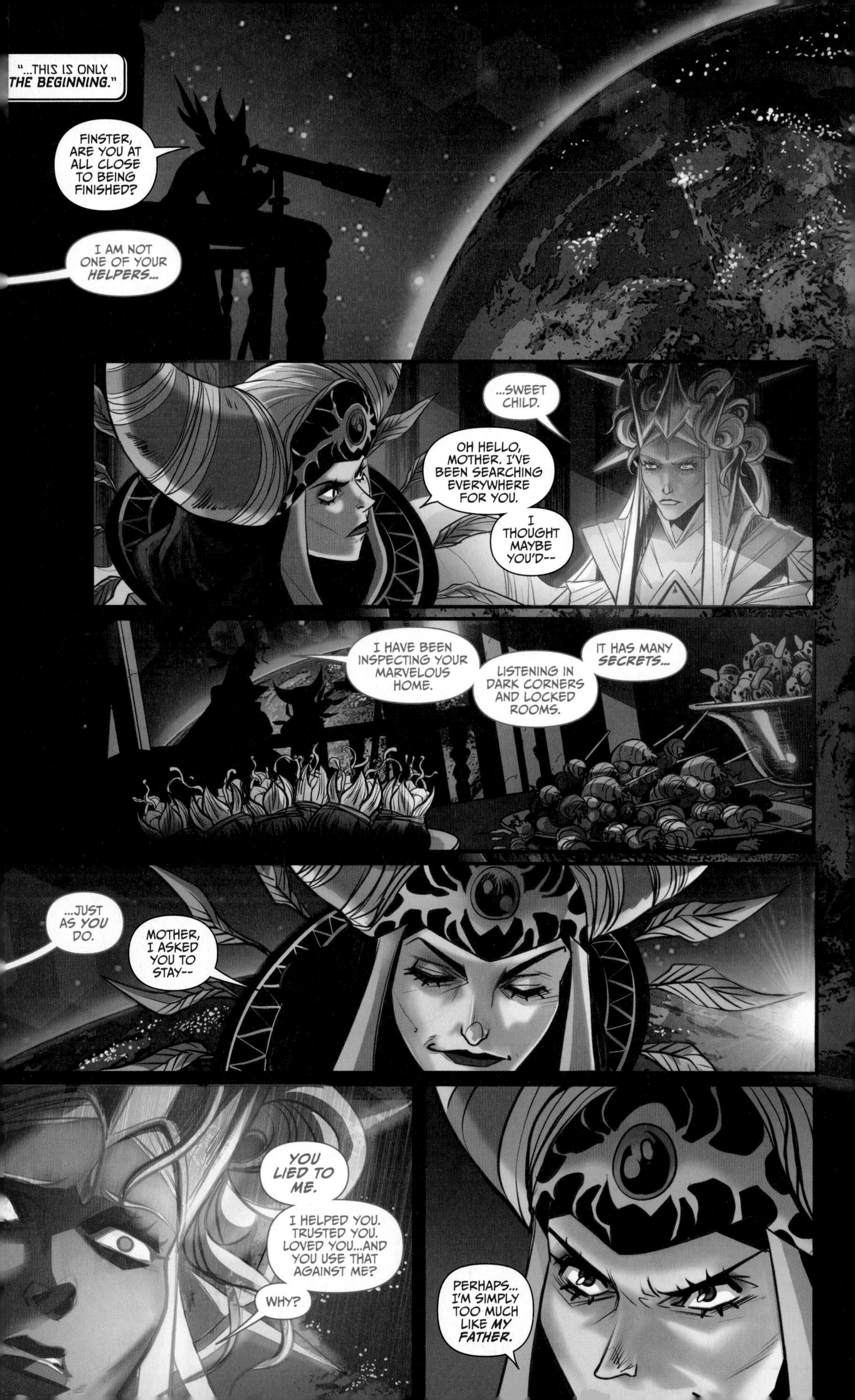
"...THIS IS ONLY THE BEGINNING."
FINSTER, ARE YOU AT ALL CLOSE TO BEING FINISHED?
I AM NOT ONE OF YOUR HELPERS...
...SWEET CHILD.
OH HELLO, MOTHER. I'VE BEEN SEARCHING EVERYWHERE FOR YOU.
I THOUGHT MAYBE YOU'D--
I HAVE BEEN INSPECTING YOUR MARVELOUS HOME.
LISTENING IN DARK CORNERS AND LOCKED ROOMS.
IT HAS MANY SECRETS...
...JUST AS YOU DO.
MOTHER, I ASKED YOU TO STAY--
YOU LIED TO ME.
I HELPED YOU. TRUSTED YOU. LOVED YOU...AND YOU USE THAT AGAINST ME?
WHY?
PERHAPS... I'M SIMPLY TOO MUCH LIKE MY FATHER.

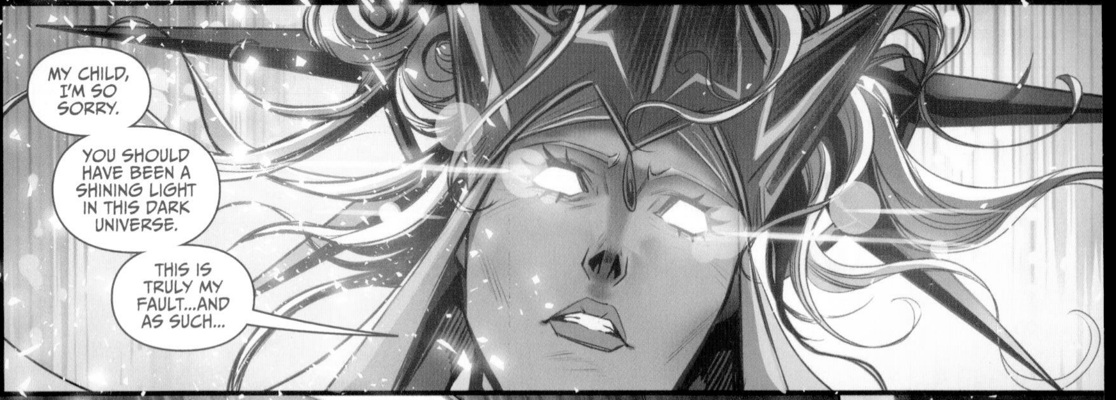
MY CHILD, I'M SO SORRY.
YOU SHOULD HAVE BEEN A SHINING LIGHT IN THIS DARK UNIVERSE.
THIS IS TRULY MY FAULT...AND AS SUCH...

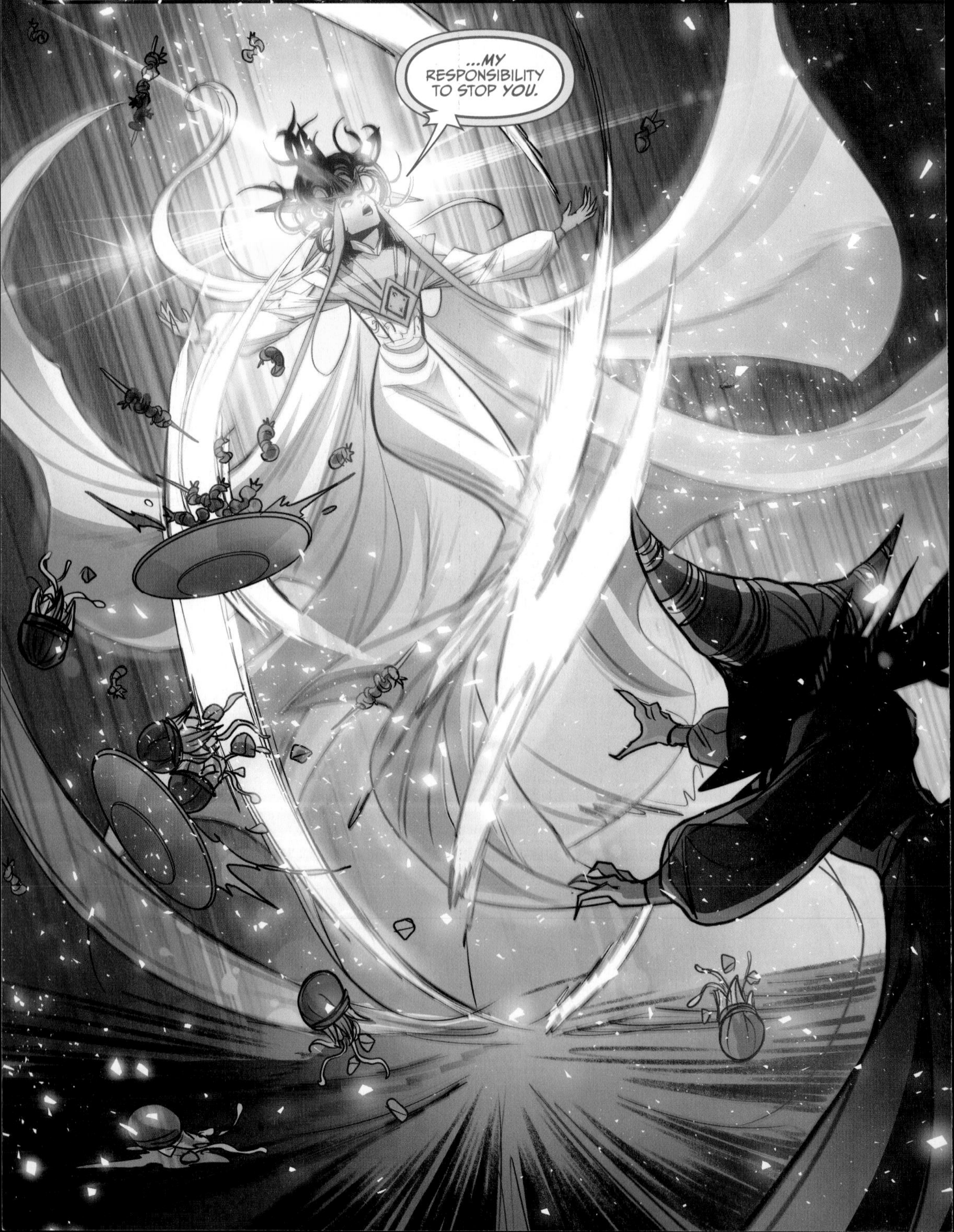
...MY RESPONSIBILITY TO STOP *YOU.*

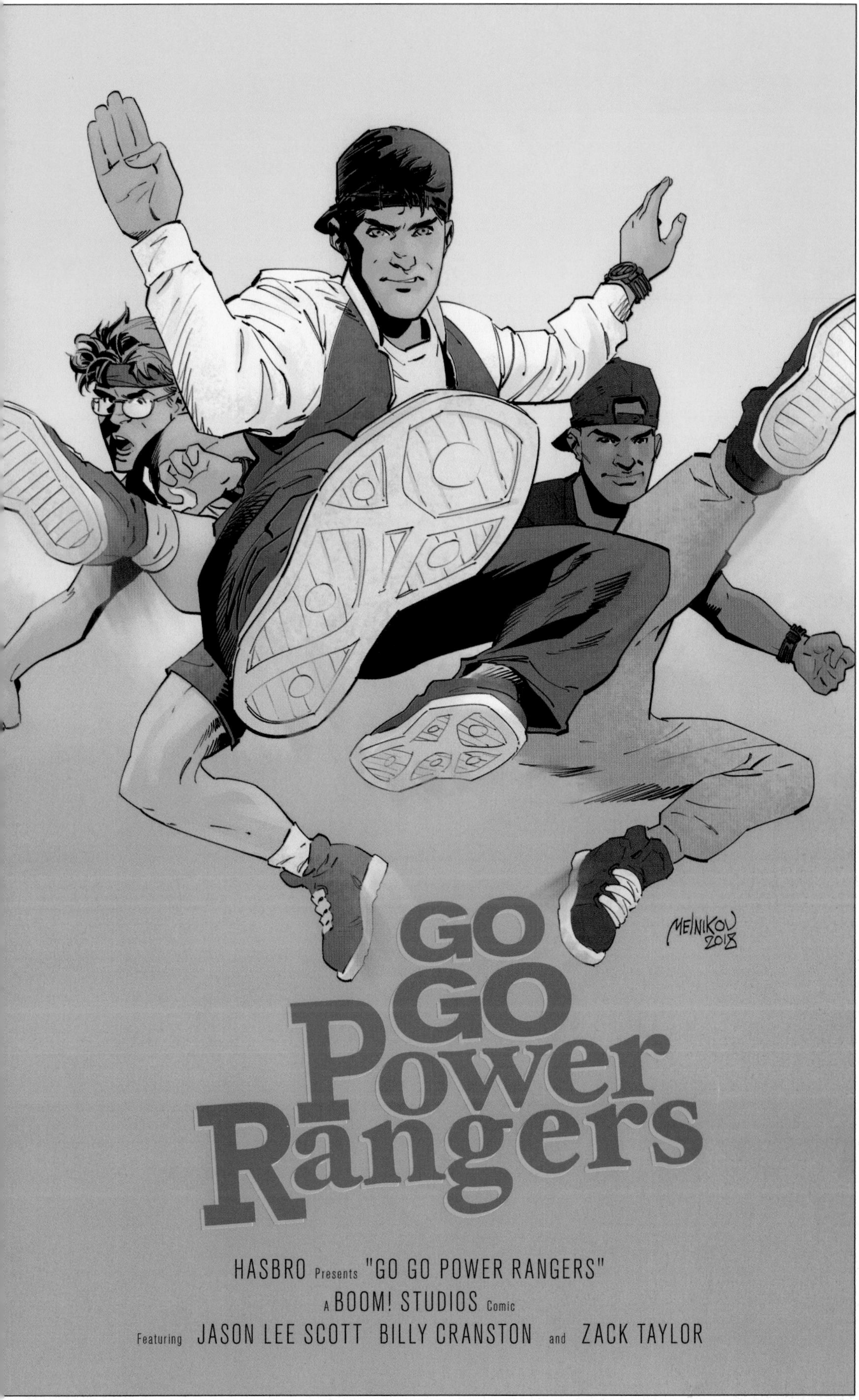
MELNIKOV 2018
GO GO Power Rangers
HASBRO Presents "GO GO POWER RANGERS"
A BOOM! STUDIOS Comic
Featuring JASON LEE SCOTT BILLY CRANSTON and ZACK TAYLOR

GLEB MELNIKOV WITH DESIGN BY **DYLAN TODD** ISSUE EIGHTEEN MOVIE HOMAGE VARIANT

MARCUS TO WITH COLORS BY **RAÚL ANGULO** ISSUE NINETEEN MAIN COVER

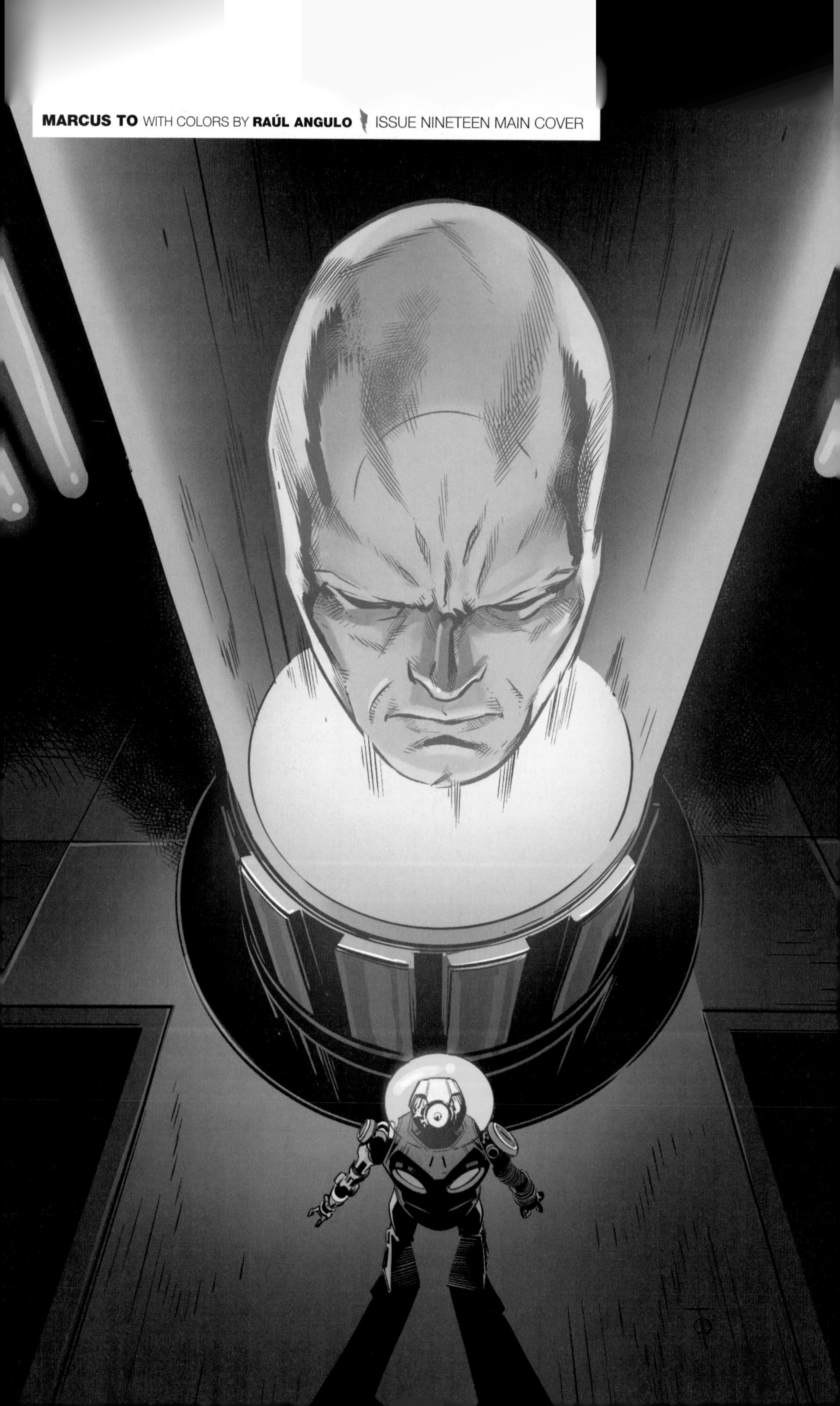

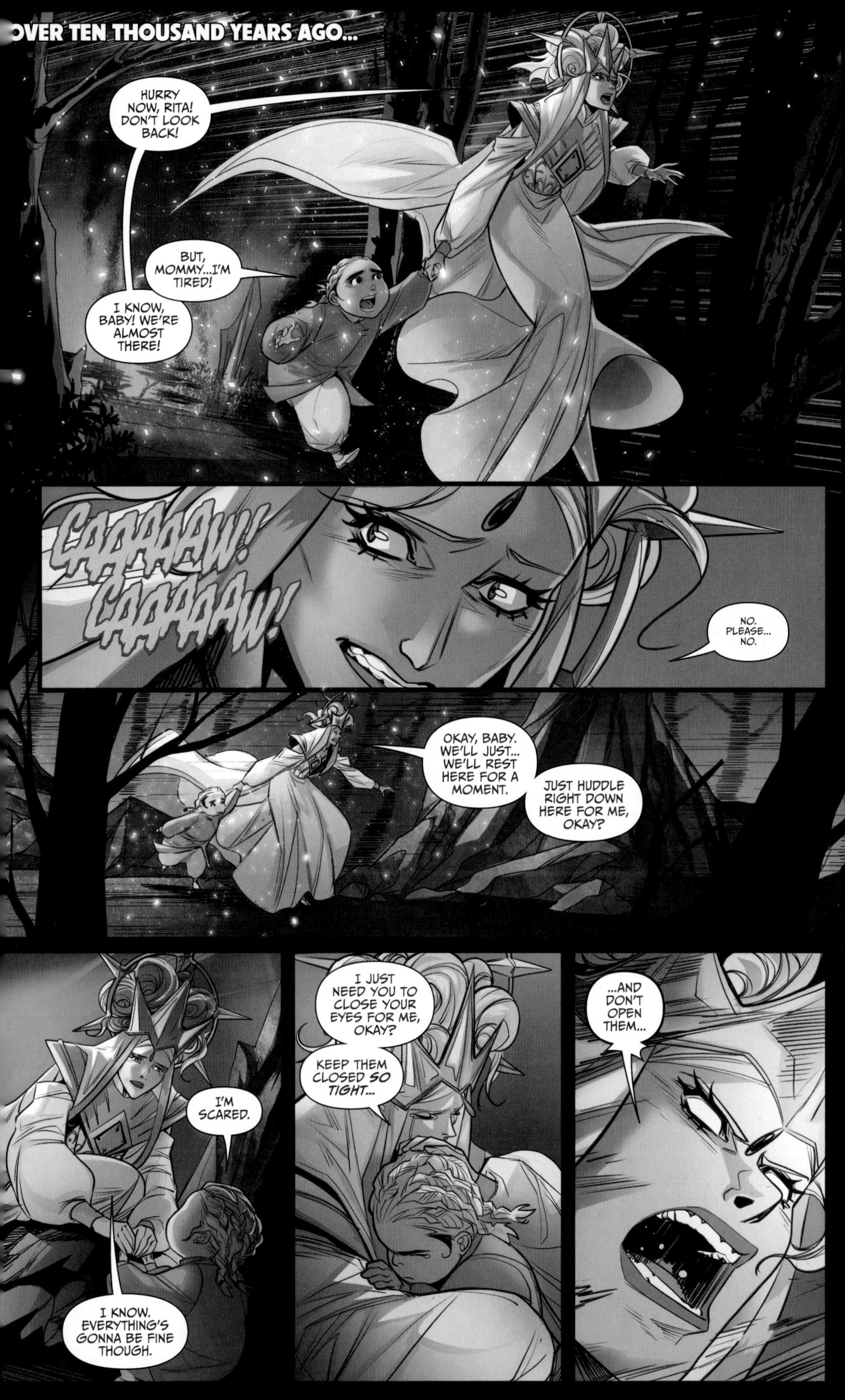
OVER TEN THOUSAND YEARS AGO...
HURRY NOW, RITA! DON'T LOOK BACK!
BUT, MOMMY...I'M TIRED!
I KNOW, BABY! WE'RE ALMOST THERE!
CAAAAAW! CAAAAAW!
NO. PLEASE... NO.
OKAY, BABY. WE'LL JUST... WE'LL REST HERE FOR A MOMENT.
JUST HUDDLE RIGHT DOWN HERE FOR ME, OKAY?
I'M SCARED.
I KNOW. EVERYTHING'S GONNA BE FINE THOUGH.
I JUST NEED YOU TO CLOSE YOUR EYES FOR ME, OKAY?
KEEP THEM CLOSED *SO TIGHT*...
...AND DON'T OPEN THEM...

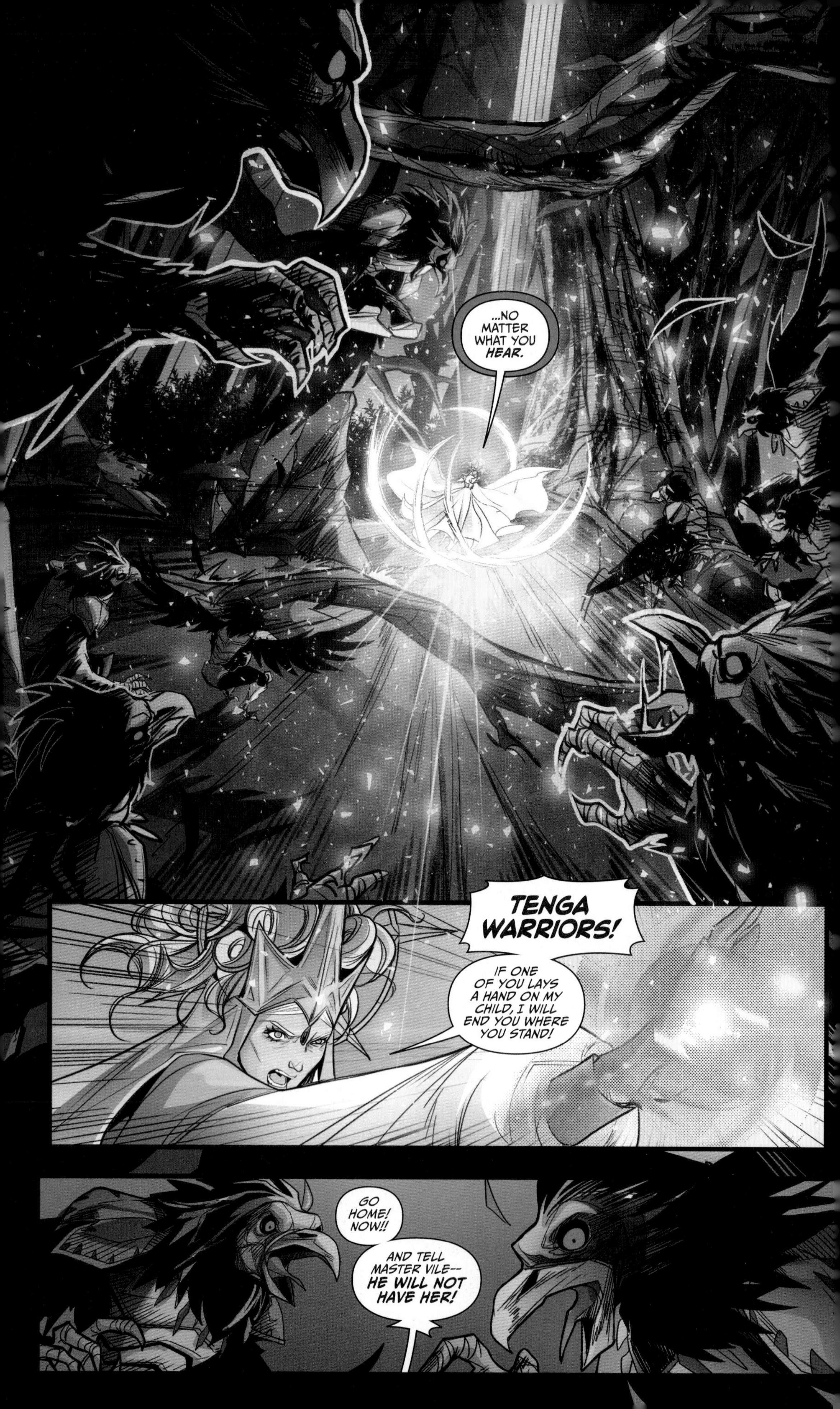

...NO MATTER WHAT YOU HEAR.
TENGA WARRIORS!
IF ONE OF YOU LAYS A HAND ON MY CHILD, I WILL END YOU WHERE YOU STAND!
GO HOME! NOW!!
AND TELL MASTER VILE-- HE WILL NOT HAVE HER!

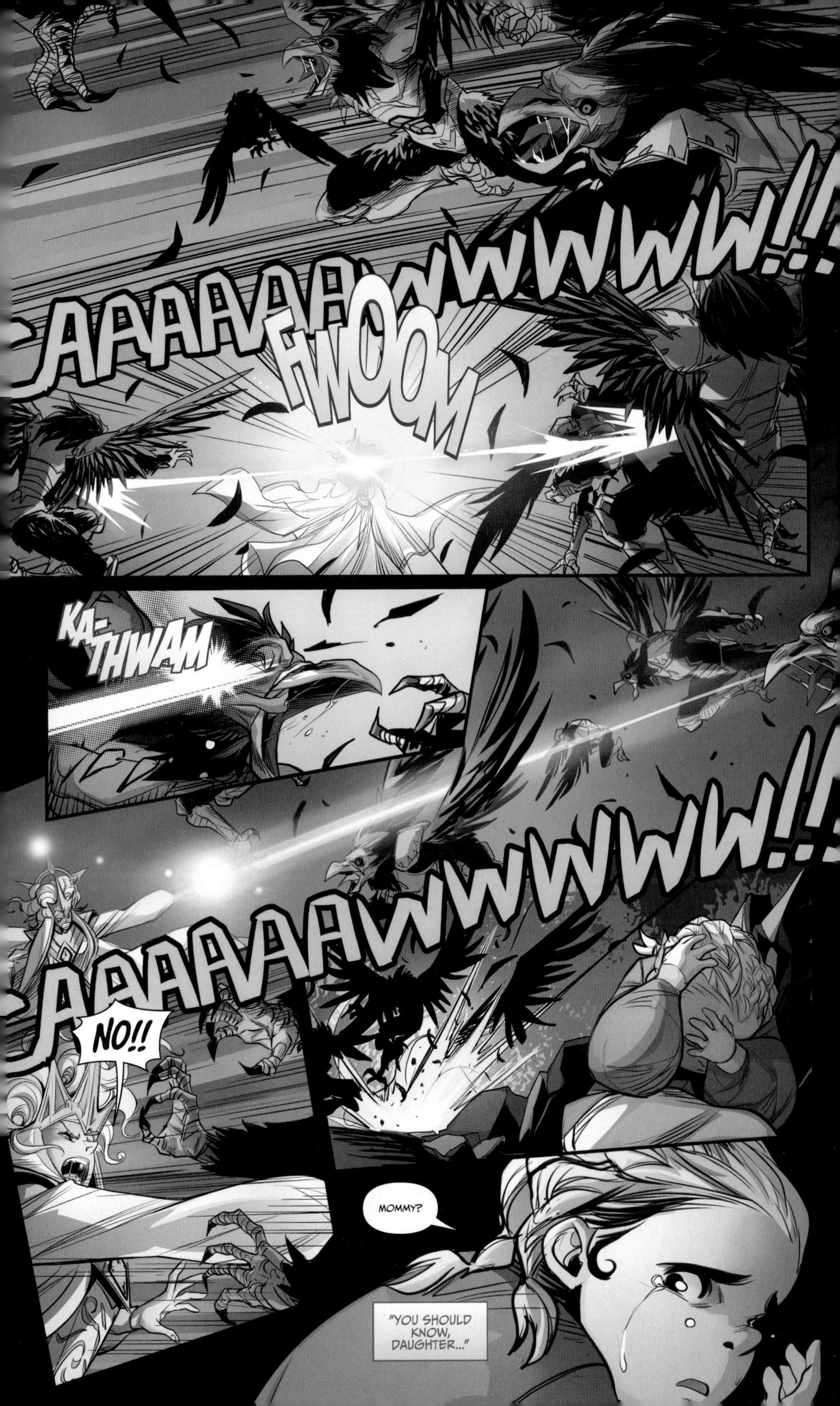
CAAAAAAWWWWWW!!!
FWOOM
KA-THWAM
CAAAAAAWWWWWW!!!
NO!!
MOMMY?
"YOU SHOULD KNOW, DAUGHTER..."

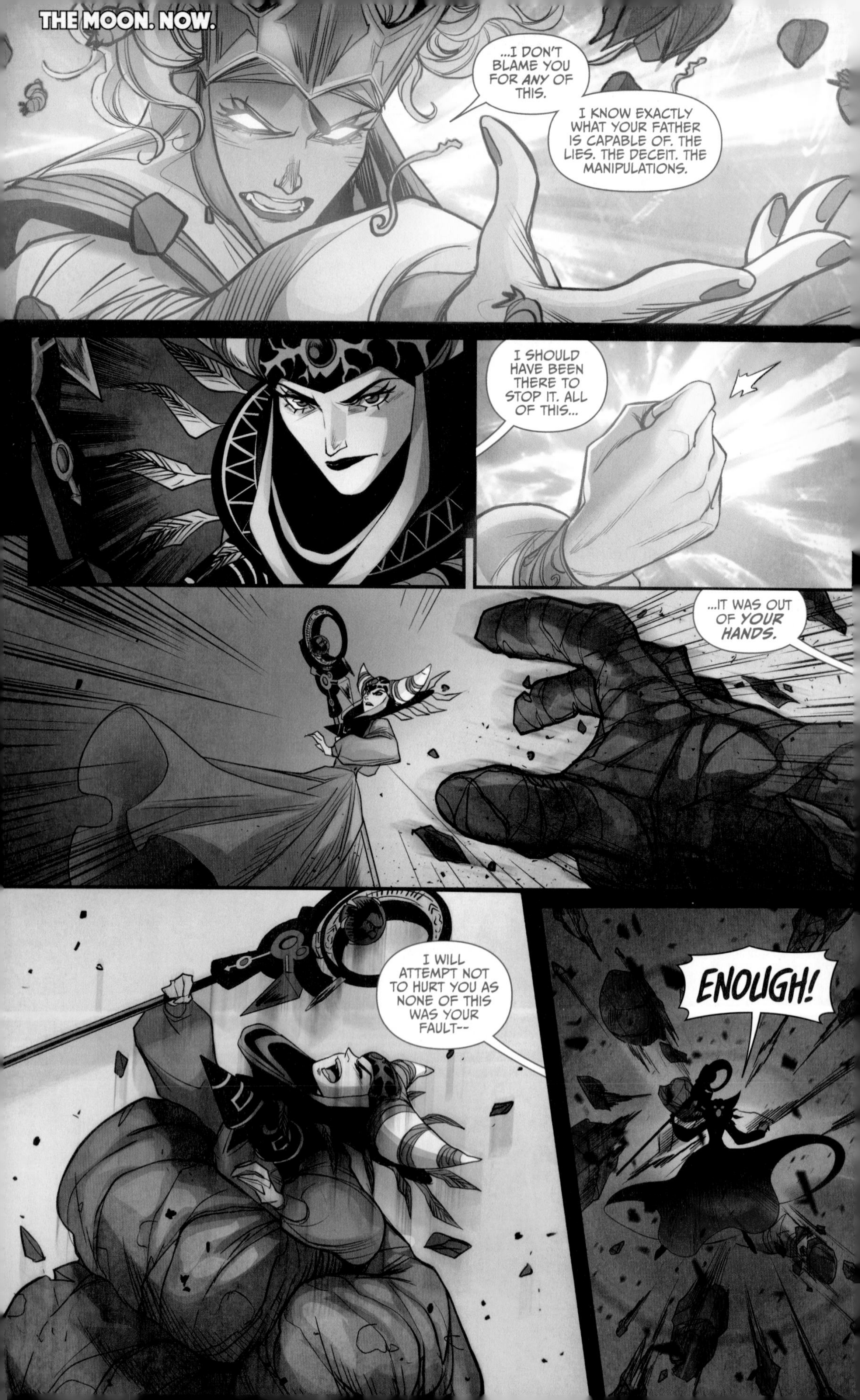
THE MOON. NOW.
...I DON'T BLAME YOU FOR ANY OF THIS.
I KNOW EXACTLY WHAT YOUR FATHER IS CAPABLE OF. THE LIES. THE DECEIT. THE MANIPULATIONS.
I SHOULD HAVE BEEN THERE TO STOP IT. ALL OF THIS...
...IT WAS OUT OF YOUR HANDS.
I WILL ATTEMPT NOT TO HURT YOU AS NONE OF THIS WAS YOUR FAULT--
ENOUGH!

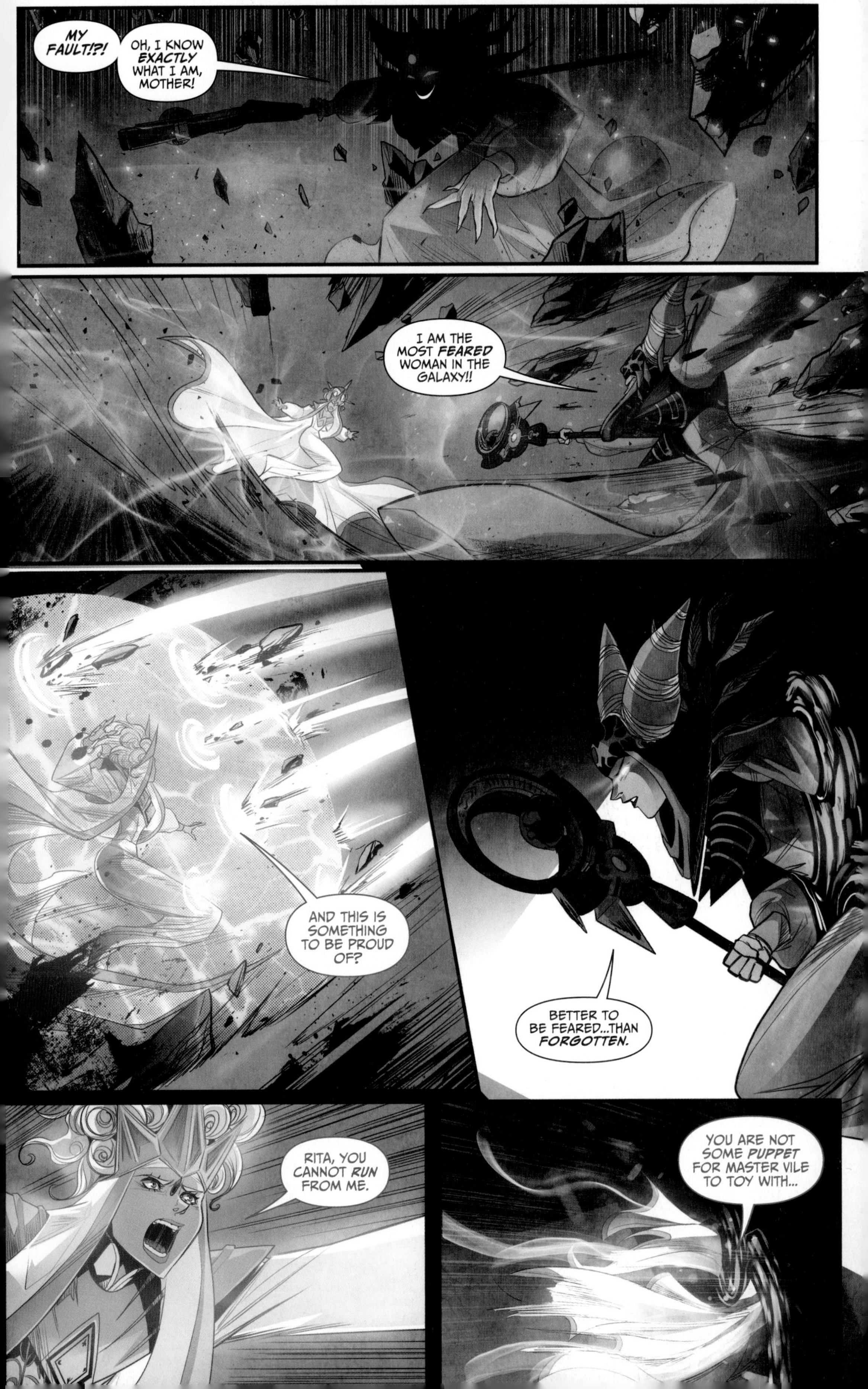
MY FAULT!?!
OH, I KNOW EXACTLY WHAT I AM, MOTHER!
I AM THE MOST FEARED WOMAN IN THE GALAXY!!
AND THIS IS SOMETHING TO BE PROUD OF?
BETTER TO BE FEARED...THAN FORGOTTEN.
RITA, YOU CANNOT RUN FROM ME.
YOU ARE NOT SOME PUPPET FOR MASTER VILE TO TOY WITH...

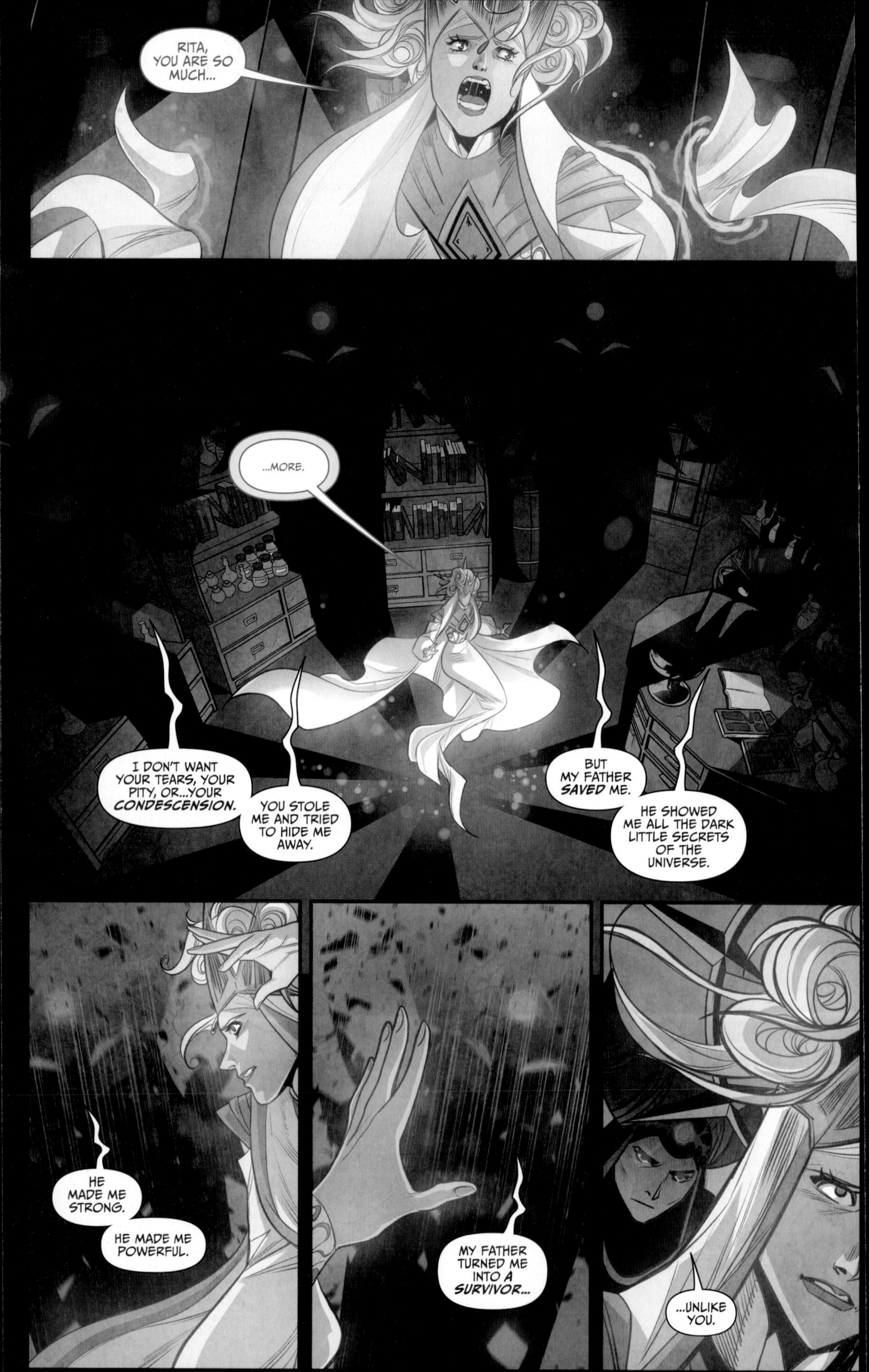
RITA, YOU ARE SO MUCH...
...MORE.
I DON'T WANT YOUR TEARS, YOUR PITY, OR...YOUR CONDESCENSION.
YOU STOLE ME AND TRIED TO HIDE ME AWAY.
BUT MY FATHER SAVED ME.
HE SHOWED ME ALL THE DARK LITTLE SECRETS OF THE UNIVERSE.
HE MADE ME STRONG.
HE MADE ME POWERFUL.
MY FATHER TURNED ME INTO A SURVIVOR...
...UNLIKE YOU.

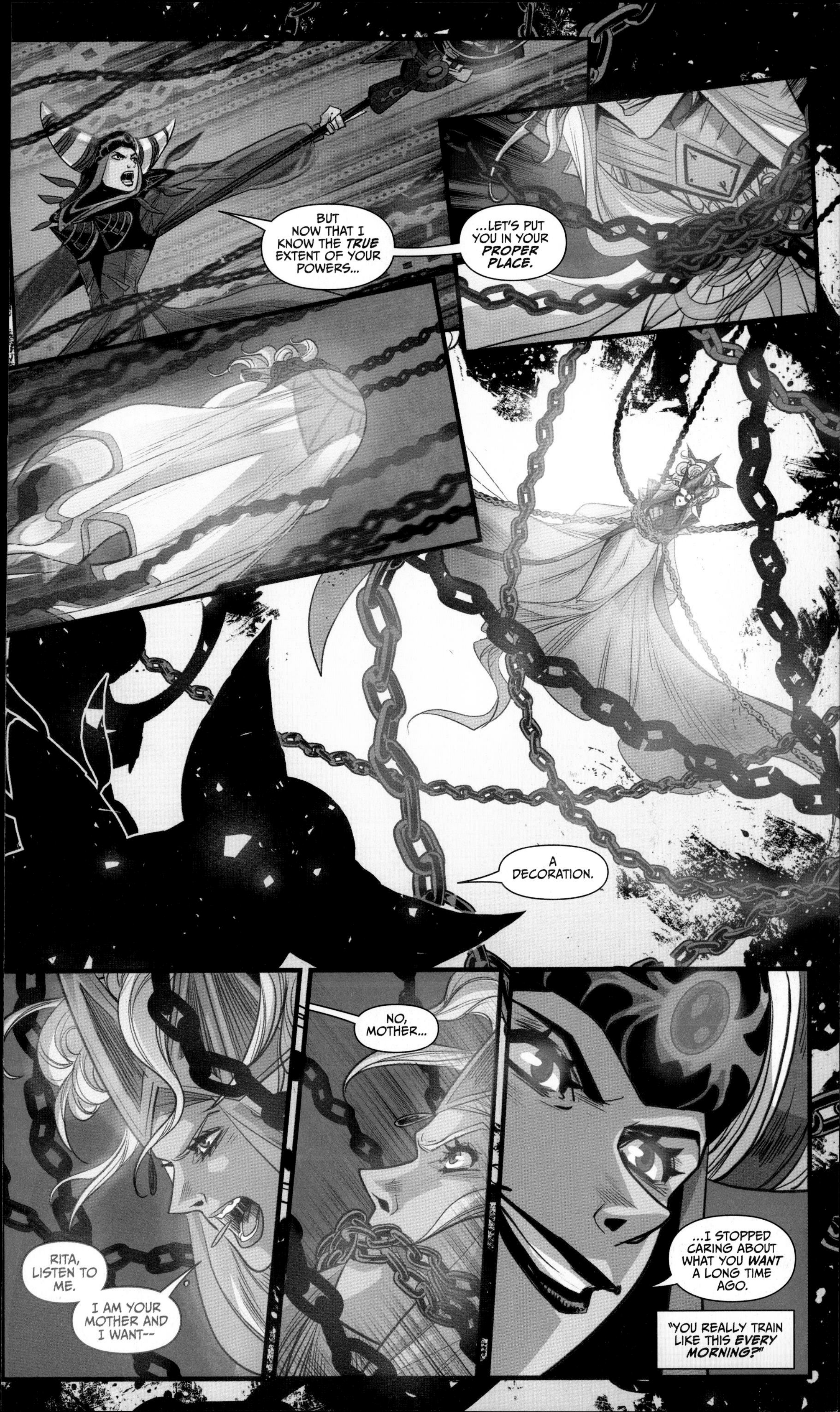
BUT NOW THAT I KNOW THE *TRUE* EXTENT OF YOUR POWERS...
...LET'S PUT YOU IN YOUR *PROPER PLACE.*
A DECORATION.
RITA, LISTEN TO ME.
I AM YOUR MOTHER AND I WANT--
NO, MOTHER...
...I STOPPED CARING ABOUT WHAT YOU *WANT* A LONG TIME AGO.
"YOU REALLY TRAIN LIKE THIS *EVERY MORNING?*"

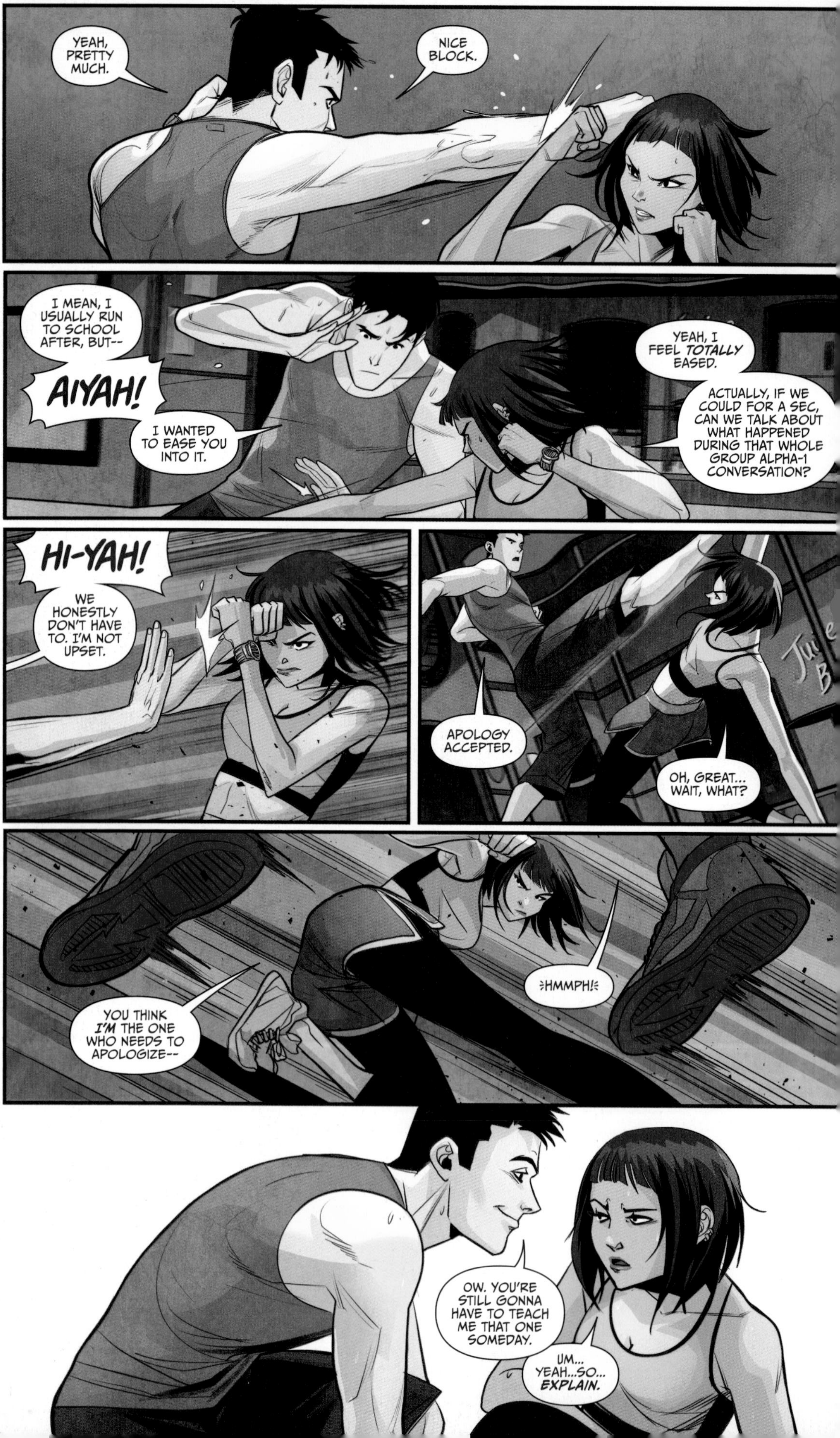
YEAH, PRETTY MUCH.
NICE BLOCK.
I MEAN, I USUALLY RUN TO SCHOOL AFTER, BUT--
AIYAH!
I WANTED TO EASE YOU INTO IT.
YEAH, I FEEL *TOTALLY* EASED.
ACTUALLY, IF WE COULD FOR A SEC, CAN WE TALK ABOUT WHAT HAPPENED DURING THAT WHOLE GROUP ALPHA-1 CONVERSATION?
HI-YAH!
WE HONESTLY DON'T HAVE TO. I'M NOT UPSET.
APOLOGY ACCEPTED.
OH, GREAT... WAIT, WHAT?
YOU THINK *I'M* THE ONE WHO NEEDS TO APOLOGIZE--
HMMPH!
OW. YOU'RE STILL GONNA HAVE TO TEACH ME THAT ONE SOMEDAY.
UM... YEAH...SO... *EXPLAIN.*

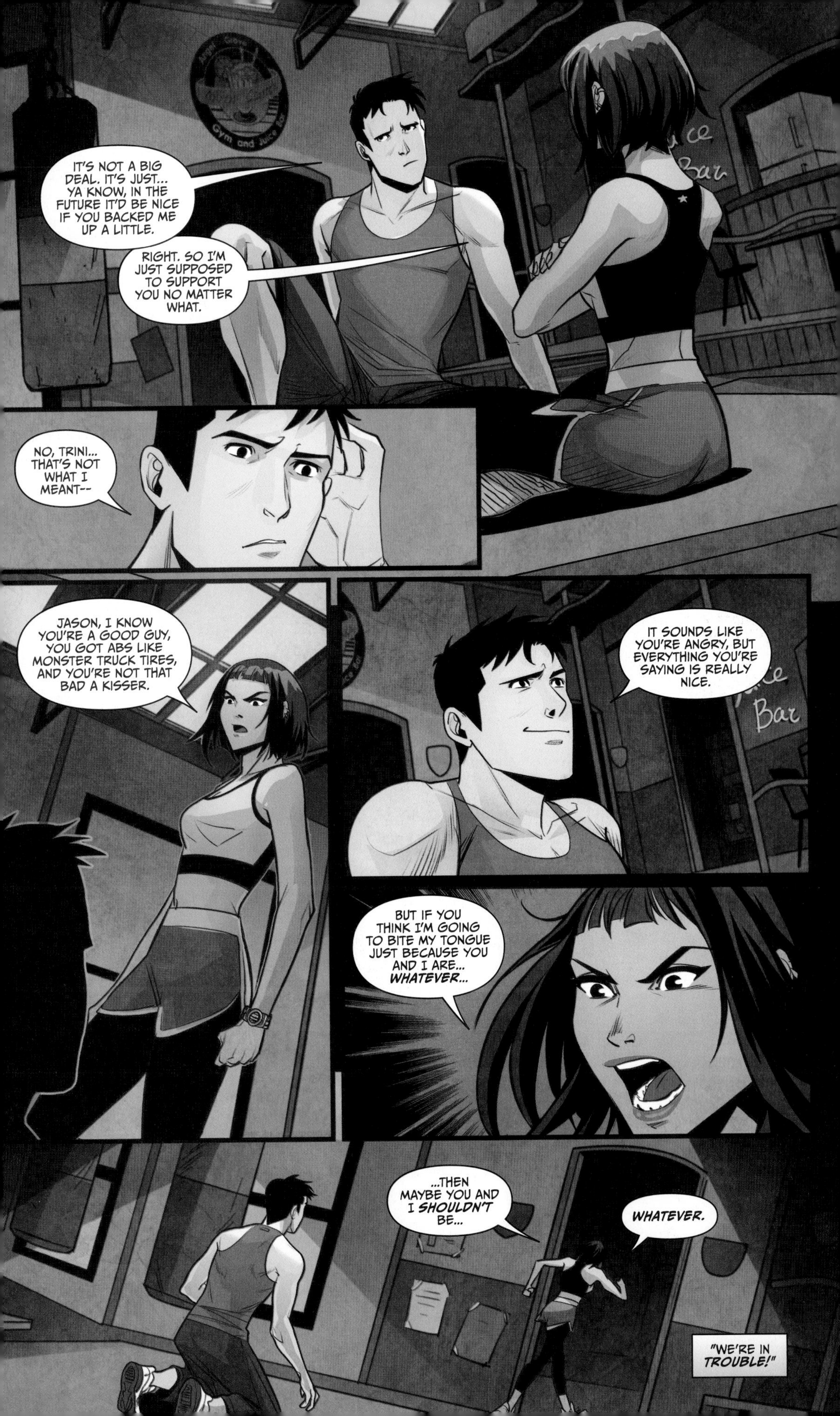
IT'S NOT A BIG DEAL. IT'S JUST... YA KNOW, IN THE FUTURE IT'D BE NICE IF YOU BACKED ME UP A LITTLE.
RIGHT. SO I'M JUST SUPPOSED TO SUPPORT YOU NO MATTER WHAT.
NO, TRINI... THAT'S NOT WHAT I MEANT--
JASON, I KNOW YOU'RE A GOOD GUY, YOU GOT ABS LIKE MONSTER TRUCK TIRES, AND YOU'RE NOT THAT BAD A KISSER.
IT SOUNDS LIKE YOU'RE ANGRY, BUT EVERYTHING YOU'RE SAYING IS REALLY NICE.
Bar
BUT IF YOU THINK I'M GOING TO BITE MY TONGUE JUST BECAUSE YOU AND I ARE... *WHATEVER*...
...THEN MAYBE YOU AND I *SHOULDN'T* BE...
WHATEVER.
"WE'RE IN *TROUBLE!*"

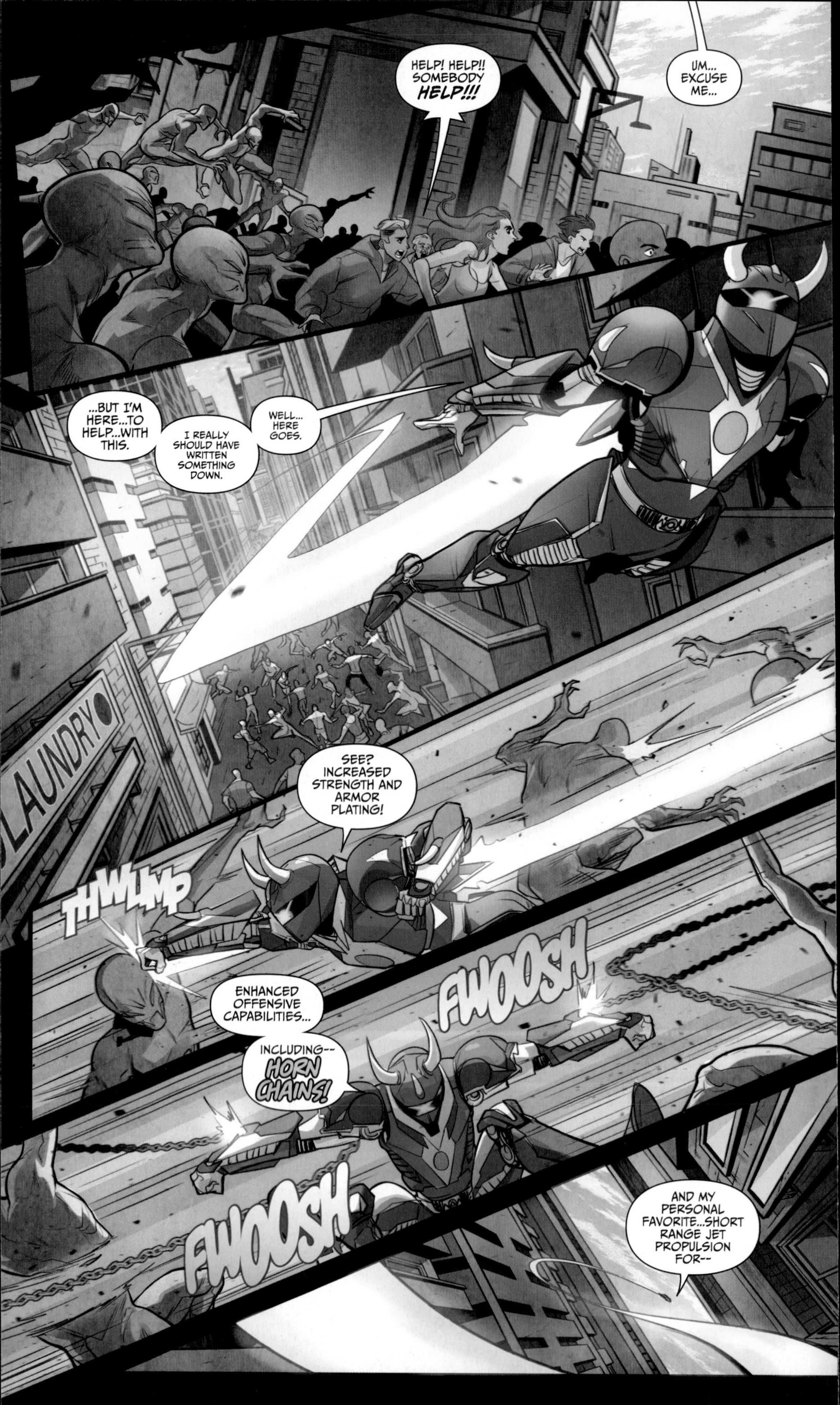

HELP! HELP!! SOMEBODY HELP!!!
UM... EXCUSE ME...
...BUT I'M HERE...TO HELP...WITH THIS.
I REALLY SHOULD HAVE WRITTEN SOMETHING DOWN.
WELL... HERE GOES.
LAUNDRY
SEE? INCREASED STRENGTH AND ARMOR PLATING!
THWUMP
FWOOSH
ENHANCED OFFENSIVE CAPABILITIES...
INCLUDING-- HORN CHAINS!
FWOOSH
AND MY PERSONAL FAVORITE...SHORT RANGE JET PROPULSION FOR--

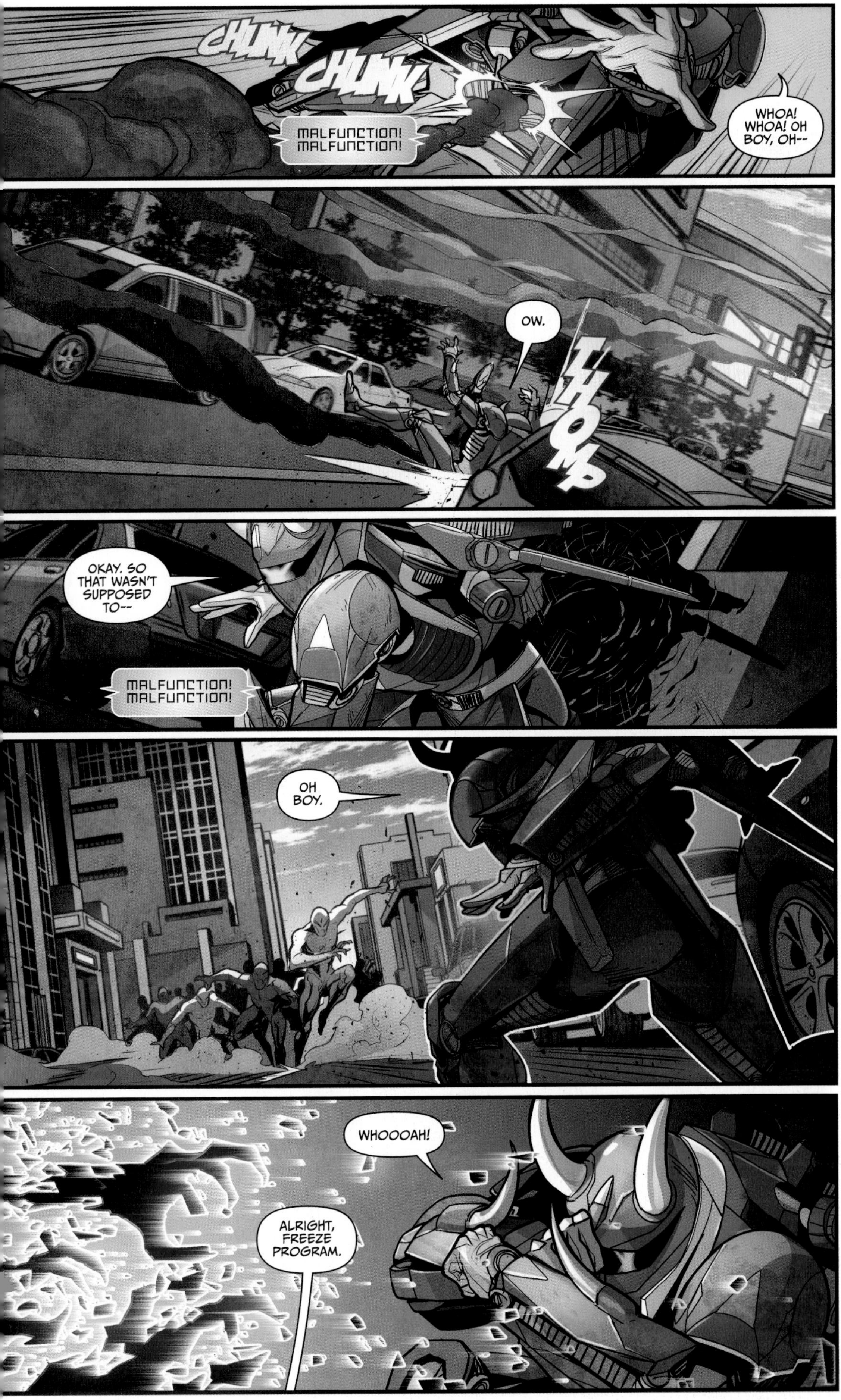
CHUNK
CHUNK
MALFUNCTION! MALFUNCTION!
WHOA! WHOA! OH BOY, OH--
OW.
THOMP
OKAY. SO THAT WASN'T SUPPOSED TO--
MALFUNCTION! MALFUNCTION!
OH BOY.
WHOOOAH!
ALRIGHT, FREEZE PROGRAM.

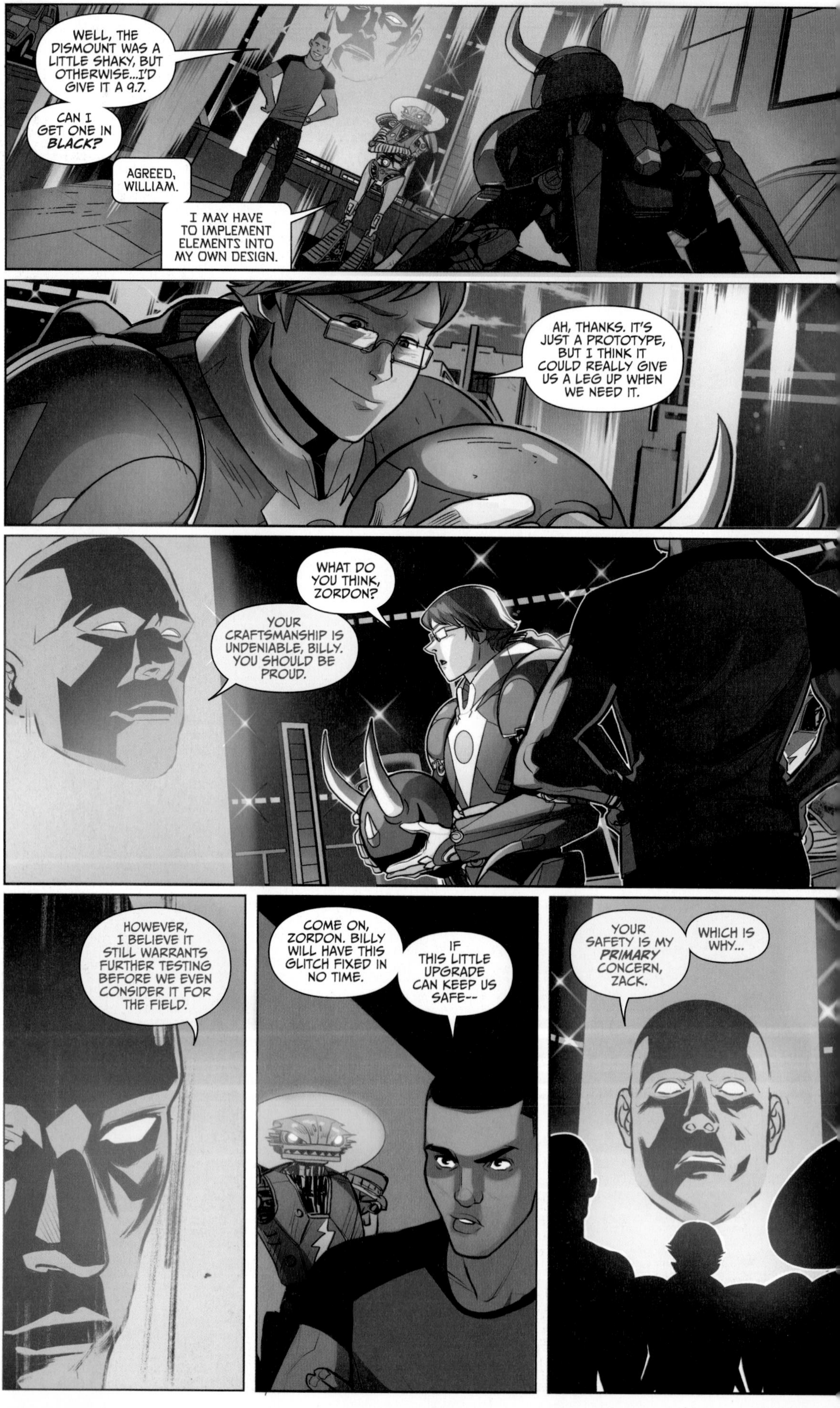

WELL, THE DISMOUNT WAS A LITTLE SHAKY, BUT OTHERWISE...I'D GIVE IT A 9.7.
CAN I GET ONE IN *BLACK?*
AGREED, WILLIAM.
I MAY HAVE TO IMPLEMENT ELEMENTS INTO MY OWN DESIGN.
AH, THANKS. IT'S JUST A PROTOTYPE, BUT I THINK IT COULD REALLY GIVE US A LEG UP WHEN WE NEED IT.
WHAT DO YOU THINK, ZORDON?
YOUR CRAFTSMANSHIP IS UNDENIABLE, BILLY. YOU SHOULD BE PROUD.
HOWEVER, I BELIEVE IT STILL WARRANTS FURTHER TESTING BEFORE WE EVEN CONSIDER IT FOR THE FIELD.
COME ON, ZORDON. BILLY WILL HAVE THIS GLITCH FIXED IN NO TIME.
IF THIS LITTLE UPGRADE CAN KEEP US SAFE--
YOUR SAFETY IS MY *PRIMARY* CONCERN, ZACK.
WHICH IS WHY...

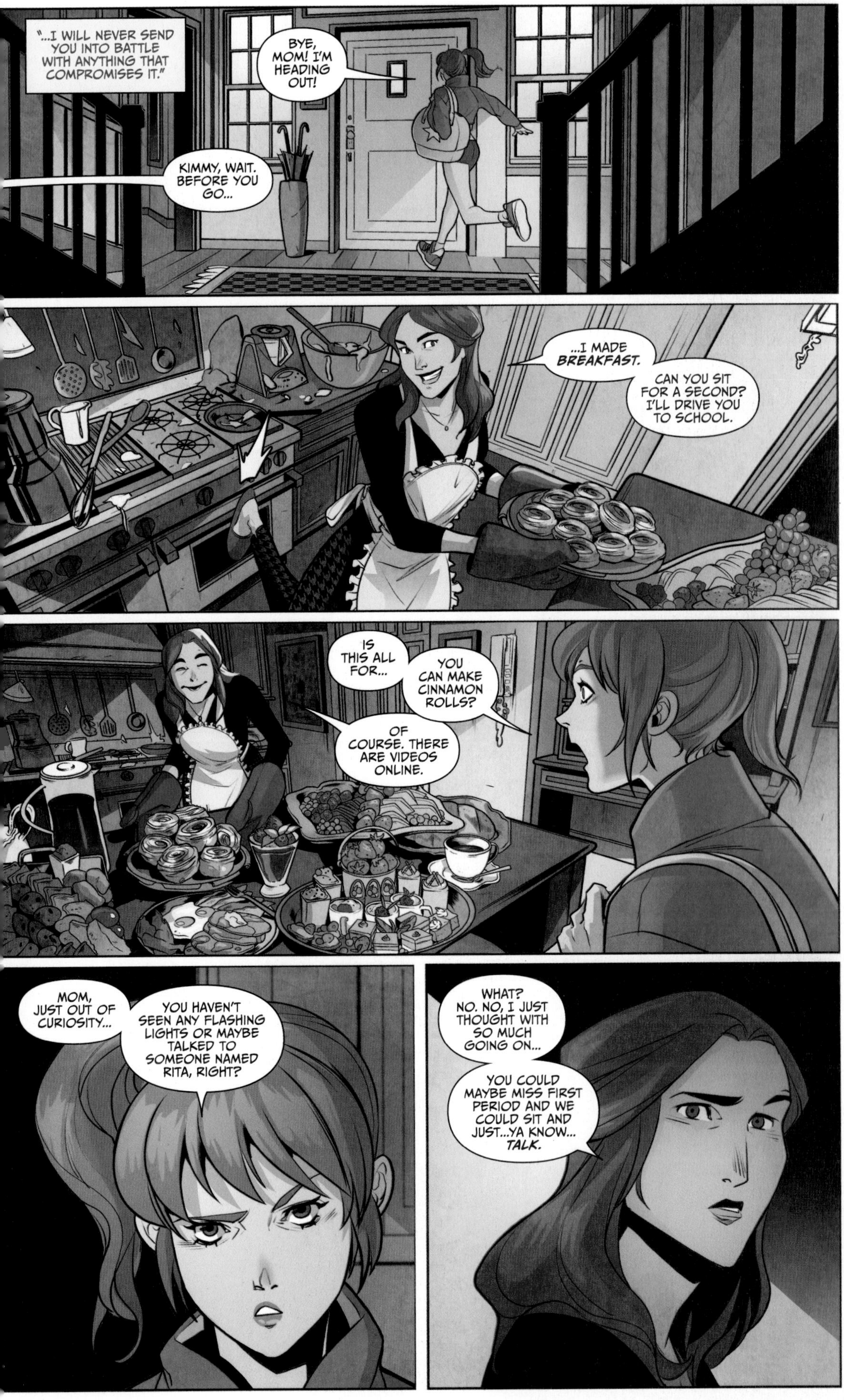
"...I WILL NEVER SEND YOU INTO BATTLE WITH ANYTHING THAT COMPROMISES IT."
BYE, MOM! I'M HEADING OUT!
KIMMY, WAIT. BEFORE YOU GO...
...I MADE BREAKFAST.
CAN YOU SIT FOR A SECOND? I'LL DRIVE YOU TO SCHOOL.
IS THIS ALL FOR...
YOU CAN MAKE CINNAMON ROLLS?
OF COURSE. THERE ARE VIDEOS ONLINE.
MOM, JUST OUT OF CURIOSITY...
YOU HAVEN'T SEEN ANY FLASHING LIGHTS OR MAYBE TALKED TO SOMEONE NAMED RITA, RIGHT?
WHAT? NO. NO, I JUST THOUGHT WITH SO MUCH GOING ON...
YOU COULD MAYBE MISS FIRST PERIOD AND WE COULD SIT AND JUST...YA KNOW... TALK.

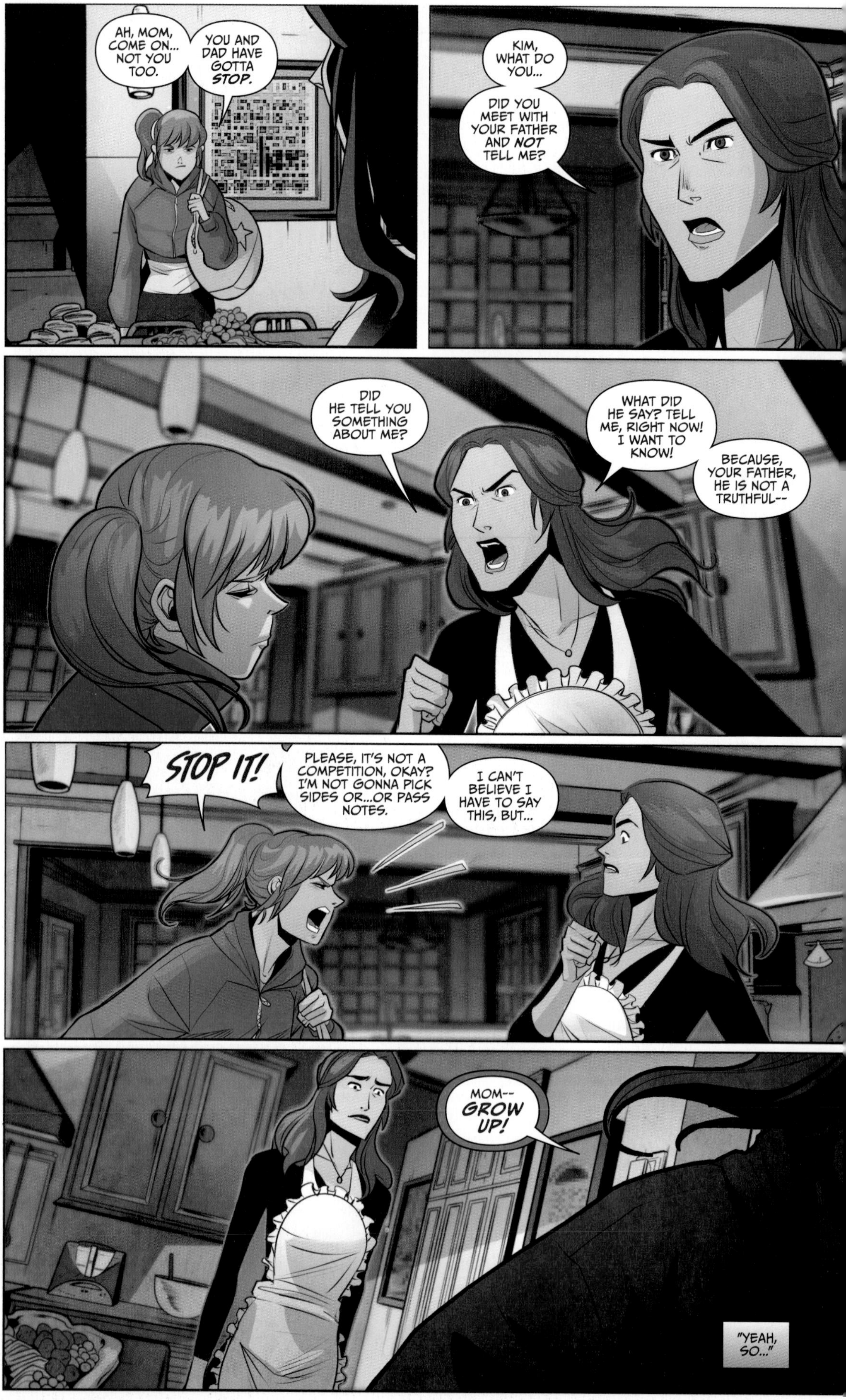
AH, MOM, COME ON... NOT YOU TOO.
YOU AND DAD HAVE GOTTA STOP.
KIM, WHAT DO YOU...
DID YOU MEET WITH YOUR FATHER AND NOT TELL ME?
DID HE TELL YOU SOMETHING ABOUT ME?
WHAT DID HE SAY? TELL ME, RIGHT NOW! I WANT TO KNOW!
BECAUSE, YOUR FATHER, HE IS NOT A TRUTHFUL--
STOP IT!
PLEASE, IT'S NOT A COMPETITION, OKAY? I'M NOT GONNA PICK SIDES OR...OR PASS NOTES.
I CAN'T BELIEVE I HAVE TO SAY THIS, BUT...
MOM-- GROW UP!
"YEAH, SO..."

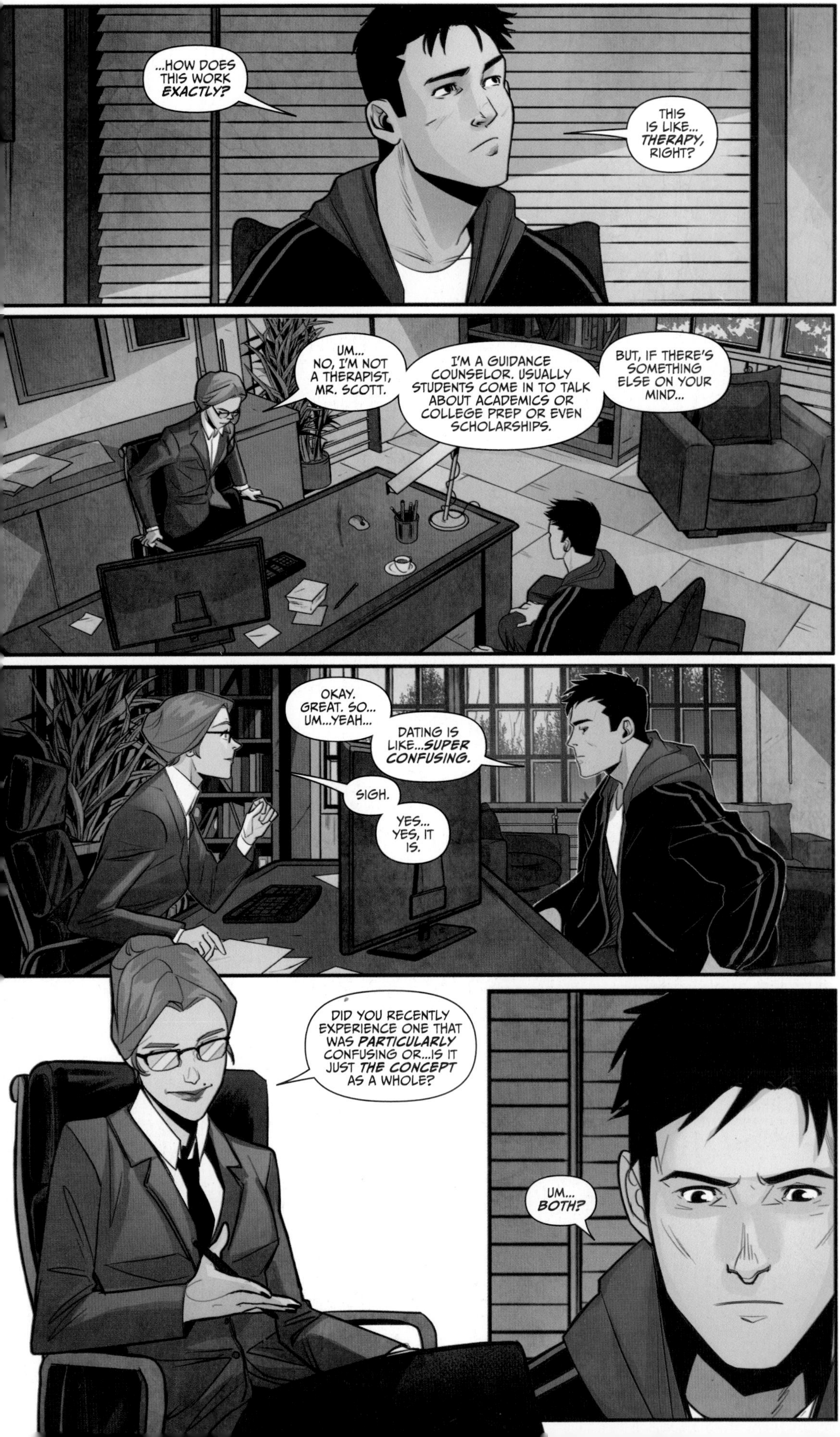
...HOW DOES THIS WORK EXACTLY?
THIS IS LIKE... THERAPY, RIGHT?
UM... NO, I'M NOT A THERAPIST, MR. SCOTT.
I'M A GUIDANCE COUNSELOR. USUALLY STUDENTS COME IN TO TALK ABOUT ACADEMICS OR COLLEGE PREP OR EVEN SCHOLARSHIPS.
BUT, IF THERE'S SOMETHING ELSE ON YOUR MIND...
OKAY. GREAT. SO... UM...YEAH...
DATING IS LIKE...SUPER CONFUSING.
SIGH.
YES... YES, IT IS.
DID YOU RECENTLY EXPERIENCE ONE THAT WAS PARTICULARLY CONFUSING OR...IS IT JUST THE CONCEPT AS A WHOLE?
UM... BOTH?

I MEAN, WE JUST STARTED... WHATEVER... SEEING EACH OTHER, I GUESS?

AND IT'S BEEN GOOD. SHE'S FUNNY AND SMART AND EXCITING...BUT, YOU KNOW *CALMING* TOO--

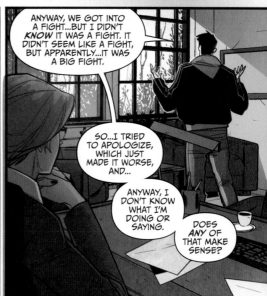

ANYWAY, WE GOT INTO A FIGHT...BUT I DIDN'T *KNOW* IT WAS A FIGHT. IT DIDN'T SEEM LIKE A FIGHT, BUT APPARENTLY...IT WAS A BIG FIGHT.

SO...I TRIED TO APOLOGIZE, WHICH JUST MADE IT WORSE, AND...

ANYWAY, I DON'T KNOW WHAT I'M DOING OR SAYING.

DOES *ANY* OF THAT MAKE SENSE?

BEGINNING A RELATIONSHIP IS DIFFICULT, JASON. ESPECIALLY AT YOUR AGE.

AS A COUNSELOR, I'D ADVISE AGAINST THEM UNTIL YOUR MID-TWENTIES...BUT, I REALIZE YOU'RE A TEENAGER, SO...

I'M GONNA TAKE A SHOT IN THE DARK AND SAY--SHE BELIEVES YOU DID SOMETHING WRONG, CORRECT?

SHE DOES... BUT, *DID I?*

IF YOU CARE ABOUT HER, IT DOESN'T *REALLY* MATTER.

YOU HAVE TO BE OPEN, HONEST, AND MOST IMPORTANTLY...

...JUST *TRY* TO FIX IT.

SOMETIMES THAT'S ENOUGH.

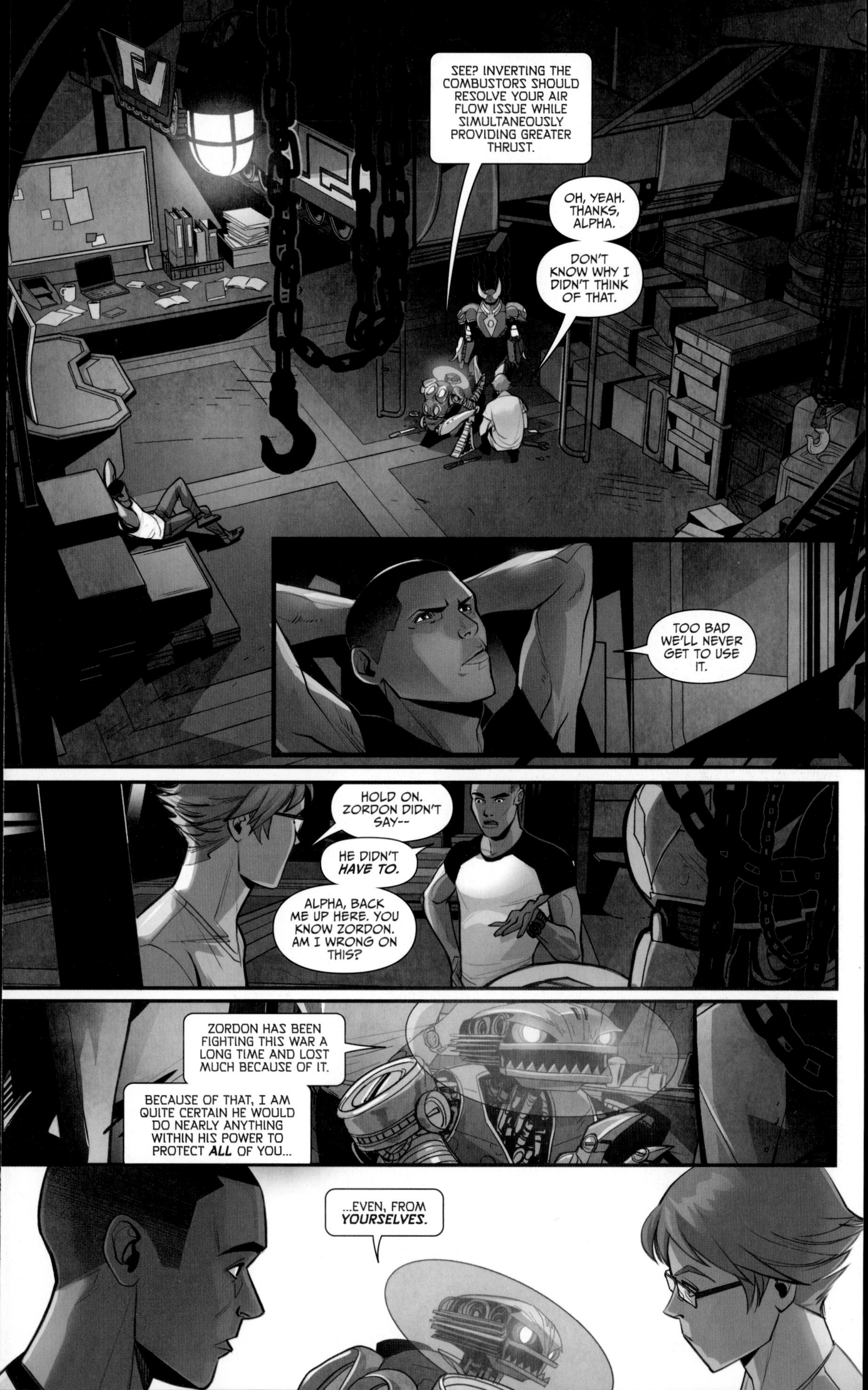
SEE? INVERTING THE COMBUSTORS SHOULD RESOLVE YOUR AIR FLOW ISSUE WHILE SIMULTANEOUSLY PROVIDING GREATER THRUST.
OH, YEAH. THANKS, ALPHA.
DON'T KNOW WHY I DIDN'T THINK OF THAT.
TOO BAD WE'LL NEVER GET TO USE IT.
HOLD ON. ZORDON DIDN'T SAY--
HE DIDN'T *HAVE TO.*
ALPHA, BACK ME UP HERE. YOU KNOW ZORDON. AM I WRONG ON THIS?
ZORDON HAS BEEN FIGHTING THIS WAR A LONG TIME AND LOST MUCH BECAUSE OF IT.
BECAUSE OF THAT, I AM QUITE CERTAIN HE WOULD DO NEARLY ANYTHING WITHIN HIS POWER TO PROTECT *ALL* OF YOU...
...EVEN, FROM *YOURSELVES.*

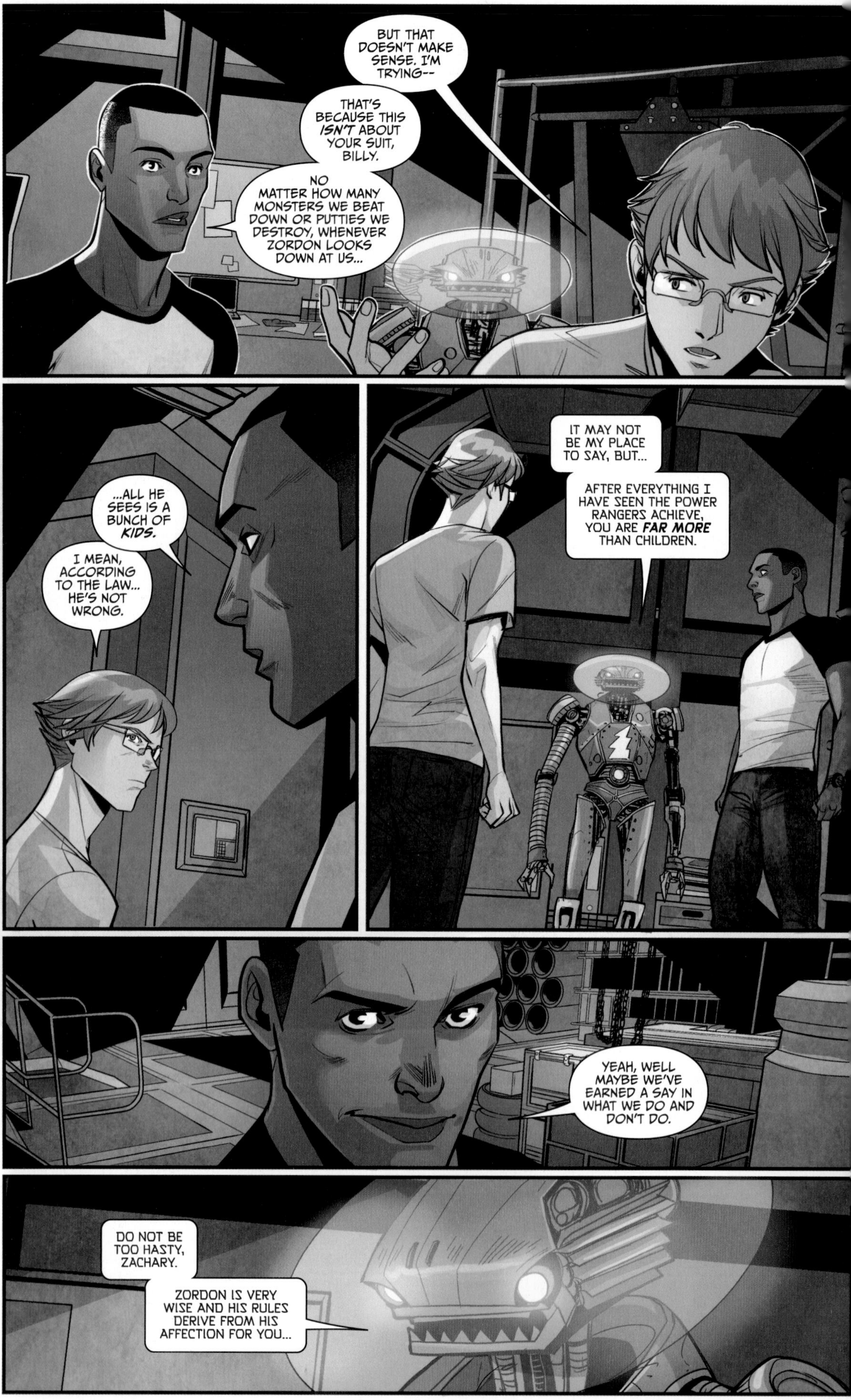
BUT THAT DOESN'T MAKE SENSE. I'M TRYING--
THAT'S BECAUSE THIS *ISN'T* ABOUT YOUR SUIT, BILLY.
NO MATTER HOW MANY MONSTERS WE BEAT DOWN OR PUTTIES WE DESTROY, WHENEVER ZORDON LOOKS DOWN AT US...
...ALL HE SEES IS A BUNCH OF *KIDS.*
I MEAN, ACCORDING TO THE LAW... HE'S NOT WRONG.
IT MAY NOT BE MY PLACE TO SAY, BUT...
AFTER EVERYTHING I HAVE SEEN THE POWER RANGERS ACHIEVE, YOU ARE ***FAR MORE*** THAN CHILDREN.
YEAH, WELL MAYBE WE'VE EARNED A SAY IN WHAT WE DO AND DON'T DO.
DO NOT BE TOO HASTY, ZACHARY.
ZORDON IS VERY WISE AND HIS RULES DERIVE FROM HIS AFFECTION FOR YOU...

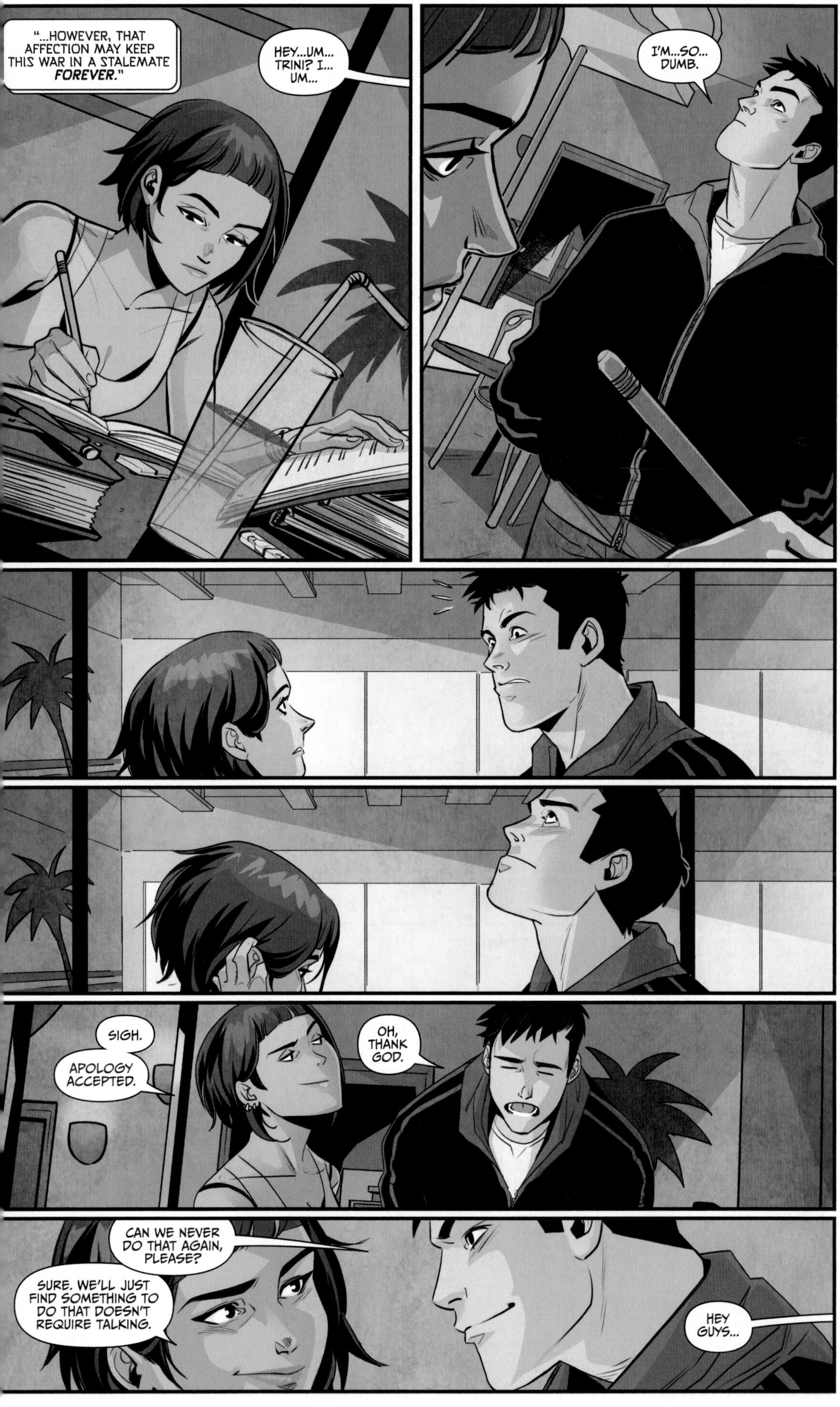
"...HOWEVER, THAT AFFECTION MAY KEEP THIS WAR IN A STALEMATE **FOREVER**."
HEY...UM... TRINI? I... UM...
I'M...SO... DUMB.
SIGH.
APOLOGY ACCEPTED.
OH, THANK GOD.
CAN WE NEVER DO THAT AGAIN, PLEASE?
SURE. WE'LL JUST FIND SOMETHING TO DO THAT DOESN'T REQUIRE TALKING.
HEY GUYS...

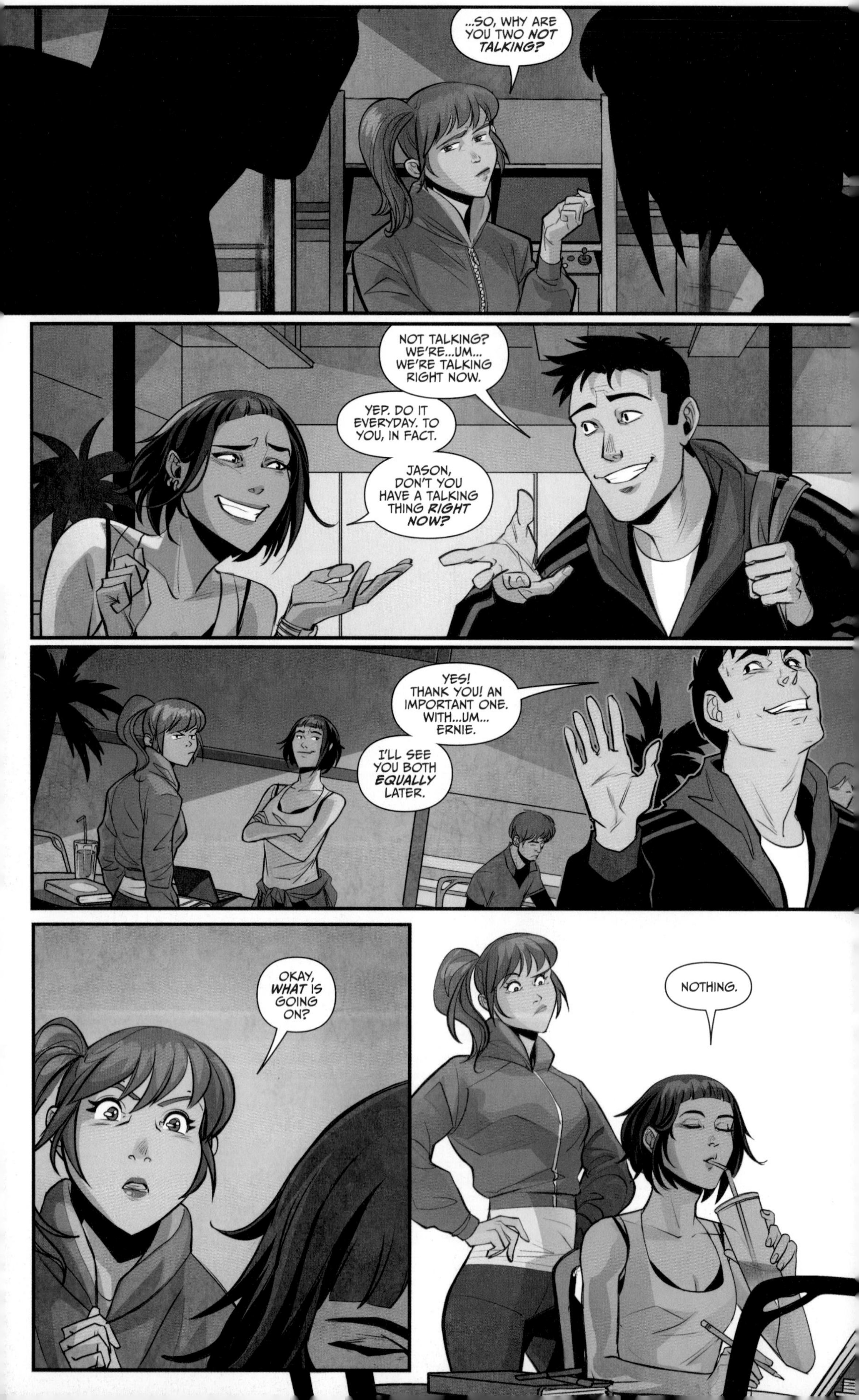
...SO, WHY ARE YOU TWO *NOT TALKING?*
NOT TALKING? WE'RE...UM... WE'RE TALKING RIGHT NOW.
YEP. DO IT EVERYDAY. TO YOU, IN FACT.
JASON, DON'T YOU HAVE A TALKING THING ***RIGHT NOW?***
YES! THANK YOU! AN IMPORTANT ONE. WITH...UM... ERNIE.
I'LL SEE YOU BOTH ***EQUALLY*** LATER.
OKAY, ***WHAT*** IS GOING ON?
NOTHING.

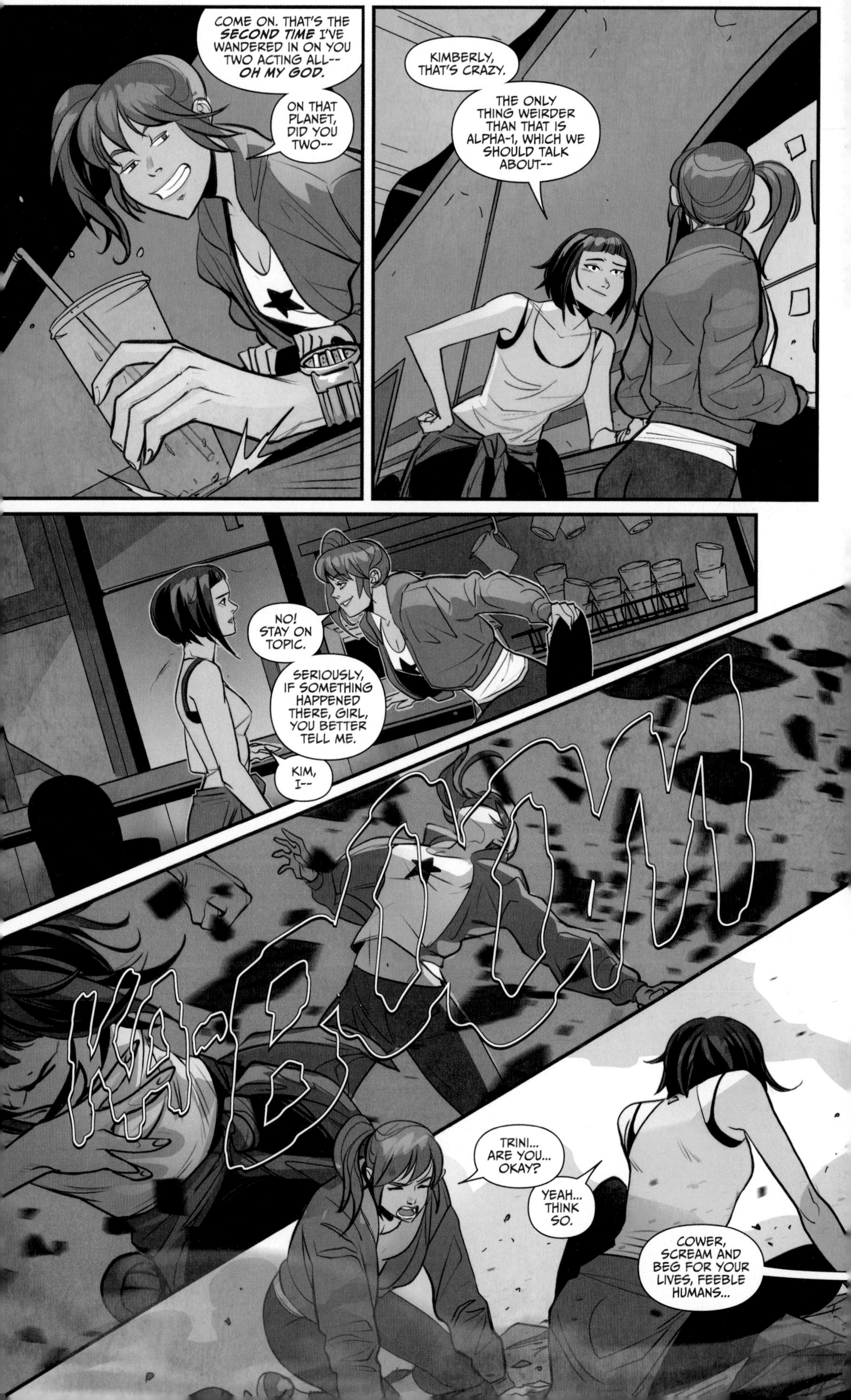
COME ON. THAT'S THE SECOND TIME I'VE WANDERED IN ON YOU TWO ACTING ALL-- OH MY GOD.
ON THAT PLANET, DID YOU TWO--
KIMBERLY, THAT'S CRAZY.
THE ONLY THING WEIRDER THAN THAT IS ALPHA-1, WHICH WE SHOULD TALK ABOUT--
NO! STAY ON TOPIC.
SERIOUSLY, IF SOMETHING HAPPENED THERE, GIRL, YOU BETTER TELL ME.
KIM, I--
KA-BOOM
TRINI... ARE YOU... OKAY?
YEAH... THINK SO.
COWER, SCREAM AND BEG FOR YOUR LIVES, FEEBLE HUMANS...

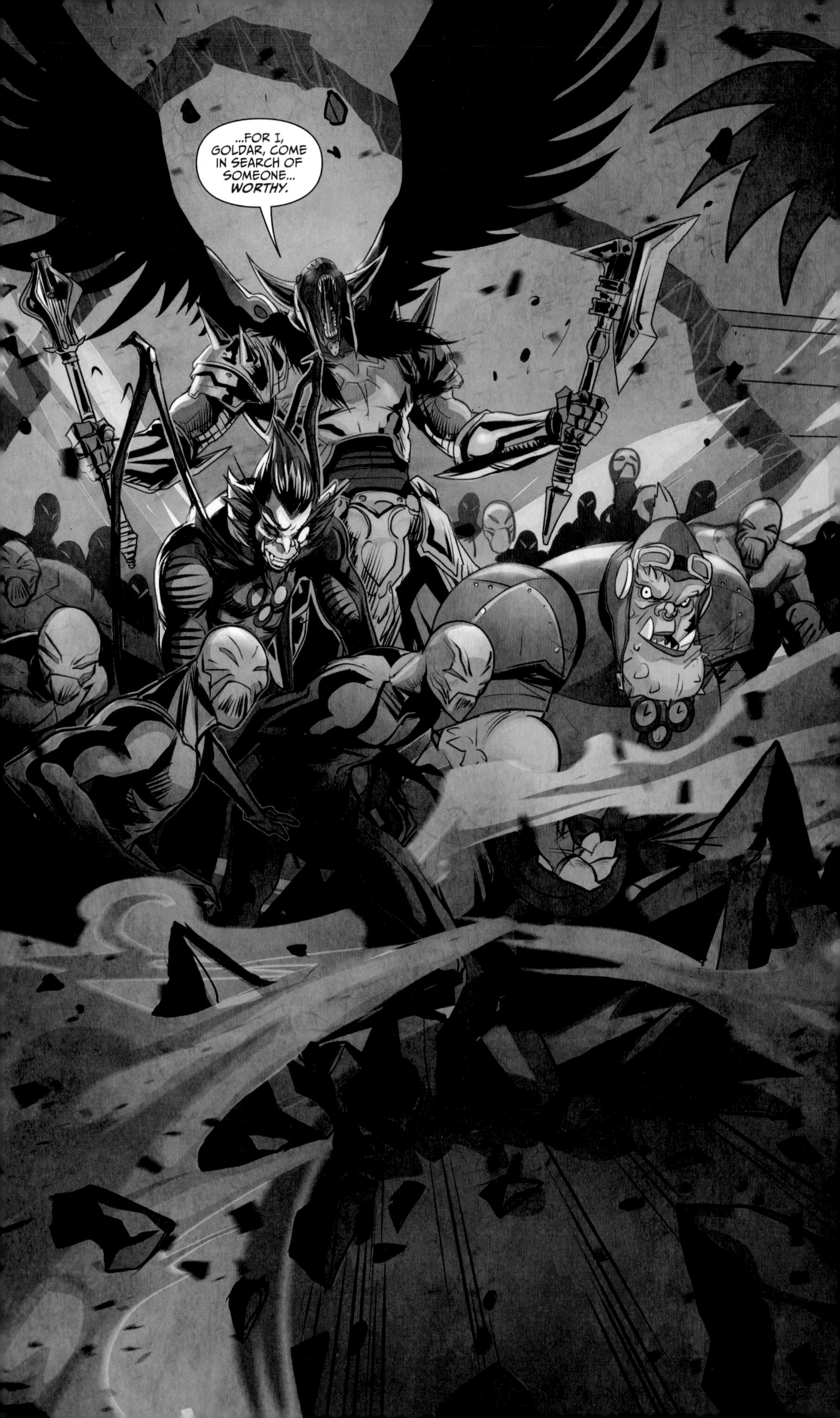
...FOR I, GOLDAR, COME IN SEARCH OF SOMEONE... *WORTHY.*

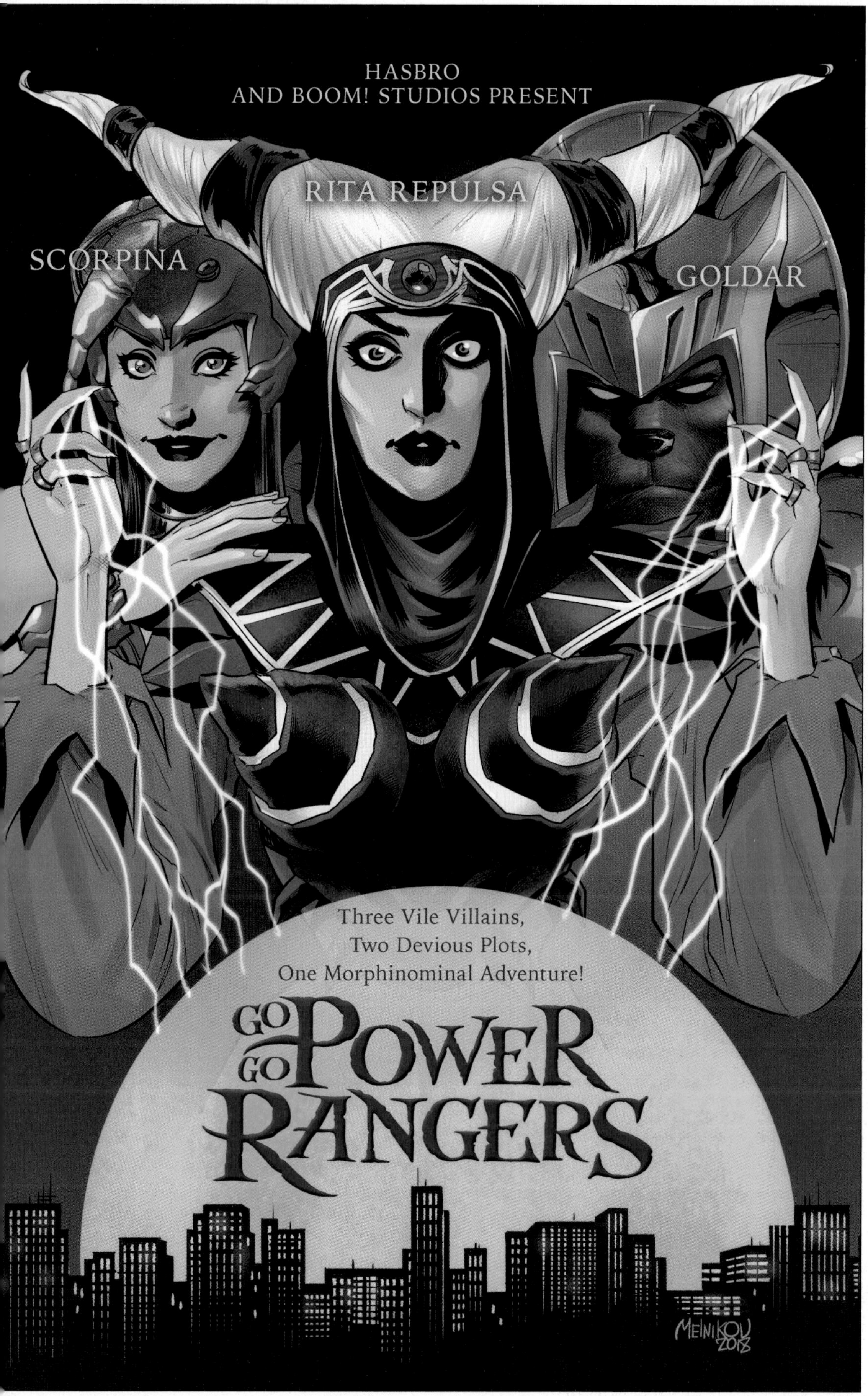

GLEB MELNIKOV WITH DESIGN BY **DYLAN TODD** ISSUE NINETEEN MOVIE HOMAGE VARIANT

TWENTY

MARCUS TO WITH COLORS BY **RAÚL ANGULO** | ISSUE TWENTY MAIN COVER

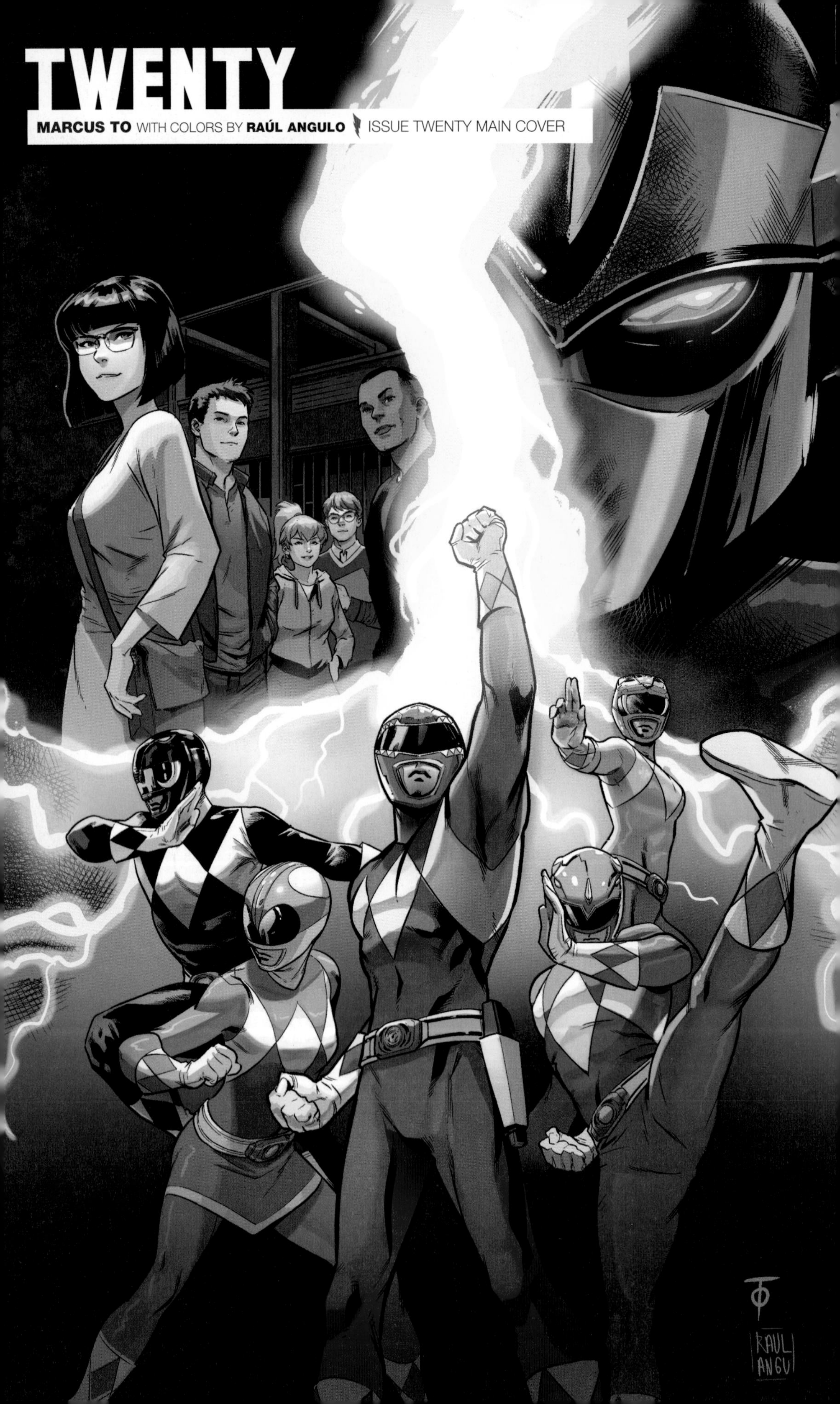
RAUL
ANGU

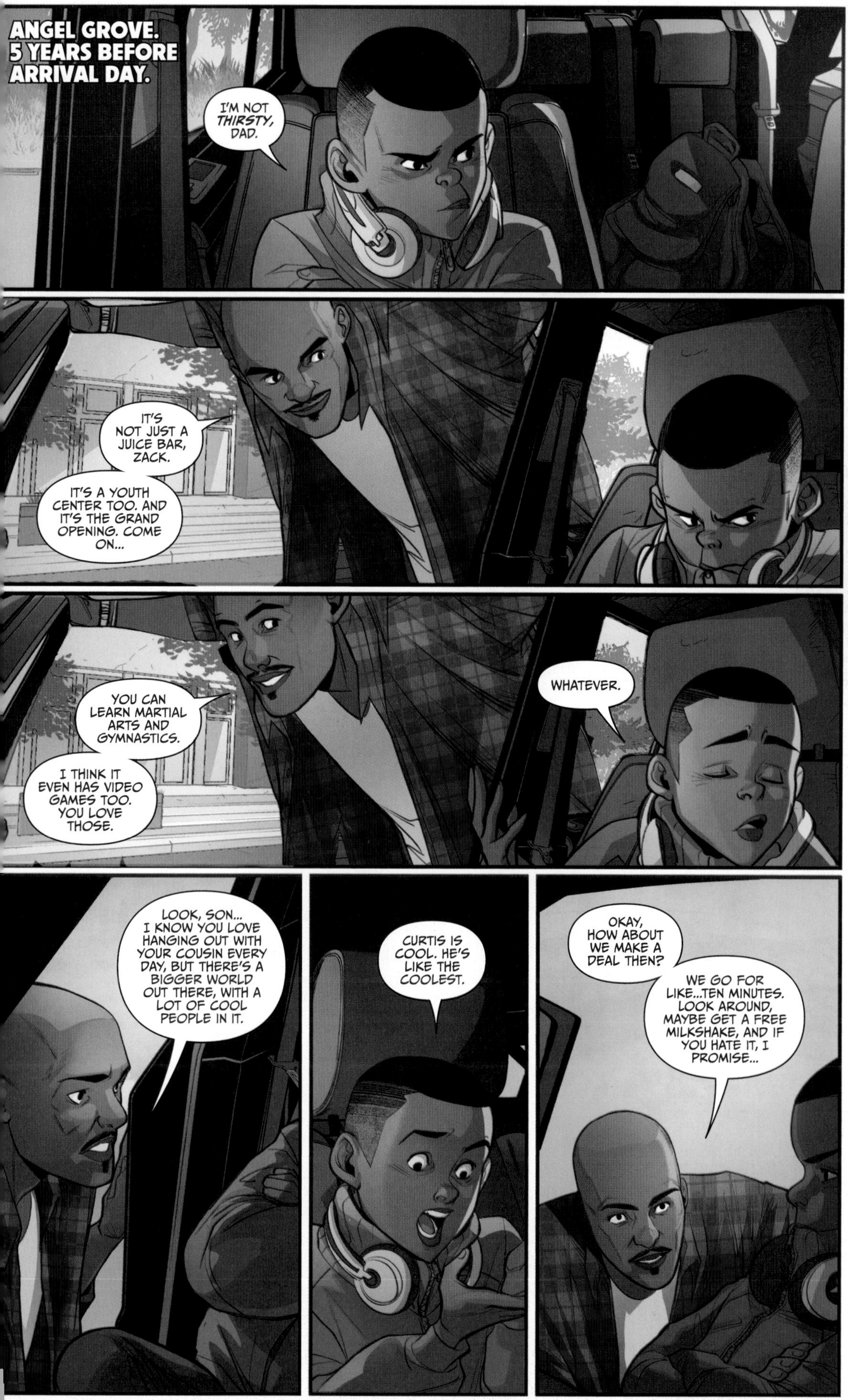
ANGEL GROVE.
5 YEARS BEFORE ARRIVAL DAY.
I'M NOT *THIRSTY,* DAD.
IT'S NOT JUST A JUICE BAR, ZACK.
IT'S A YOUTH CENTER TOO. AND IT'S THE GRAND OPENING. COME ON...
YOU CAN LEARN MARTIAL ARTS AND GYMNASTICS.
I THINK IT EVEN HAS VIDEO GAMES TOO. YOU LOVE THOSE.
WHATEVER.
LOOK, SON... I KNOW YOU LOVE HANGING OUT WITH YOUR COUSIN EVERY DAY, BUT THERE'S A BIGGER WORLD OUT THERE, WITH A LOT OF COOL PEOPLE IN IT.
CURTIS IS COOL. HE'S LIKE THE COOLEST.
OKAY, HOW ABOUT WE MAKE A DEAL THEN?
WE GO FOR LIKE...TEN MINUTES. LOOK AROUND, MAYBE GET A FREE MILKSHAKE, AND IF YOU HATE IT, I PROMISE...

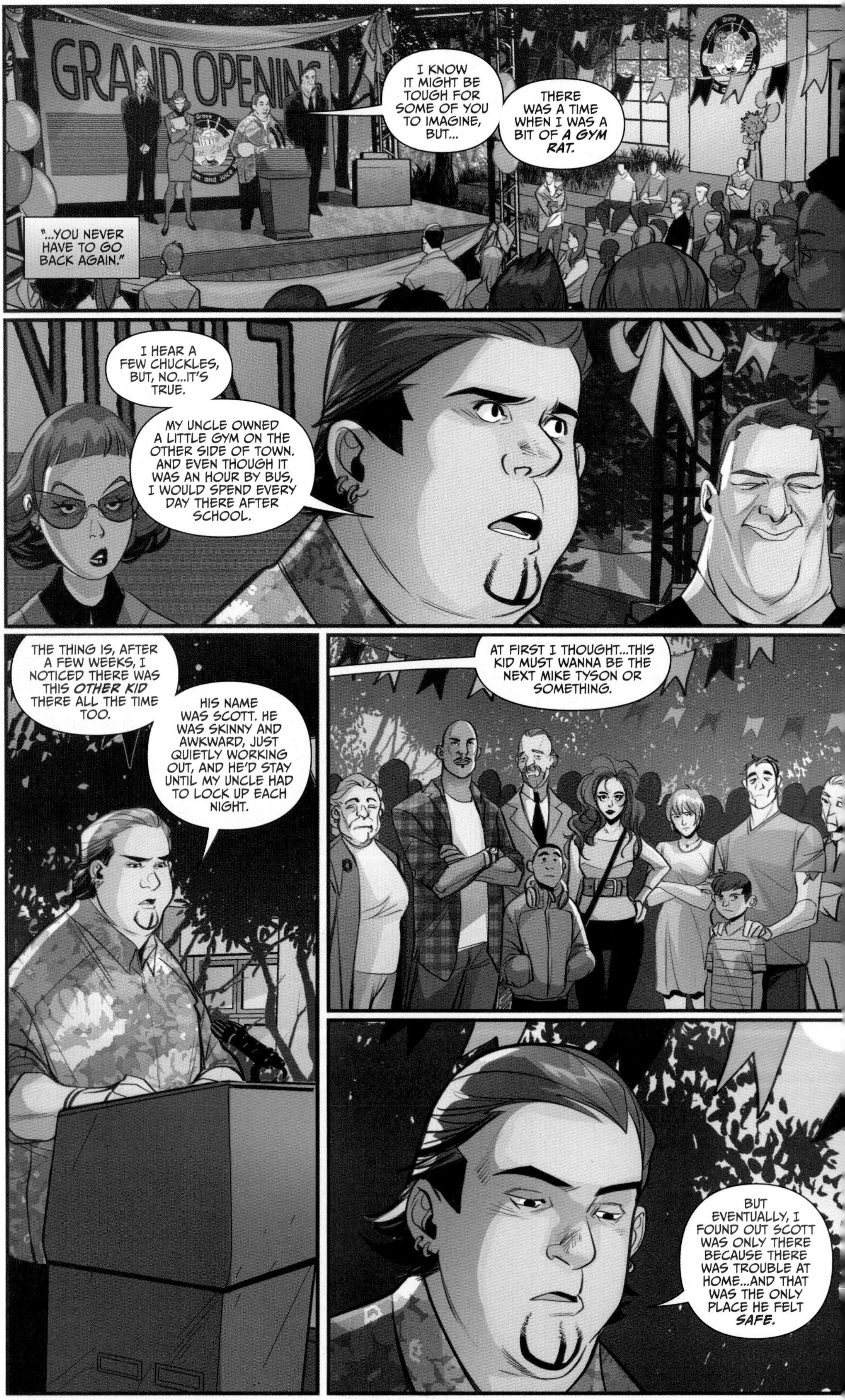
GRAND OPENING
"...YOU NEVER HAVE TO GO BACK AGAIN."
I KNOW IT MIGHT BE TOUGH FOR SOME OF YOU TO IMAGINE, BUT...
THERE WAS A TIME WHEN I WAS A BIT OF *A GYM RAT.*
I HEAR A FEW CHUCKLES, BUT, NO...IT'S TRUE.
MY UNCLE OWNED A LITTLE GYM ON THE OTHER SIDE OF TOWN. AND EVEN THOUGH IT WAS AN HOUR BY BUS, I WOULD SPEND EVERY DAY THERE AFTER SCHOOL.
THE THING IS, AFTER A FEW WEEKS, I NOTICED THERE WAS THIS *OTHER KID* THERE ALL THE TIME TOO.
HIS NAME WAS SCOTT. HE WAS SKINNY AND AWKWARD, JUST QUIETLY WORKING OUT, AND HE'D STAY UNTIL MY UNCLE HAD TO LOCK UP EACH NIGHT.
AT FIRST I THOUGHT...THIS KID MUST WANNA BE THE NEXT MIKE TYSON OR SOMETHING.
BUT EVENTUALLY, I FOUND OUT SCOTT WAS ONLY THERE BECAUSE THERE WAS TROUBLE AT HOME...AND THAT WAS THE ONLY PLACE HE FELT *SAFE.*

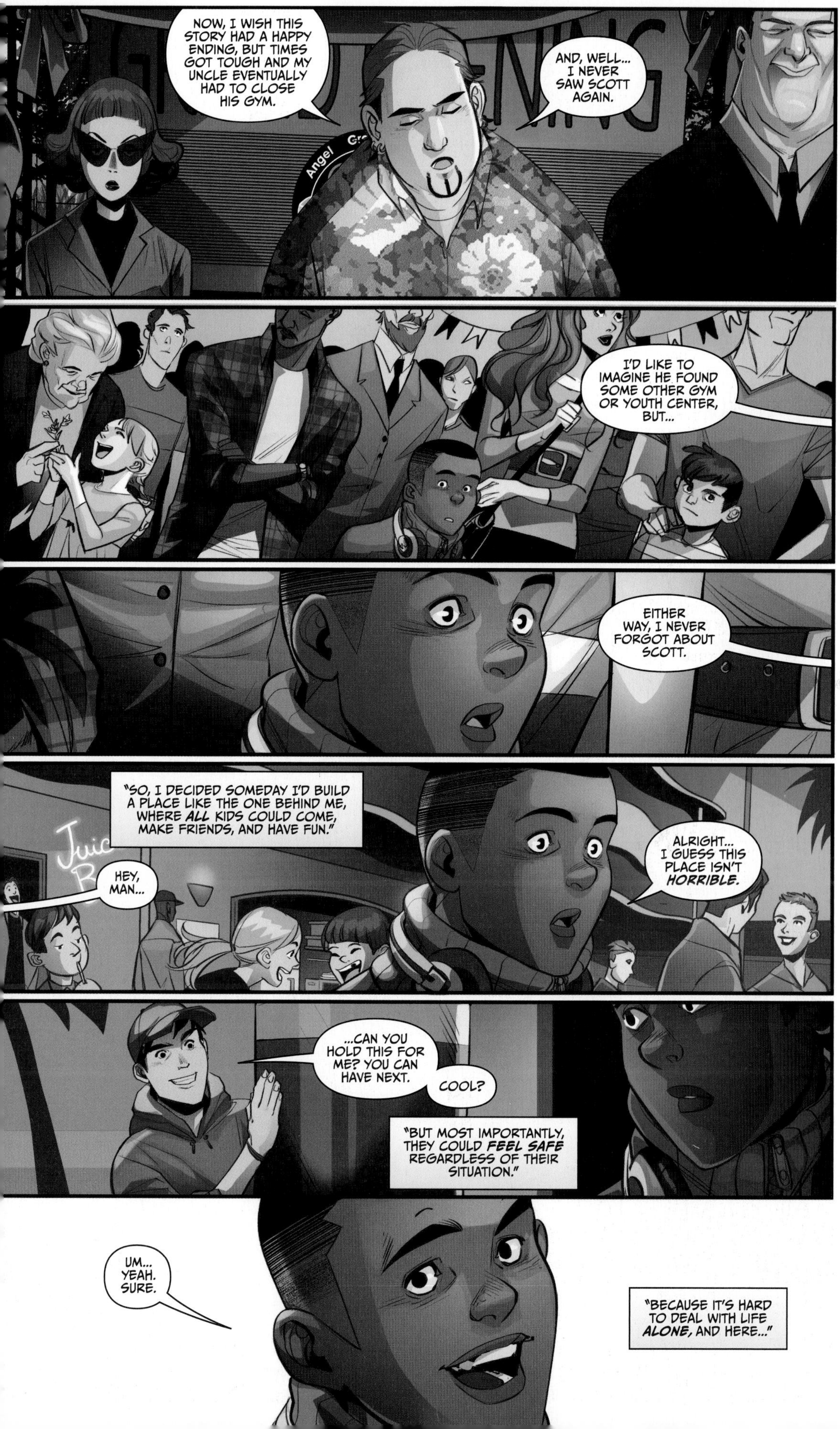
NOW, I WISH THIS STORY HAD A HAPPY ENDING, BUT TIMES GOT TOUGH AND MY UNCLE EVENTUALLY HAD TO CLOSE HIS GYM.
AND, WELL... I NEVER SAW SCOTT AGAIN.
I'D LIKE TO IMAGINE HE FOUND SOME OTHER GYM OR YOUTH CENTER, BUT...
EITHER WAY, I NEVER FORGOT ABOUT SCOTT.
"SO, I DECIDED SOMEDAY I'D BUILD A PLACE LIKE THE ONE BEHIND ME, WHERE *ALL* KIDS COULD COME, MAKE FRIENDS, AND HAVE FUN."
HEY, MAN...
ALRIGHT... I GUESS THIS PLACE ISN'T *HORRIBLE.*
...CAN YOU HOLD THIS FOR ME? YOU CAN HAVE NEXT.
COOL?
"BUT MOST IMPORTANTLY, THEY COULD *FEEL SAFE* REGARDLESS OF THEIR SITUATION."
UM... YEAH. SURE.
"BECAUSE IT'S HARD TO DEAL WITH LIFE *ALONE,* AND HERE..."

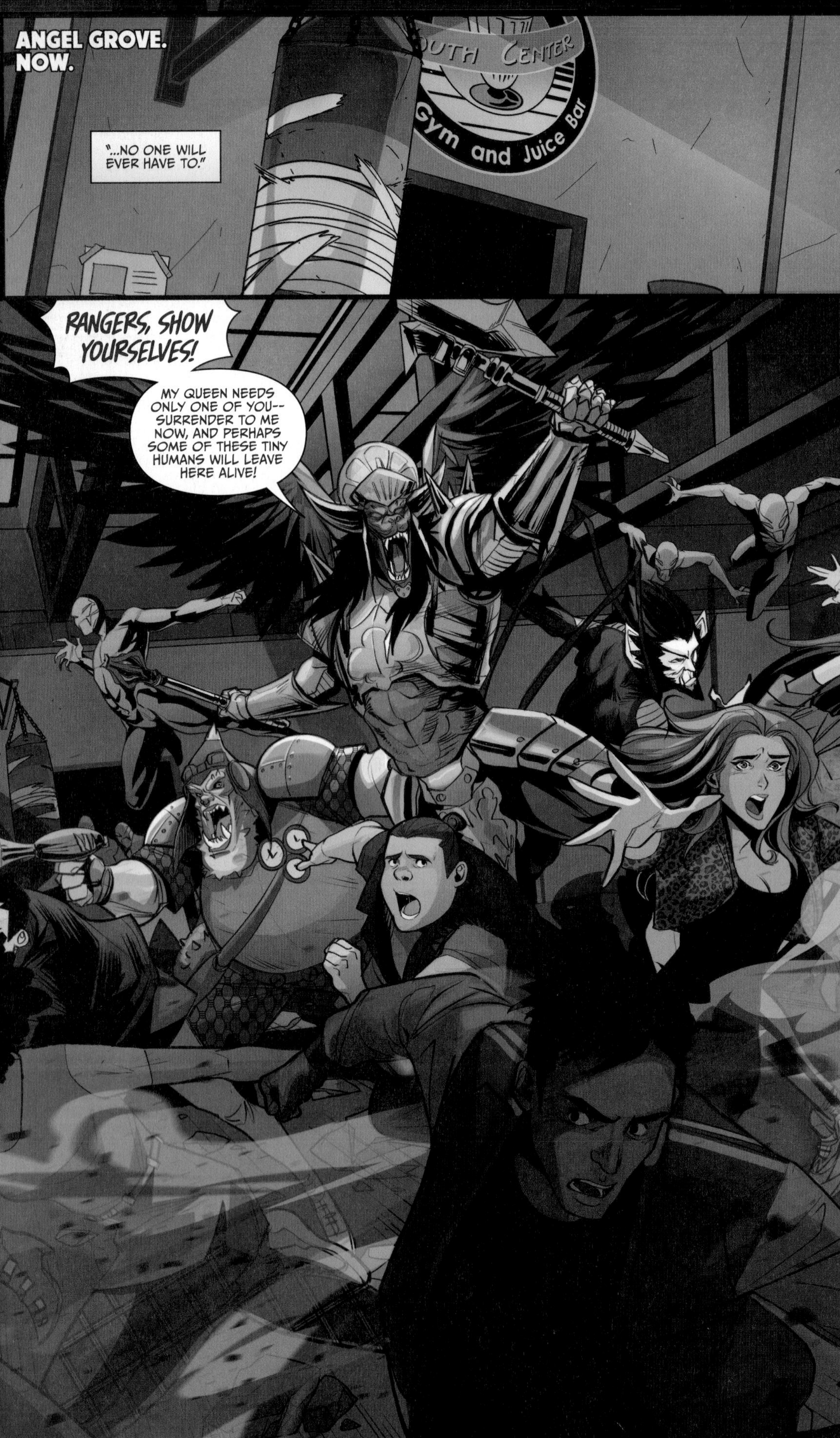

ANGEL GROVE.
NOW.
"...NO ONE WILL EVER HAVE TO."
Gym and Juice Bar
RANGERS, SHOW YOURSELVES!
MY QUEEN NEEDS ONLY ONE OF YOU-- SURRENDER TO ME NOW, AND PERHAPS SOME OF THESE TINY HUMANS WILL LEAVE HERE ALIVE!

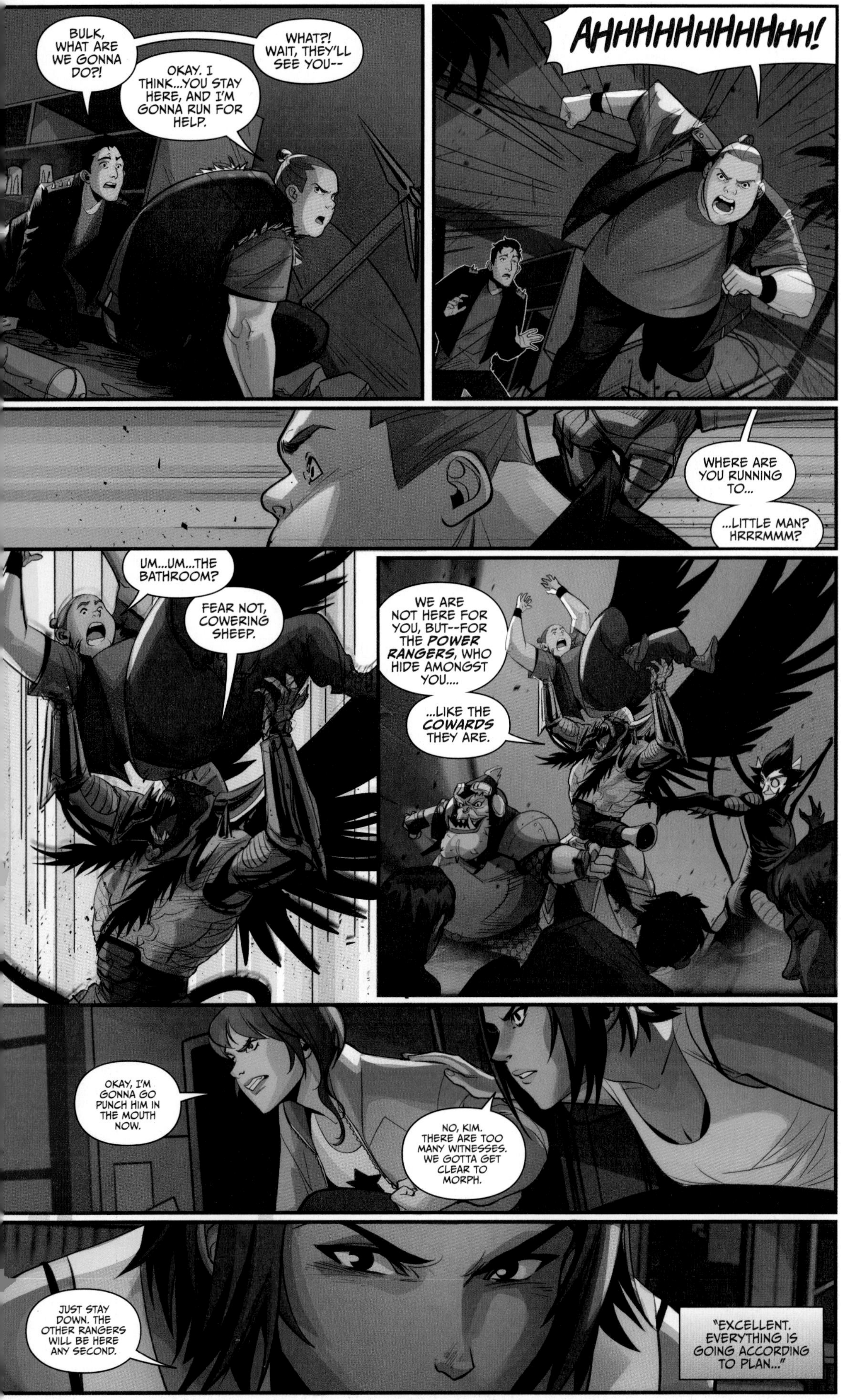
BULK, WHAT ARE WE GONNA DO?!
OKAY. I THINK...YOU STAY HERE, AND I'M GONNA RUN FOR HELP.
WHAT?! WAIT, THEY'LL SEE YOU--
AHHHHHHHHHHH!
WHERE ARE YOU RUNNING TO...
...LITTLE MAN? HRRRMMM?
UM...UM...THE BATHROOM?
FEAR NOT, COWERING SHEEP.
WE ARE NOT HERE FOR YOU, BUT--FOR THE POWER RANGERS, WHO HIDE AMONGST YOU....
...LIKE THE COWARDS THEY ARE.
OKAY, I'M GONNA GO PUNCH HIM IN THE MOUTH NOW.
NO, KIM. THERE ARE TOO MANY WITNESSES. WE GOTTA GET CLEAR TO MORPH.
JUST STAY DOWN. THE OTHER RANGERS WILL BE HERE ANY SECOND.
"EXCELLENT. EVERYTHING IS GOING ACCORDING TO PLAN..."

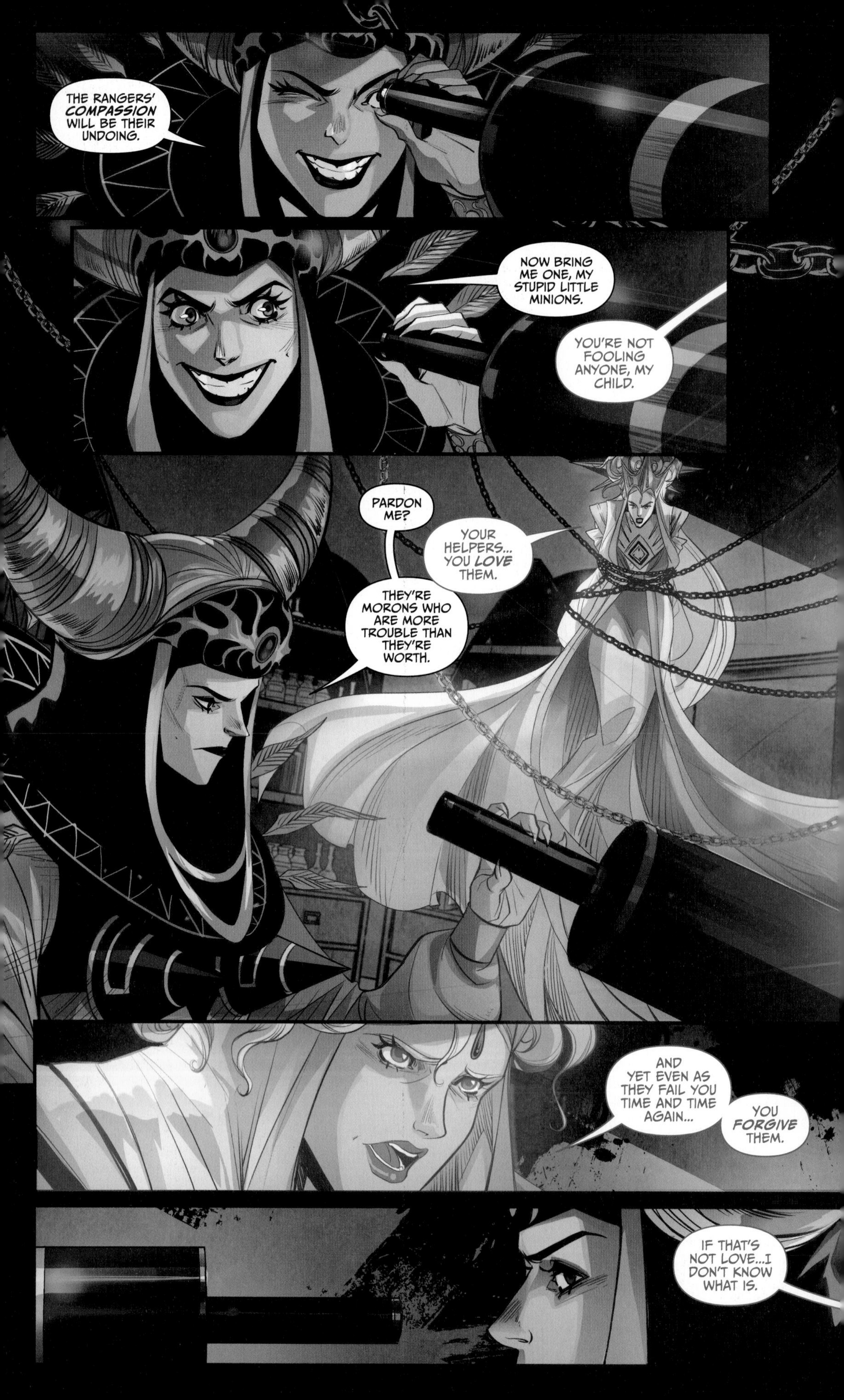
THE RANGERS' *COMPASSION* WILL BE THEIR UNDOING.
NOW BRING ME ONE, MY STUPID LITTLE MINIONS.
YOU'RE NOT FOOLING ANYONE, MY CHILD.
PARDON ME?
YOUR HELPERS... YOU *LOVE* THEM.
THEY'RE MORONS WHO ARE MORE TROUBLE THAN THEY'RE WORTH.
AND YET EVEN AS THEY FAIL YOU TIME AND TIME AGAIN...
YOU *FORGIVE* THEM.
IF THAT'S NOT LOVE...I DON'T KNOW WHAT IS.

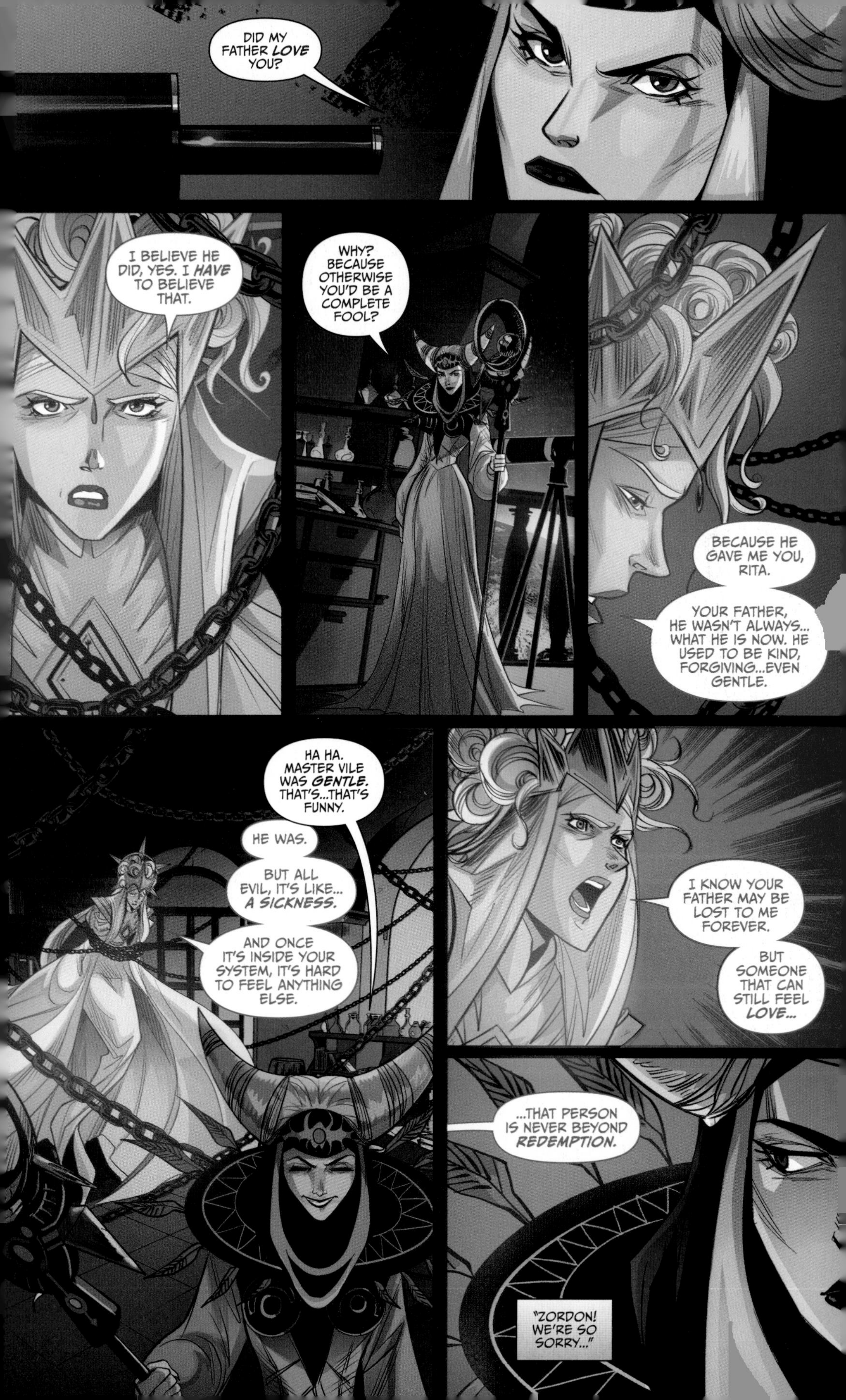
DID MY FATHER LOVE YOU?
I BELIEVE HE DID, YES. I HAVE TO BELIEVE THAT.
WHY? BECAUSE OTHERWISE YOU'D BE A COMPLETE FOOL?
BECAUSE HE GAVE ME YOU, RITA.
YOUR FATHER, HE WASN'T ALWAYS... WHAT HE IS NOW. HE USED TO BE KIND, FORGIVING...EVEN GENTLE.
HA HA. MASTER VILE WAS GENTLE. THAT'S...THAT'S FUNNY.
HE WAS.
BUT ALL EVIL, IT'S LIKE... A SICKNESS.
AND ONCE IT'S INSIDE YOUR SYSTEM, IT'S HARD TO FEEL ANYTHING ELSE.
I KNOW YOUR FATHER MAY BE LOST TO ME FOREVER.
BUT SOMEONE THAT CAN STILL FEEL LOVE...
...THAT PERSON IS NEVER BEYOND REDEMPTION.
"ZORDON! WE'RE SO SORRY..."

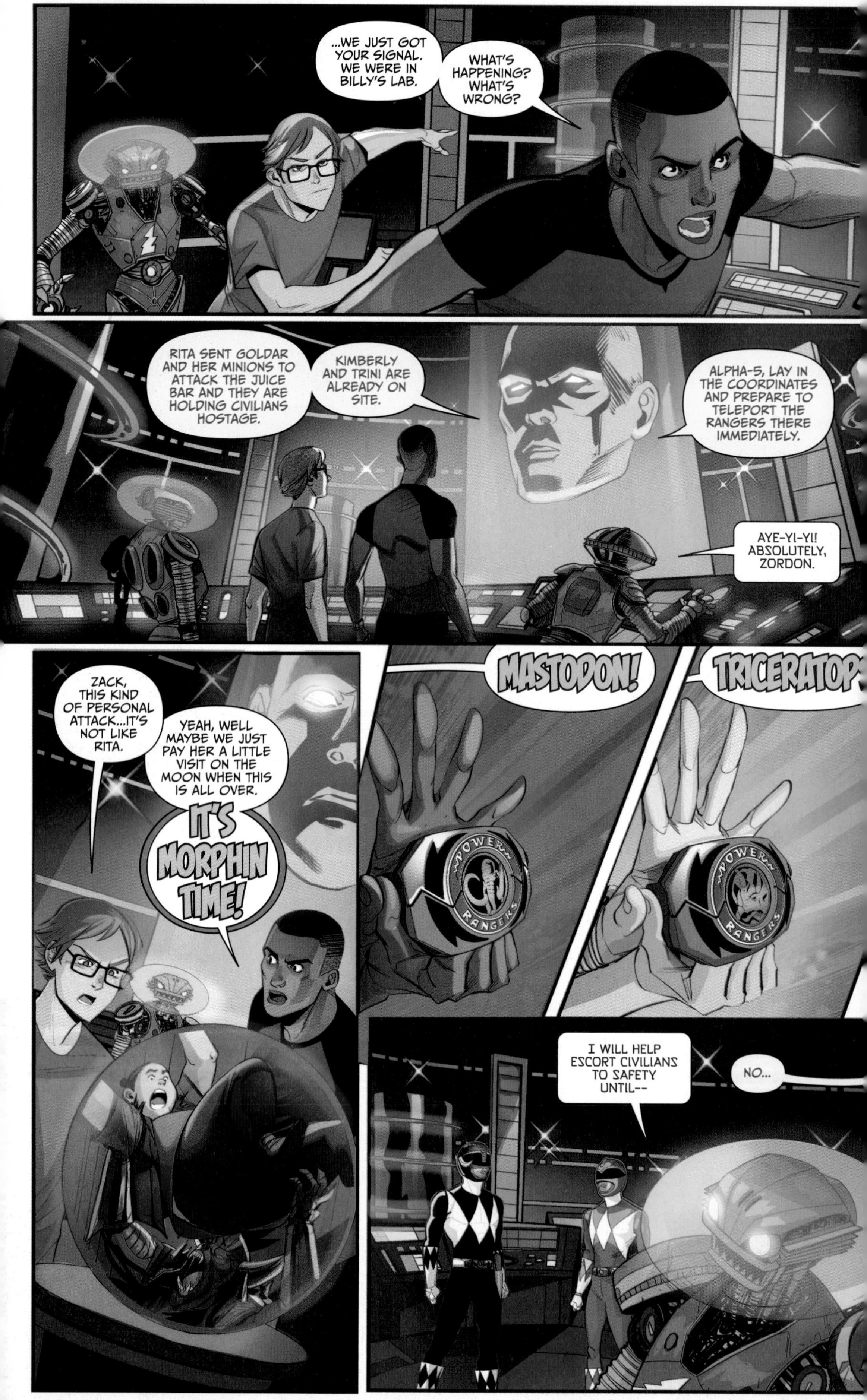
...WE JUST GOT YOUR SIGNAL. WE WERE IN BILLY'S LAB.
WHAT'S HAPPENING? WHAT'S WRONG?
RITA SENT GOLDAR AND HER MINIONS TO ATTACK THE JUICE BAR AND THEY ARE HOLDING CIVILIANS HOSTAGE.
KIMBERLY AND TRINI ARE ALREADY ON SITE.
ALPHA-5, LAY IN THE COORDINATES AND PREPARE TO TELEPORT THE RANGERS THERE IMMEDIATELY.
AYE-YI-YI! ABSOLUTELY, ZORDON.
ZACK, THIS KIND OF PERSONAL ATTACK...IT'S NOT LIKE RITA.
YEAH, WELL MAYBE WE JUST PAY HER A LITTLE VISIT ON THE MOON WHEN THIS IS ALL OVER.
IT'S MORPHIN TIME!
MASTODON!
POWER RANGERS
TRICERATOP
POWER RANGERS
I WILL HELP ESCORT CIVILIANS TO SAFETY UNTIL--
NO...

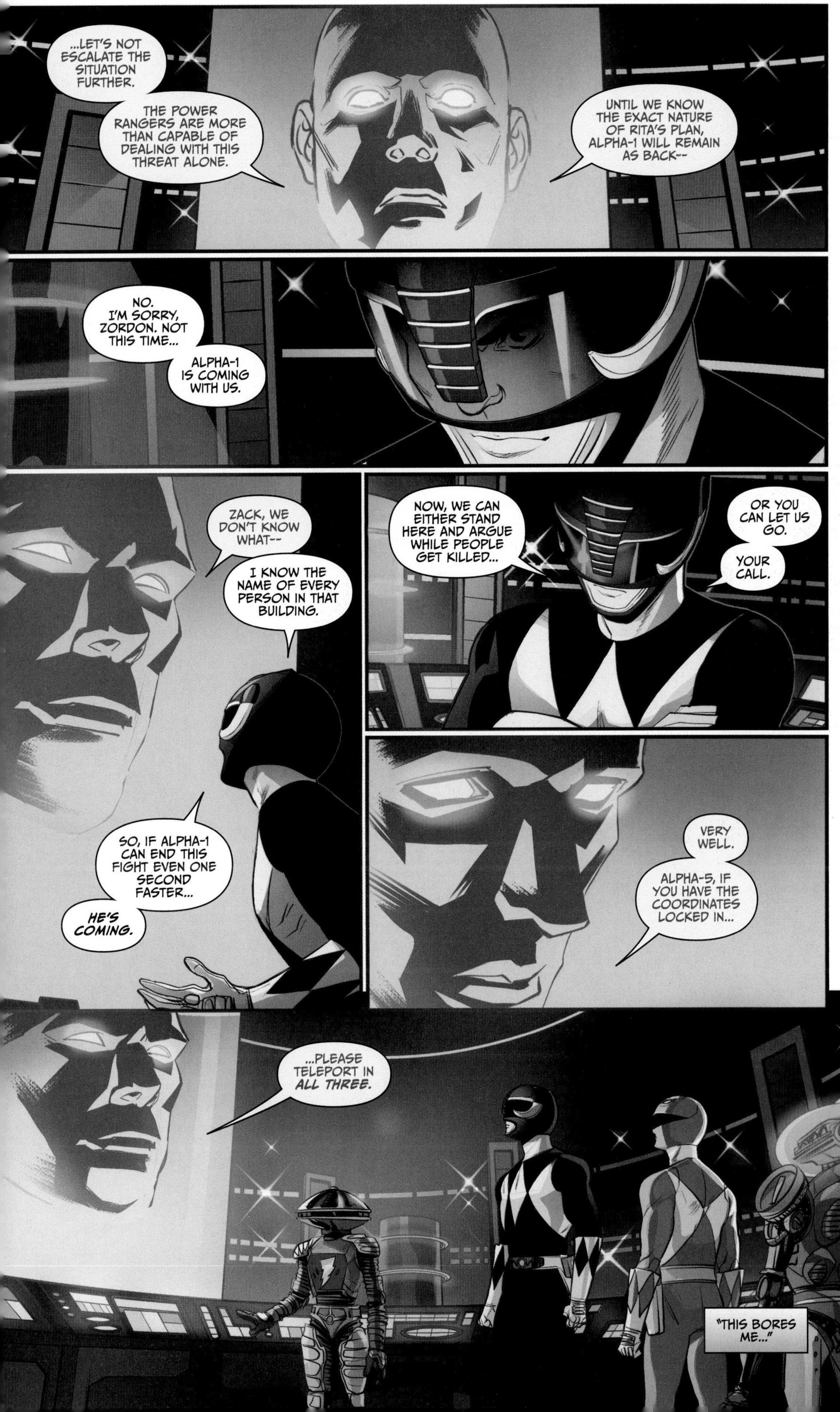

...LET'S NOT ESCALATE THE SITUATION FURTHER.
THE POWER RANGERS ARE MORE THAN CAPABLE OF DEALING WITH THIS THREAT ALONE.
UNTIL WE KNOW THE EXACT NATURE OF RITA'S PLAN, ALPHA-1 WILL REMAIN AS BACK--
NO. I'M SORRY, ZORDON. NOT THIS TIME...
ALPHA-1 IS COMING WITH US.
ZACK, WE DON'T KNOW WHAT--
I KNOW THE NAME OF EVERY PERSON IN THAT BUILDING.
SO, IF ALPHA-1 CAN END THIS FIGHT EVEN ONE SECOND FASTER...
HE'S COMING.
NOW, WE CAN EITHER STAND HERE AND ARGUE WHILE PEOPLE GET KILLED...
OR YOU CAN LET US GO.
YOUR CALL.
VERY WELL.
ALPHA-5, IF YOU HAVE THE COORDINATES LOCKED IN...
...PLEASE TELEPORT IN *ALL THREE.*
"THIS BORES ME..."

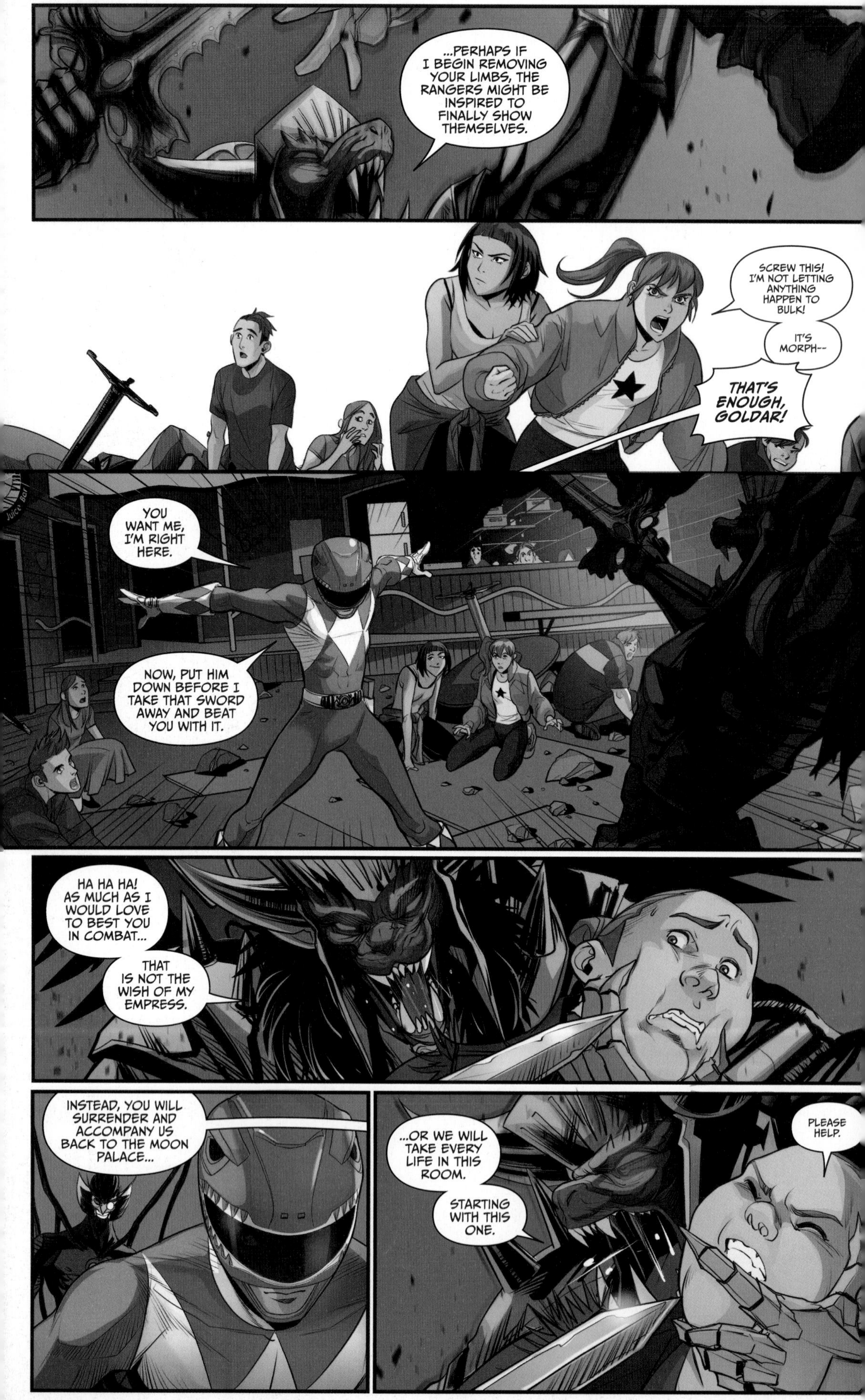
...PERHAPS IF I BEGIN REMOVING YOUR LIMBS, THE RANGERS MIGHT BE INSPIRED TO FINALLY SHOW THEMSELVES.
SCREW THIS! I'M NOT LETTING ANYTHING HAPPEN TO BULK!
IT'S MORPH--
THAT'S ENOUGH, GOLDAR!
Juice Bar
YOU WANT ME, I'M RIGHT HERE.
NOW, PUT HIM DOWN BEFORE I TAKE THAT SWORD AWAY AND BEAT YOU WITH IT.
HA HA HA! AS MUCH AS I WOULD LOVE TO BEST YOU IN COMBAT...
THAT IS NOT THE WISH OF MY EMPRESS.
INSTEAD, YOU WILL SURRENDER AND ACCOMPANY US BACK TO THE MOON PALACE...
...OR WE WILL TAKE EVERY LIFE IN THIS ROOM.
STARTING WITH THIS ONE.
PLEASE HELP.

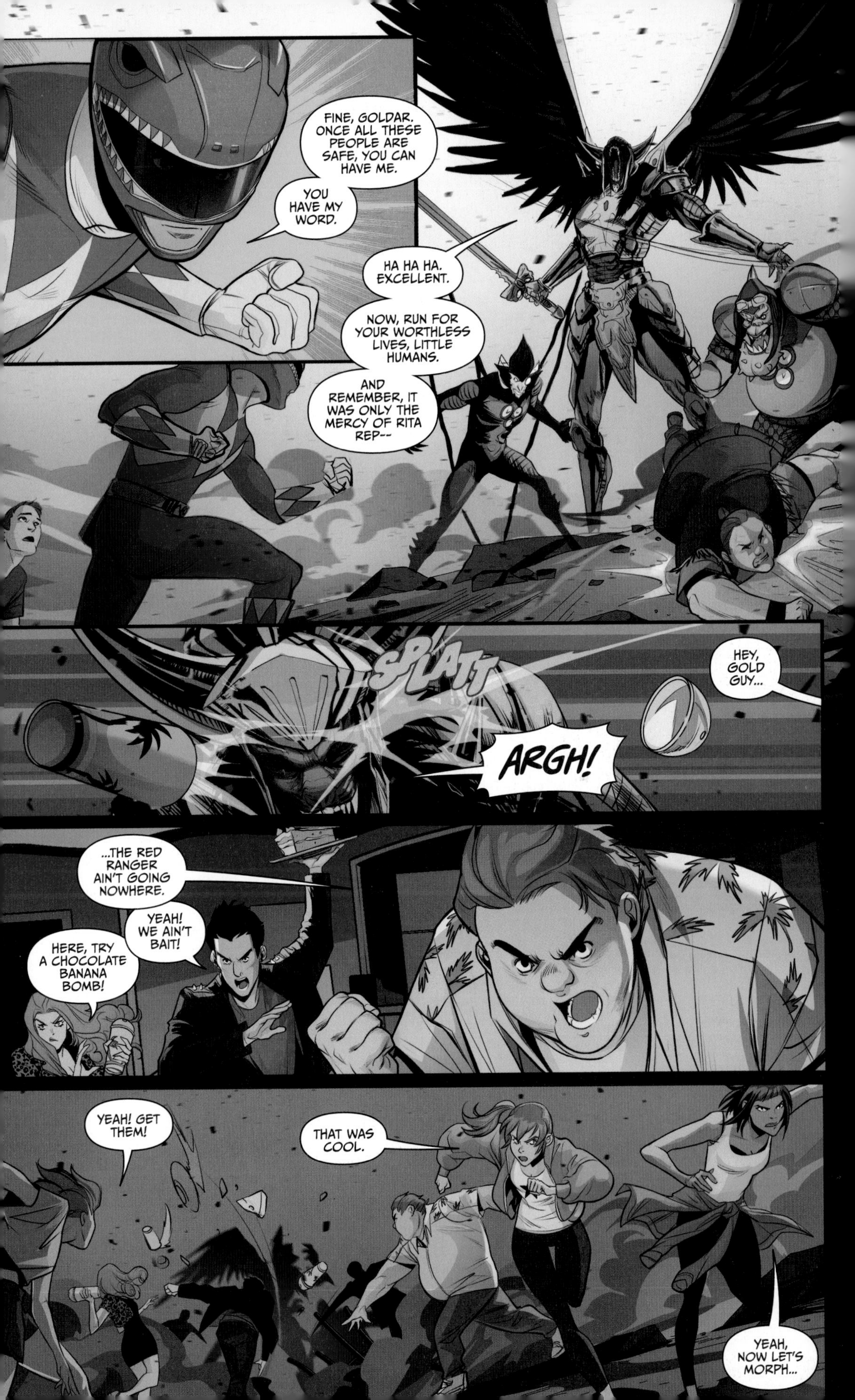
FINE, GOLDAR. ONCE ALL THESE PEOPLE ARE SAFE, YOU CAN HAVE ME.
YOU HAVE MY WORD.
HA HA HA. EXCELLENT.
NOW, RUN FOR YOUR WORTHLESS LIVES, LITTLE HUMANS.
AND REMEMBER, IT WAS ONLY THE MERCY OF RITA REP--
SPLATT
HEY, GOLD GUY...
ARGH!
...THE RED RANGER AIN'T GOING NOWHERE.
YEAH! WE AIN'T BAIT!
HERE, TRY A CHOCOLATE BANANA BOMB!
YEAH! GET THEM!
THAT WAS COOL.
YEAH, NOW LET'S MORPH...

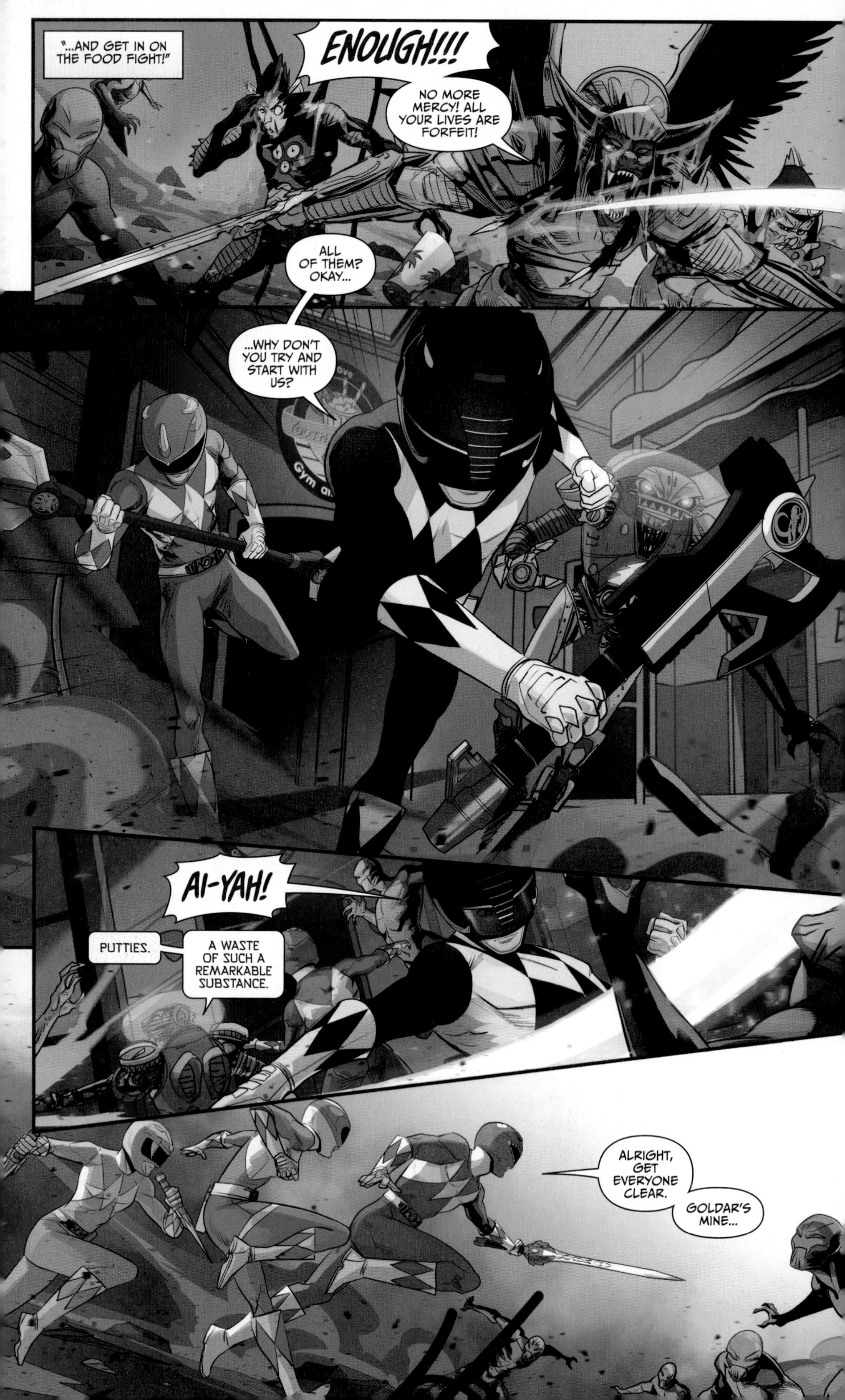
"...AND GET IN ON THE FOOD FIGHT!"
ENOUGH!!!
NO MORE MERCY! ALL YOUR LIVES ARE FORFEIT!
ALL OF THEM? OKAY...
...WHY DON'T YOU TRY AND START WITH US?
AI-YAH!
PUTTIES.
A WASTE OF SUCH A REMARKABLE SUBSTANCE.
ALRIGHT, GET EVERYONE CLEAR.
GOLDAR'S MINE...

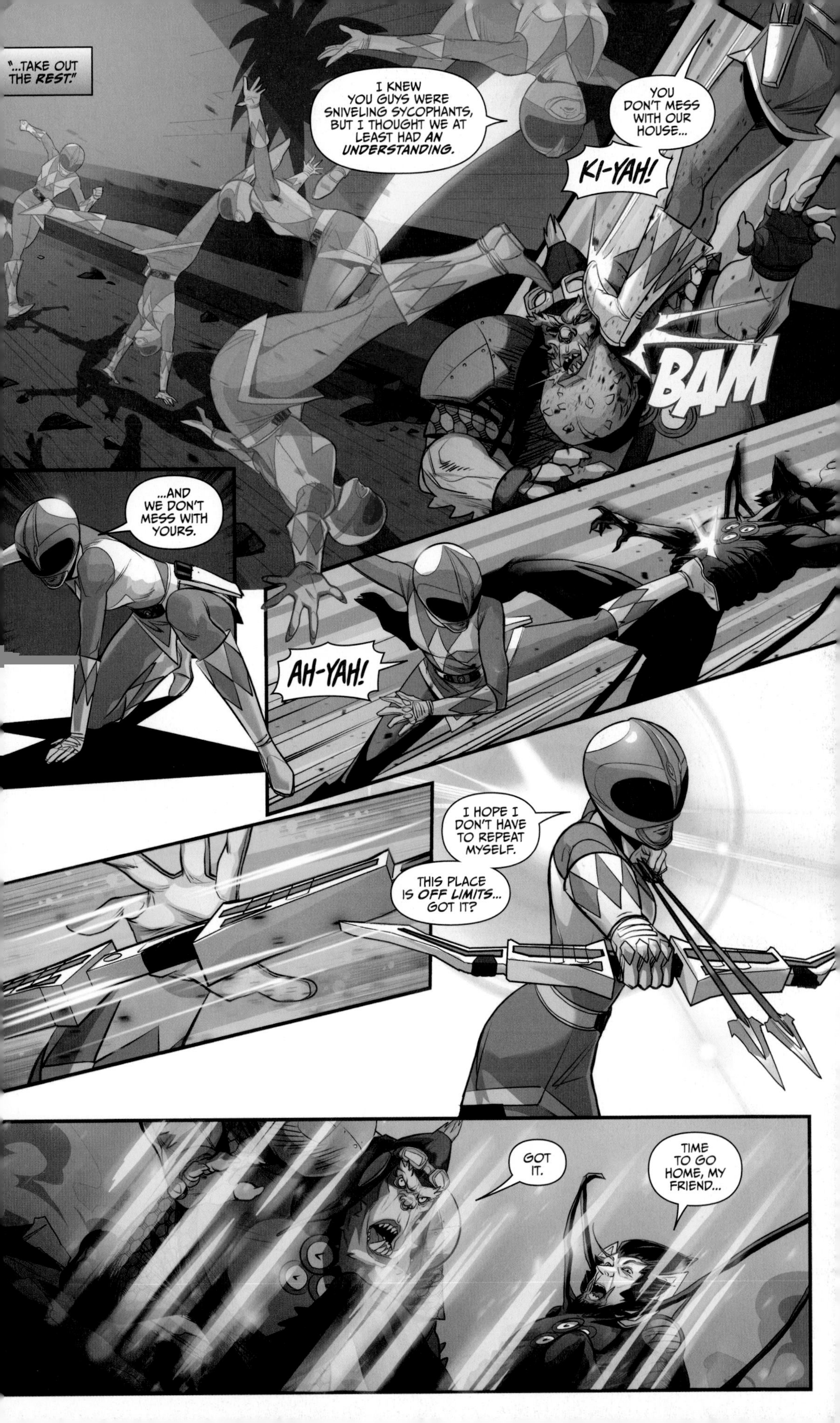

"...TAKE OUT THE REST."
I KNEW YOU GUYS WERE SNIVELING SYCOPHANTS, BUT I THOUGHT WE AT LEAST HAD AN UNDERSTANDING.
YOU DON'T MESS WITH OUR HOUSE...
KI-YAH!
BAM
...AND WE DON'T MESS WITH YOURS.
AH-YAH!
I HOPE I DON'T HAVE TO REPEAT MYSELF.
THIS PLACE IS OFF LIMITS... GOT IT?
GOT IT.
TIME TO GO HOME, MY FRIEND...

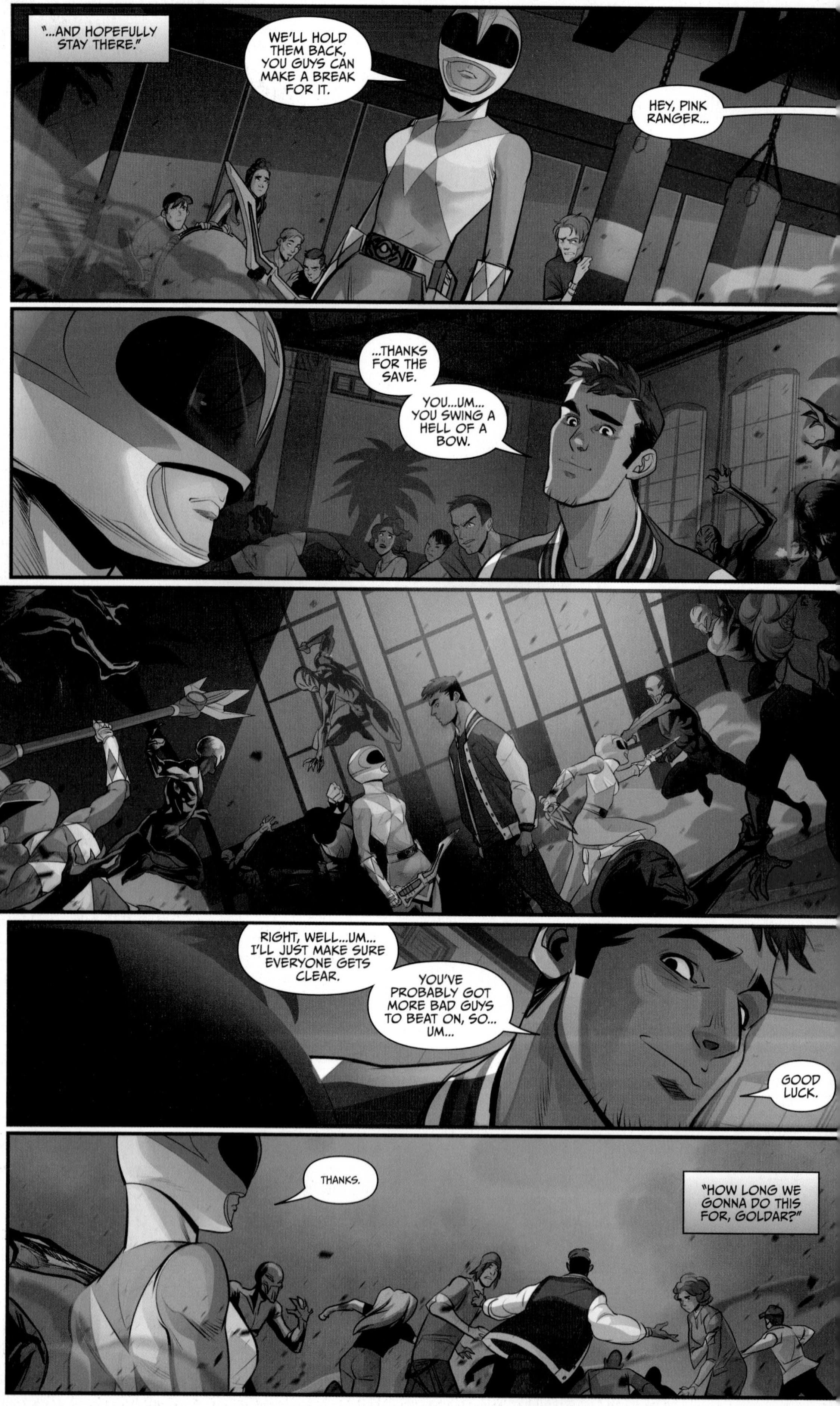
"...AND HOPEFULLY STAY THERE."
WE'LL HOLD THEM BACK, YOU GUYS CAN MAKE A BREAK FOR IT.
HEY, PINK RANGER...
...THANKS FOR THE SAVE.
YOU...UM... YOU SWING A HELL OF A BOW.
RIGHT, WELL...UM... I'LL JUST MAKE SURE EVERYONE GETS CLEAR.
YOU'VE PROBABLY GOT MORE BAD GUYS TO BEAT ON, SO... UM...
GOOD LUCK.
THANKS.
"HOW LONG WE GONNA DO THIS FOR, GOLDAR?"

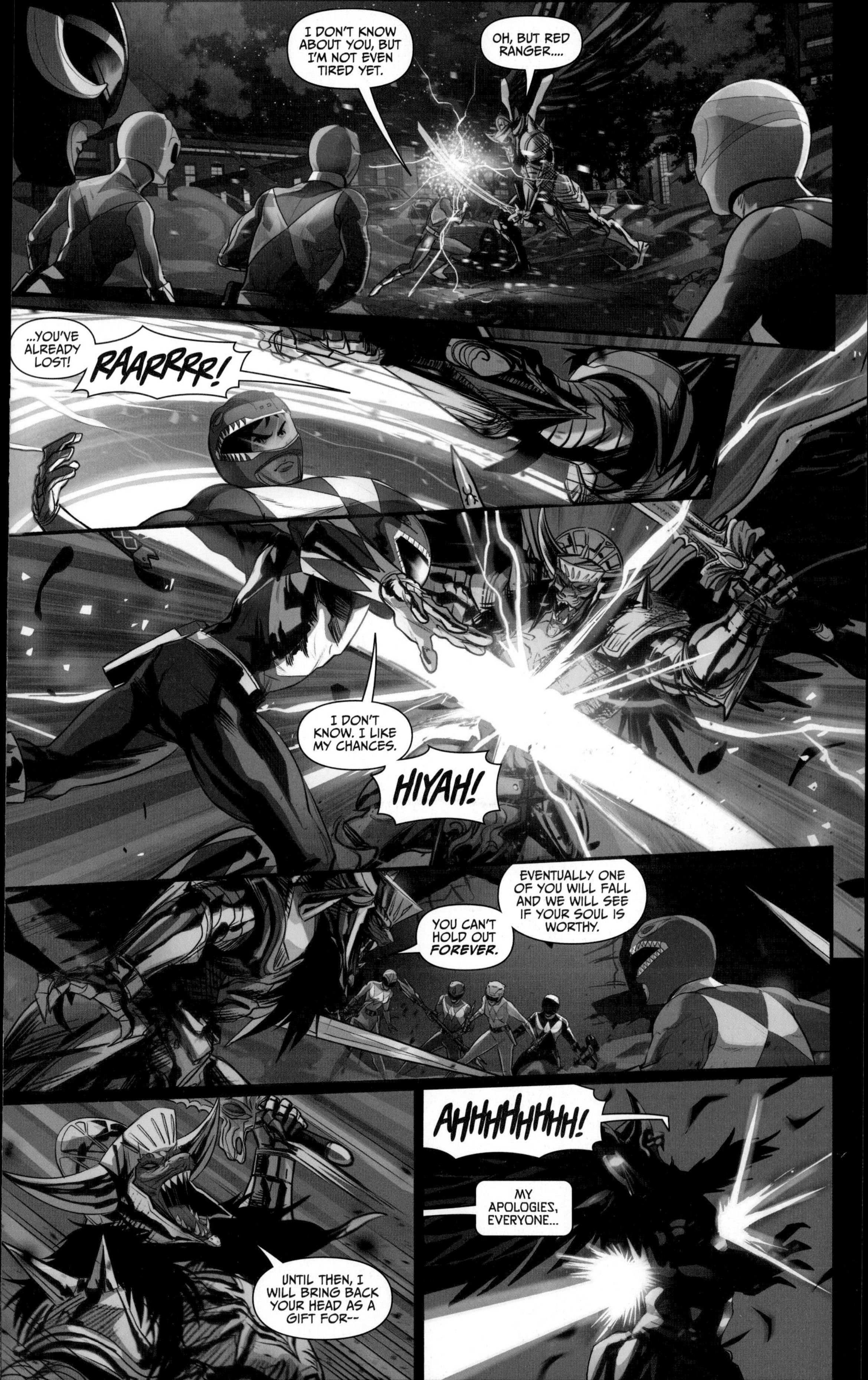
I DON'T KNOW ABOUT YOU, BUT I'M NOT EVEN TIRED YET.
OH, BUT RED RANGER....
...YOU'VE ALREADY LOST!
RAARRRR!
I DON'T KNOW. I LIKE MY CHANCES.
HIYAH!
EVENTUALLY ONE OF YOU WILL FALL AND WE WILL SEE IF YOUR SOUL IS WORTHY.
YOU CAN'T HOLD OUT FOREVER.
UNTIL THEN, I WILL BRING BACK YOUR HEAD AS A GIFT FOR--
AHHHHHHHH!
MY APOLOGIES, EVERYONE...

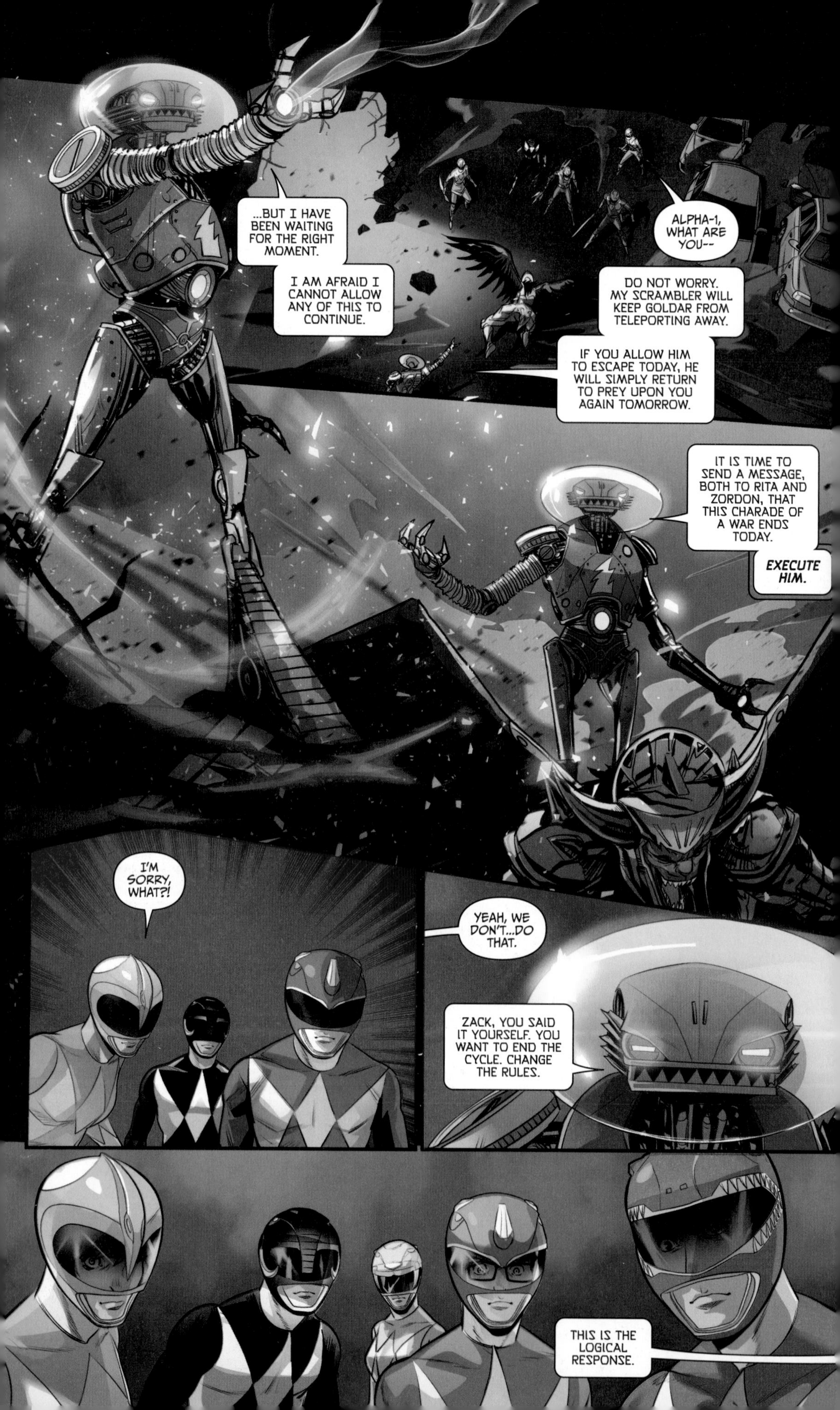
...BUT I HAVE BEEN WAITING FOR THE RIGHT MOMENT.
I AM AFRAID I CANNOT ALLOW ANY OF THIS TO CONTINUE.
ALPHA-1, WHAT ARE YOU--
DO NOT WORRY. MY SCRAMBLER WILL KEEP GOLDAR FROM TELEPORTING AWAY.
IF YOU ALLOW HIM TO ESCAPE TODAY, HE WILL SIMPLY RETURN TO PREY UPON YOU AGAIN TOMORROW.
IT IS TIME TO SEND A MESSAGE, BOTH TO RITA AND ZORDON, THAT THIS CHARADE OF A WAR ENDS TODAY.
EXECUTE HIM.
I'M SORRY, WHAT?!
YEAH, WE DON'T...DO THAT.
ZACK, YOU SAID IT YOURSELF. YOU WANT TO END THE CYCLE. CHANGE THE RULES.
THIS IS THE LOGICAL RESPONSE.

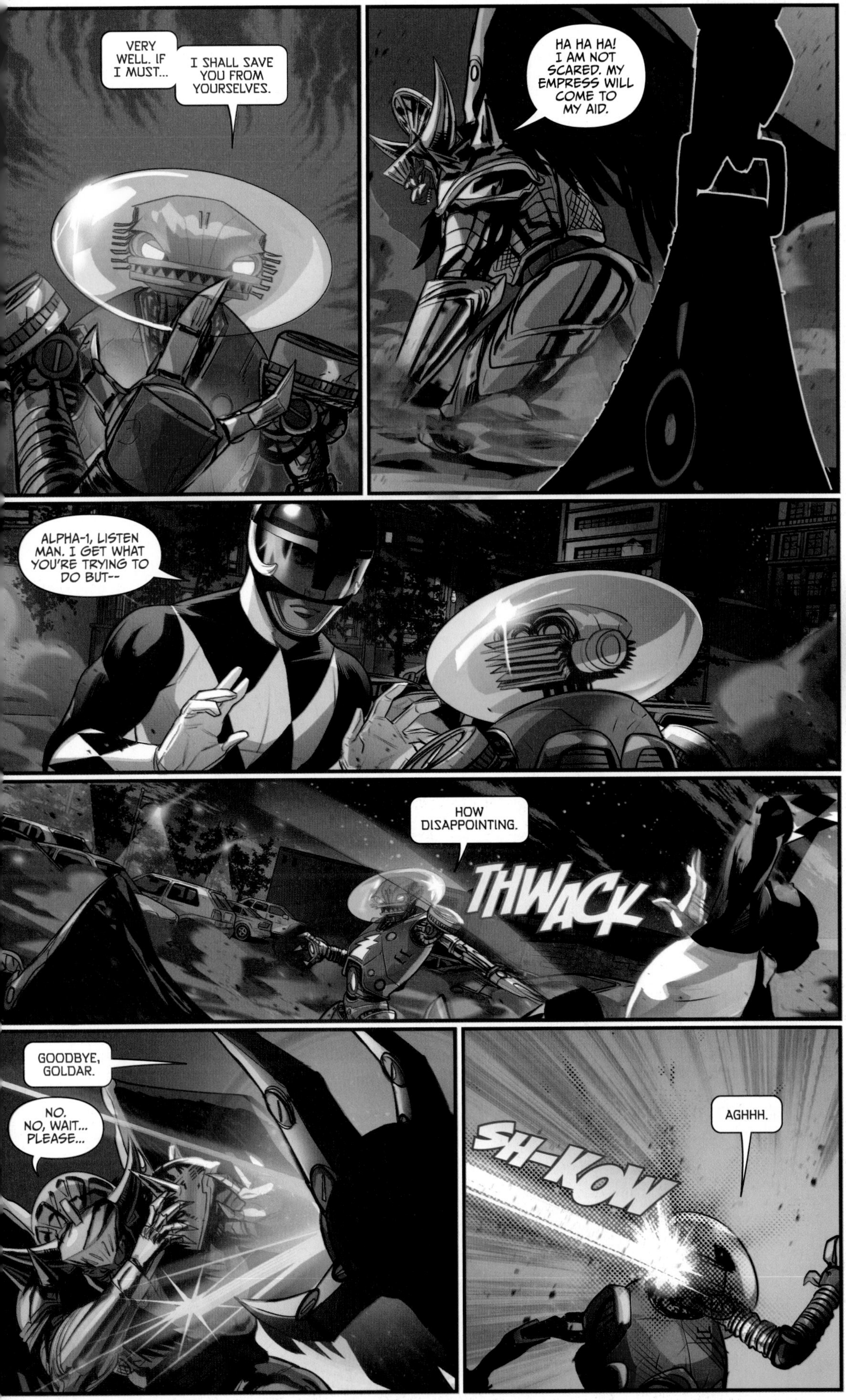

VERY WELL. IF I MUST...
I SHALL SAVE YOU FROM YOURSELVES.
HA HA HA! I AM NOT SCARED. MY EMPRESS WILL COME TO MY AID.
ALPHA-1, LISTEN MAN. I GET WHAT YOU'RE TRYING TO DO BUT--
HOW DISAPPOINTING.
THWACK
GOODBYE, GOLDAR.
NO. NO, WAIT... PLEASE...
SH-KOW
AGHHH.

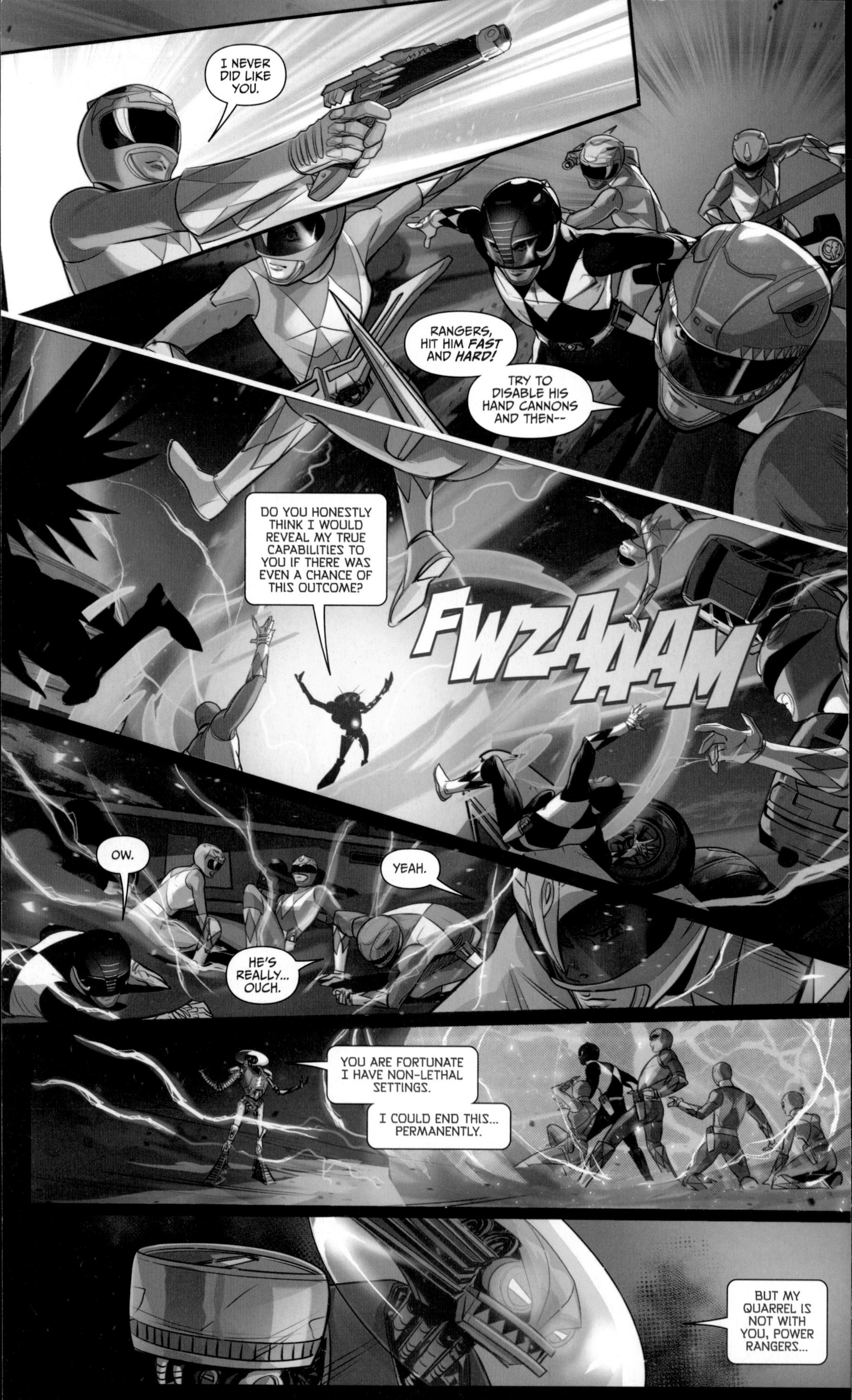
I NEVER DID LIKE YOU.
RANGERS, HIT HIM FAST AND HARD!
TRY TO DISABLE HIS HAND CANNONS AND THEN--
DO YOU HONESTLY THINK I WOULD REVEAL MY TRUE CAPABILITIES TO YOU IF THERE WAS EVEN A CHANCE OF THIS OUTCOME?
FWZAAAM
OW.
YEAH.
HE'S REALLY... OUCH.
YOU ARE FORTUNATE I HAVE NON-LETHAL SETTINGS.
I COULD END THIS... PERMANENTLY.
BUT MY QUARREL IS NOT WITH YOU, POWER RANGERS...

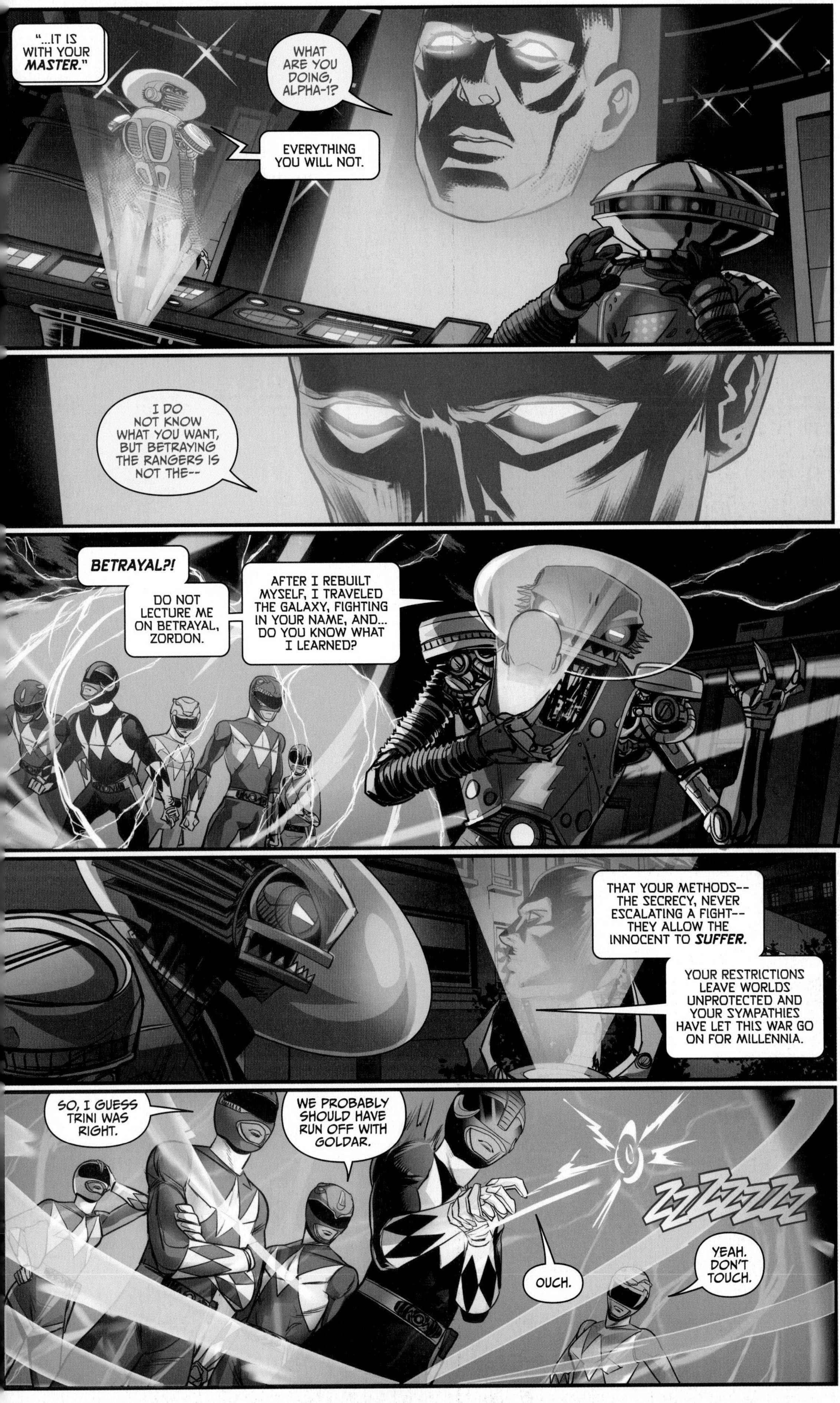
"...IT IS WITH YOUR *MASTER.*"
WHAT ARE YOU DOING, ALPHA-1?
EVERYTHING YOU WILL NOT.
I DO NOT KNOW WHAT YOU WANT, BUT BETRAYING THE RANGERS IS NOT THE--
BETRAYAL?!
DO NOT LECTURE ME ON BETRAYAL, ZORDON.
AFTER I REBUILT MYSELF, I TRAVELED THE GALAXY, FIGHTING IN YOUR NAME, AND... DO YOU KNOW WHAT I LEARNED?
THAT YOUR METHODS-- THE SECRECY, NEVER ESCALATING A FIGHT-- THEY ALLOW THE INNOCENT TO *SUFFER.*
YOUR RESTRICTIONS LEAVE WORLDS UNPROTECTED AND YOUR SYMPATHIES HAVE LET THIS WAR GO ON FOR MILLENNIA.
SO, I GUESS TRINI WAS RIGHT.
WE PROBABLY SHOULD HAVE RUN OFF WITH GOLDAR.
ZZZZZZ
OUCH.
YEAH. DON'T TOUCH.

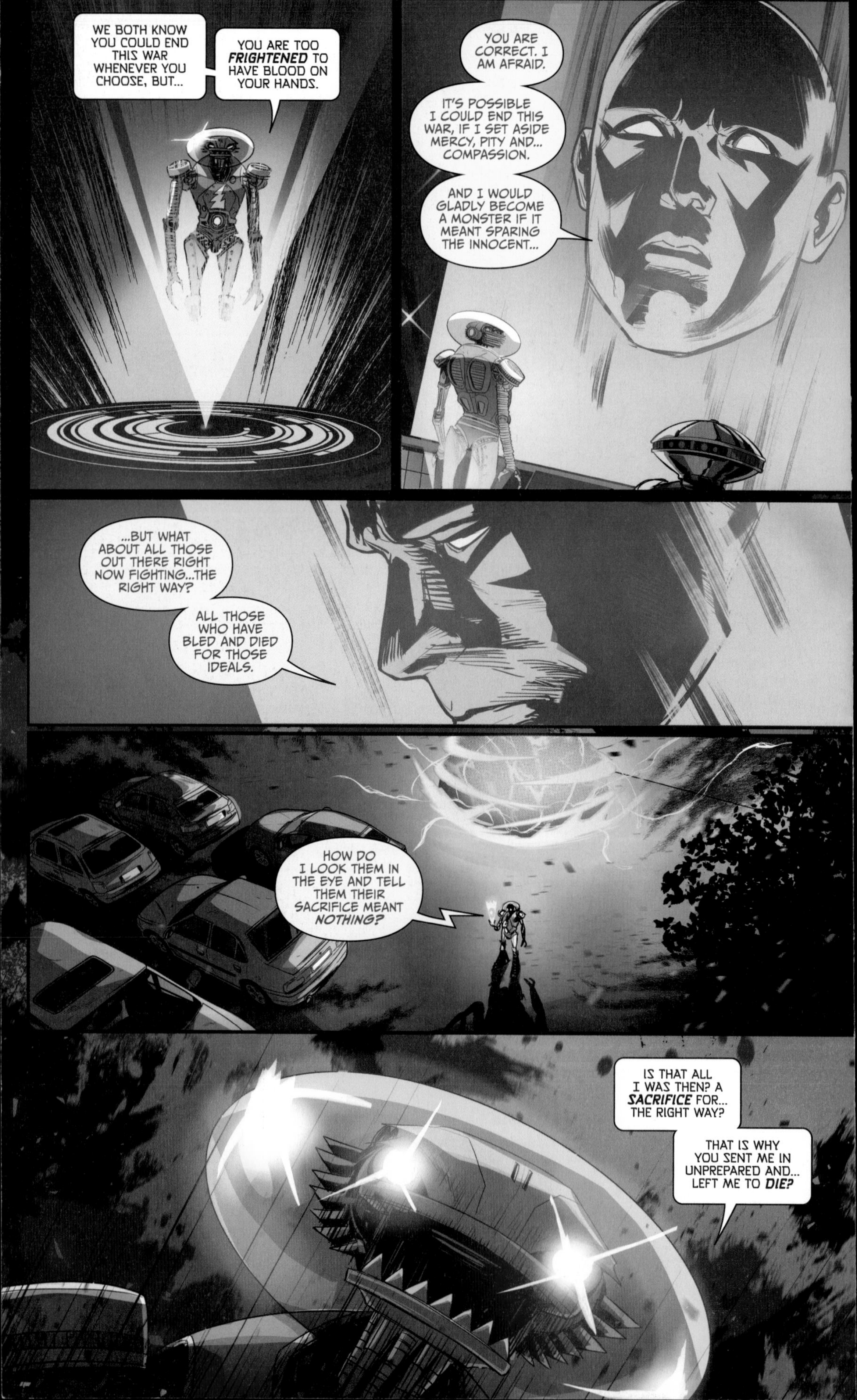

WE BOTH KNOW YOU COULD END THIS WAR WHENEVER YOU CHOOSE, BUT...
YOU ARE TOO FRIGHTENED TO HAVE BLOOD ON YOUR HANDS.
YOU ARE CORRECT. I AM AFRAID.
IT'S POSSIBLE I COULD END THIS WAR, IF I SET ASIDE MERCY, PITY AND... COMPASSION.
AND I WOULD GLADLY BECOME A MONSTER IF IT MEANT SPARING THE INNOCENT...
...BUT WHAT ABOUT ALL THOSE OUT THERE RIGHT NOW FIGHTING...THE RIGHT WAY?
ALL THOSE WHO HAVE BLED AND DIED FOR THOSE IDEALS.
HOW DO I LOOK THEM IN THE EYE AND TELL THEM THEIR SACRIFICE MEANT NOTHING?
IS THAT ALL I WAS THEN? A SACRIFICE FOR... THE RIGHT WAY?
THAT IS WHY YOU SENT ME IN UNPREPARED AND... LEFT ME TO DIE?

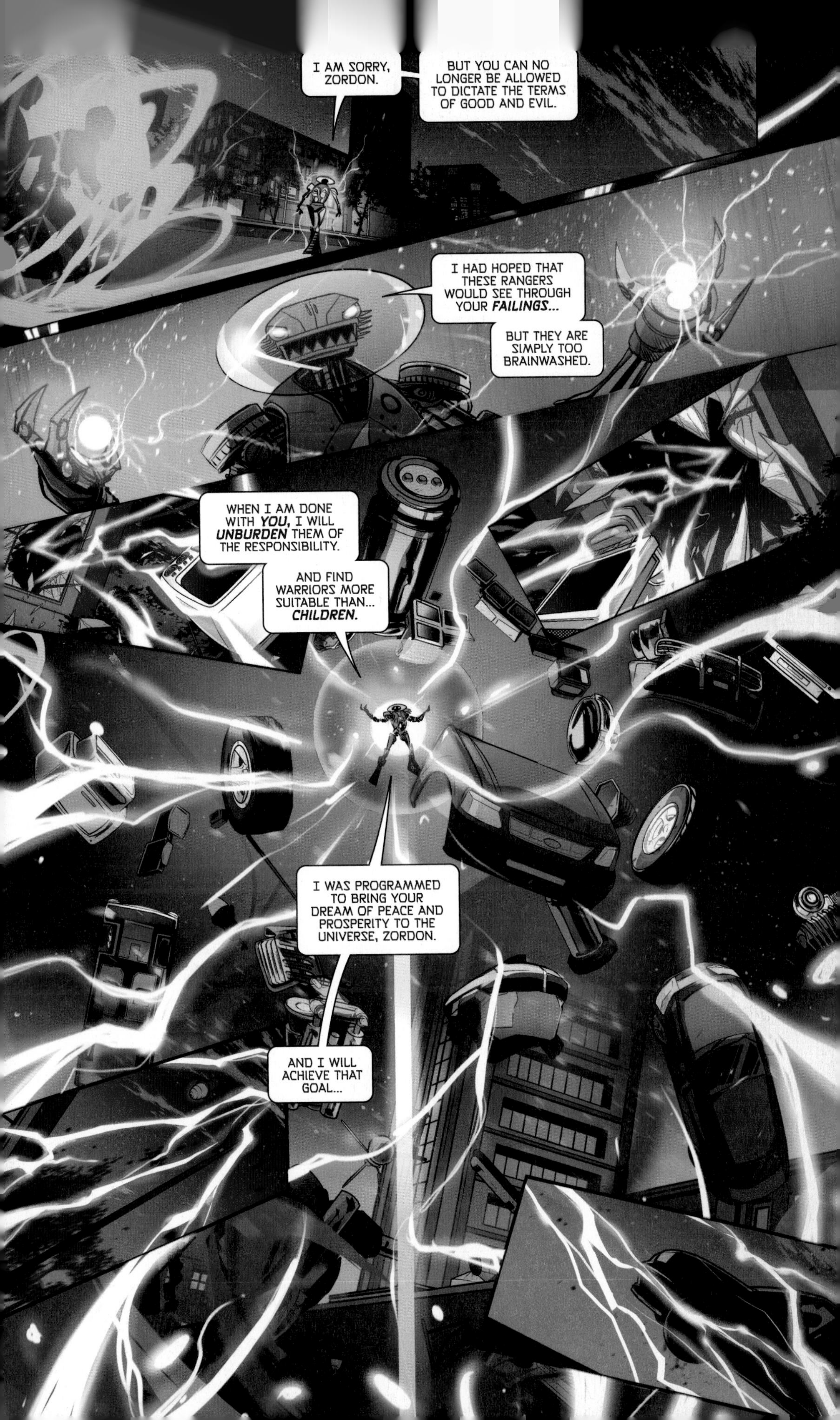
I AM SORRY, ZORDON.
BUT YOU CAN NO LONGER BE ALLOWED TO DICTATE THE TERMS OF GOOD AND EVIL.
I HAD HOPED THAT THESE RANGERS WOULD SEE THROUGH YOUR *FAILINGS...*
BUT THEY ARE SIMPLY TOO BRAINWASHED.
WHEN I AM DONE WITH *YOU,* I WILL *UNBURDEN* THEM OF THE RESPONSIBILITY.
AND FIND WARRIORS MORE SUITABLE THAN... *CHILDREN.*
I WAS PROGRAMMED TO BRING YOUR DREAM OF PEACE AND PROSPERITY TO THE UNIVERSE, ZORDON.
AND I WILL ACHIEVE THAT GOAL...

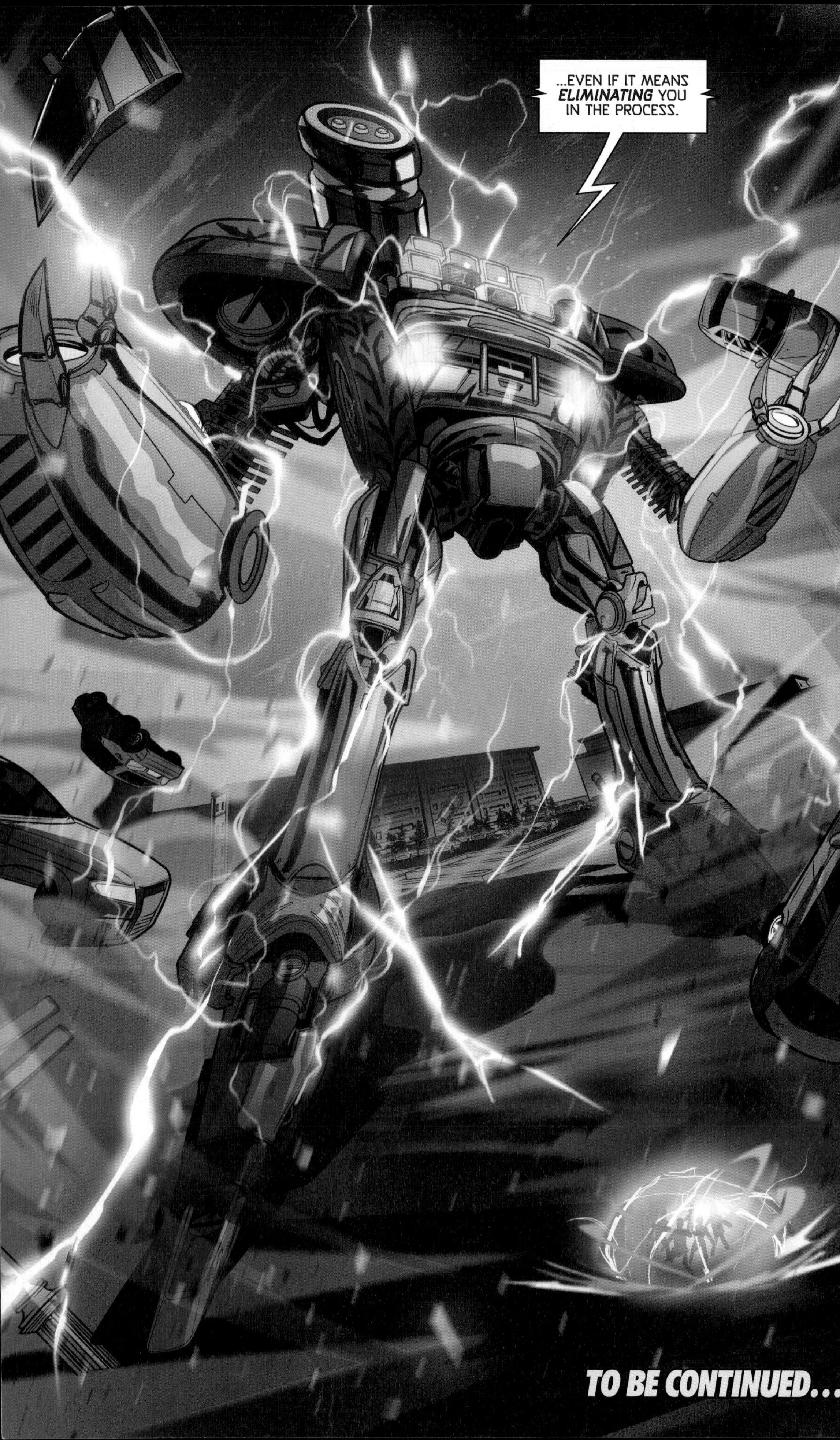
...EVEN IF IT MEANS ELIMINATING YOU IN THE PROCESS.
TO BE CONTINUED...

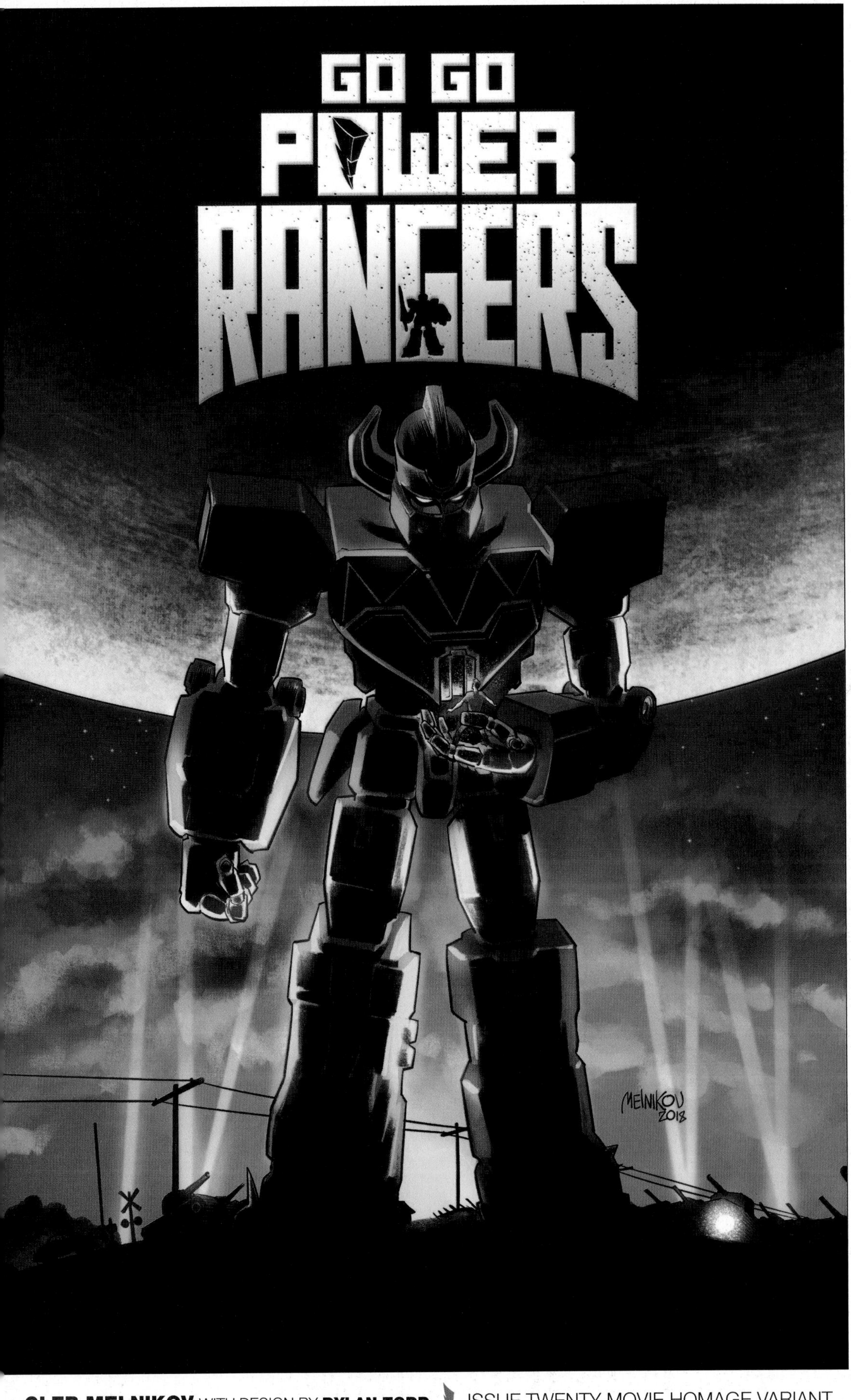
GO GO
POWER
RANGERS
MELNIKOV
2018

GLEB MELNIKOV WITH DESIGN BY **DYLAN TODD** ISSUE TWENTY MOVIE HOMAGE VARIANT

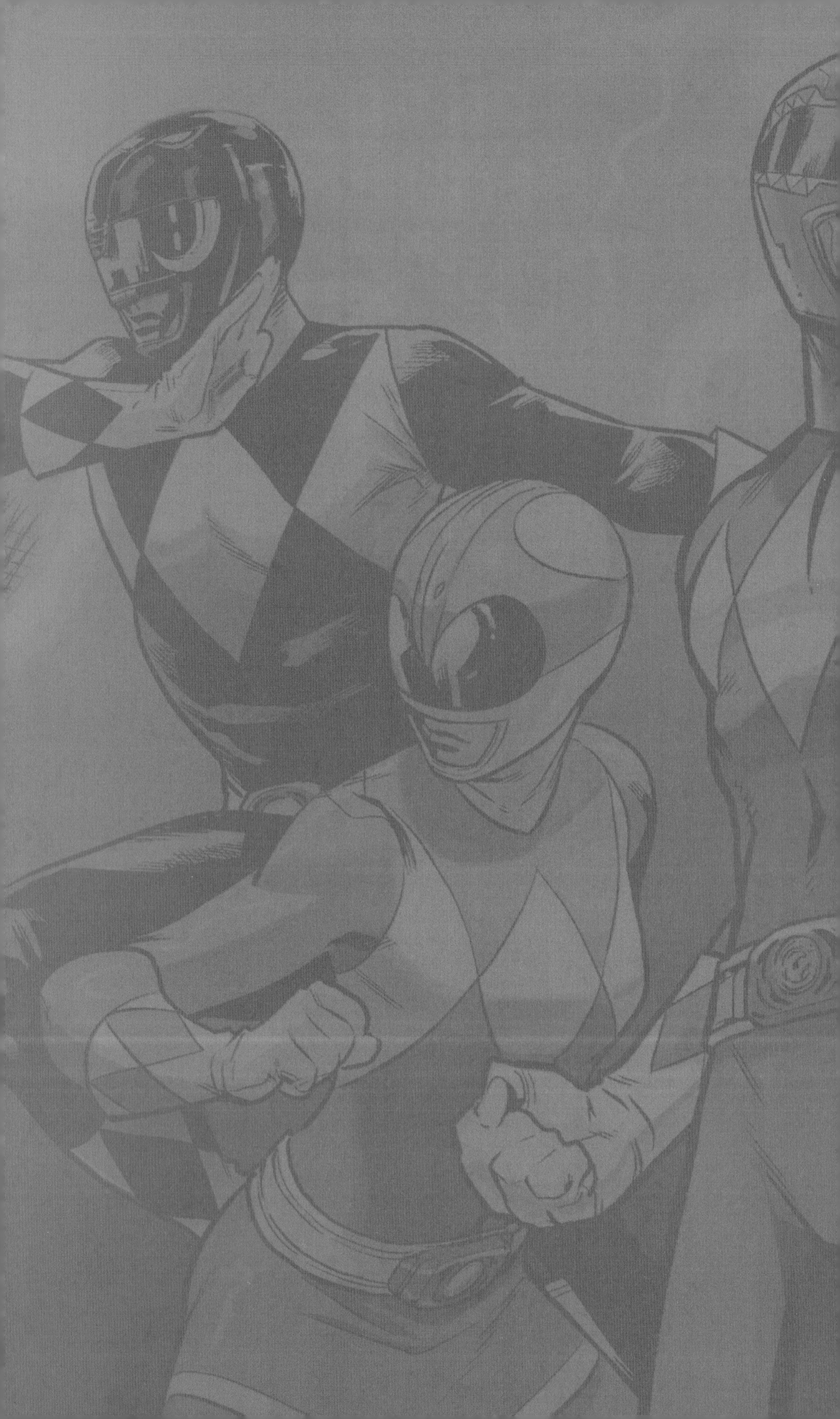

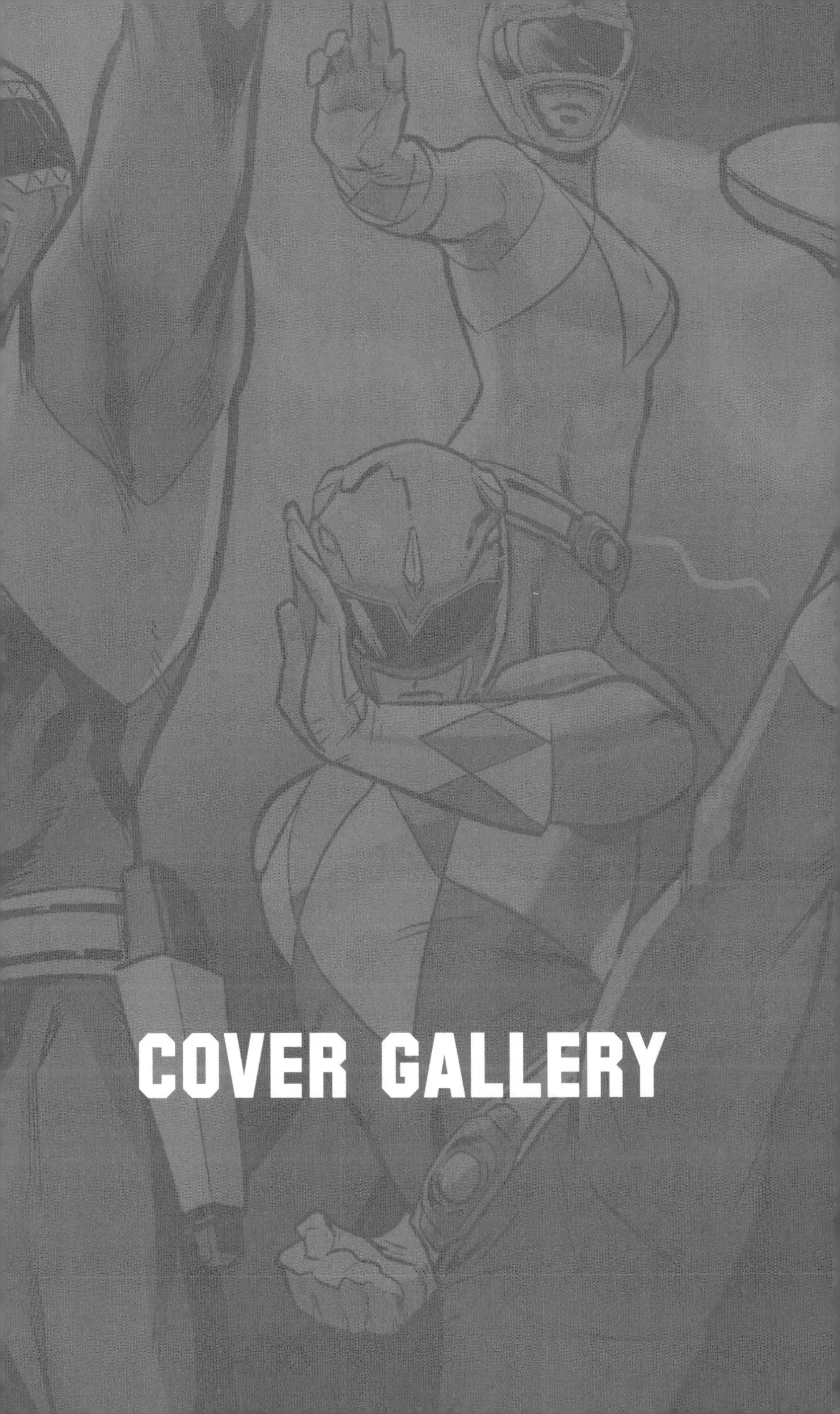

COVER GALLERY

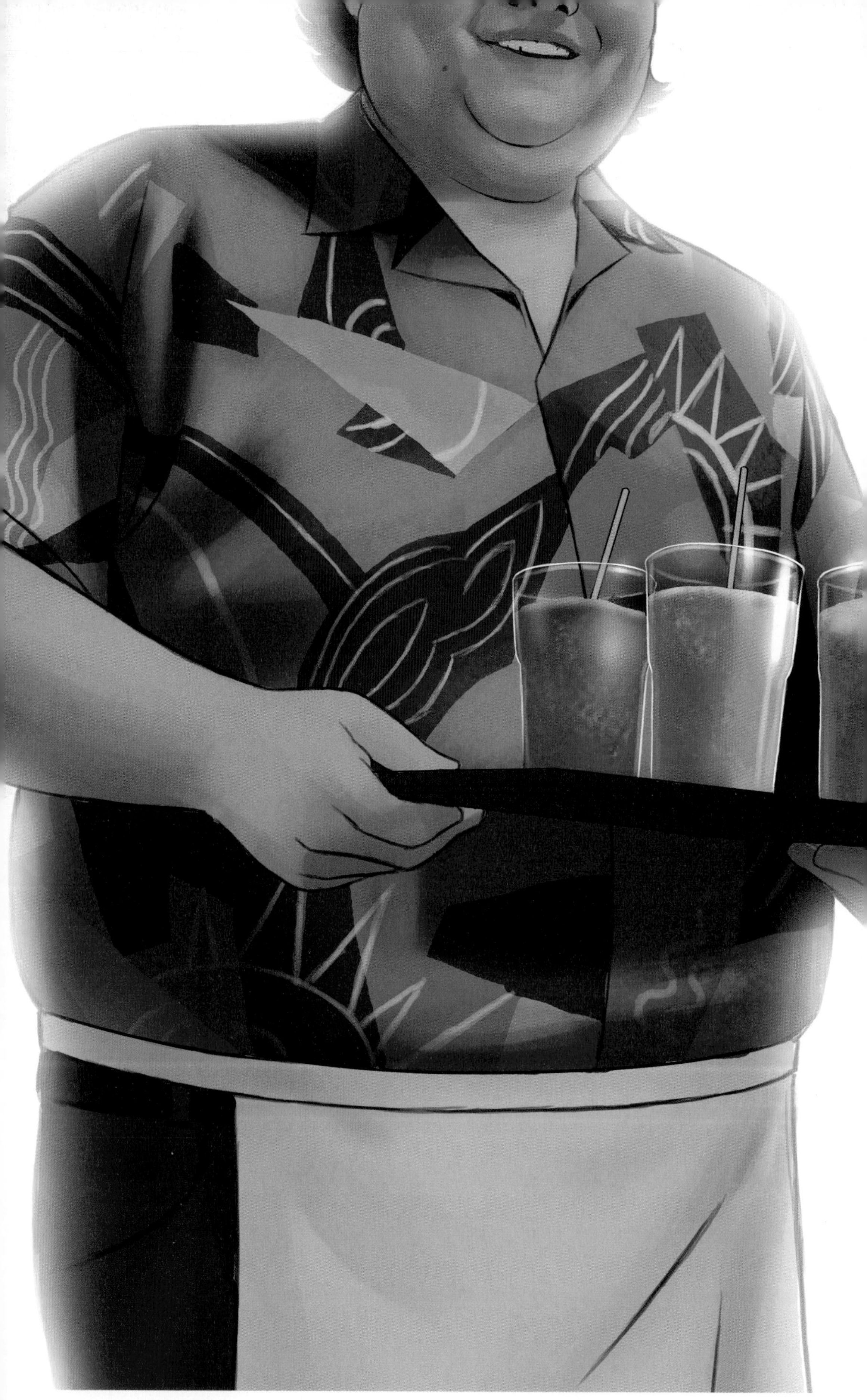

MIGUEL MERCADO | ISSUE SEVENTEEN CHARACTER VARIANT

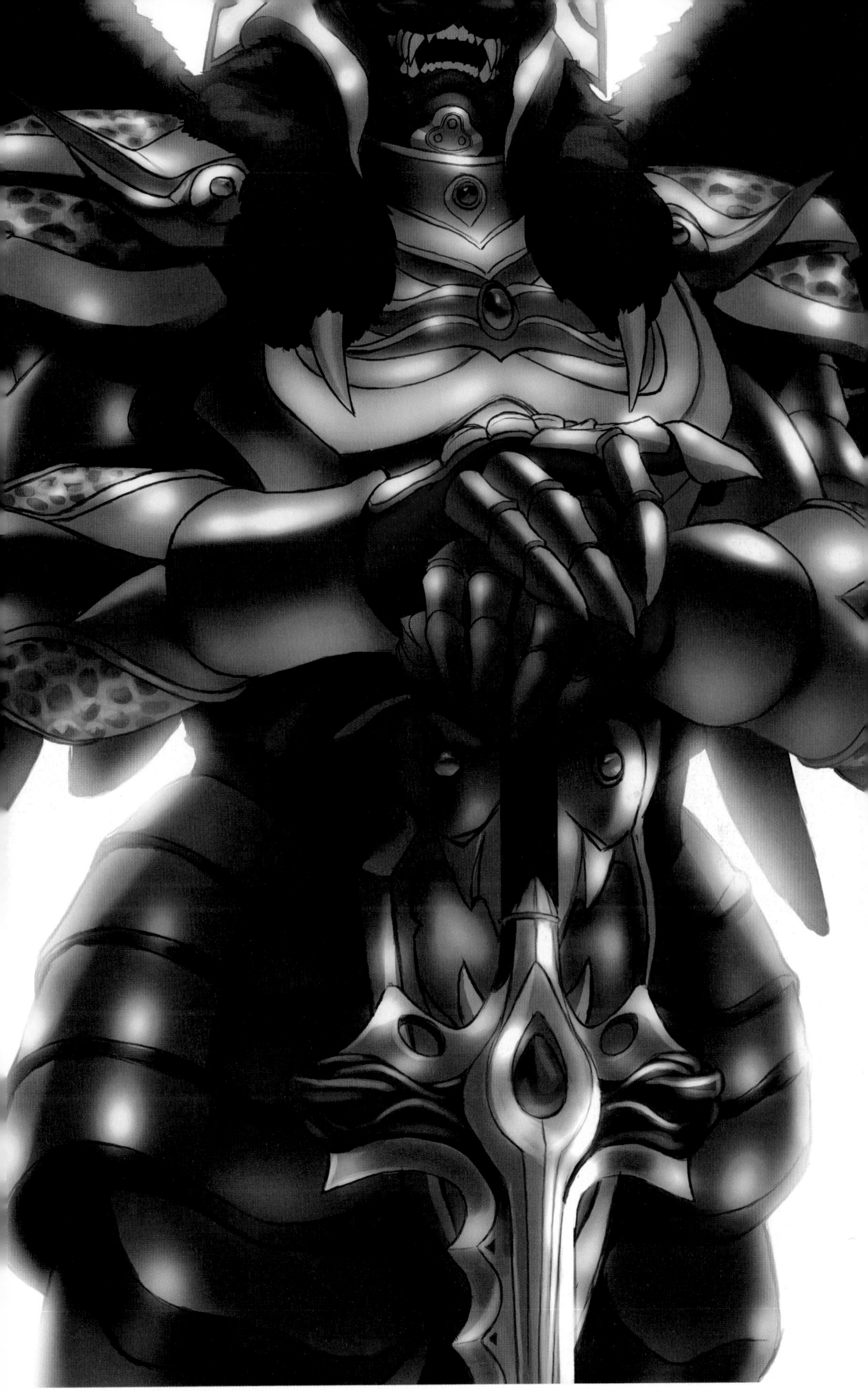

MIGUEL MERCADO ISSUE EIGHTEEN CHARACTER VARIANT

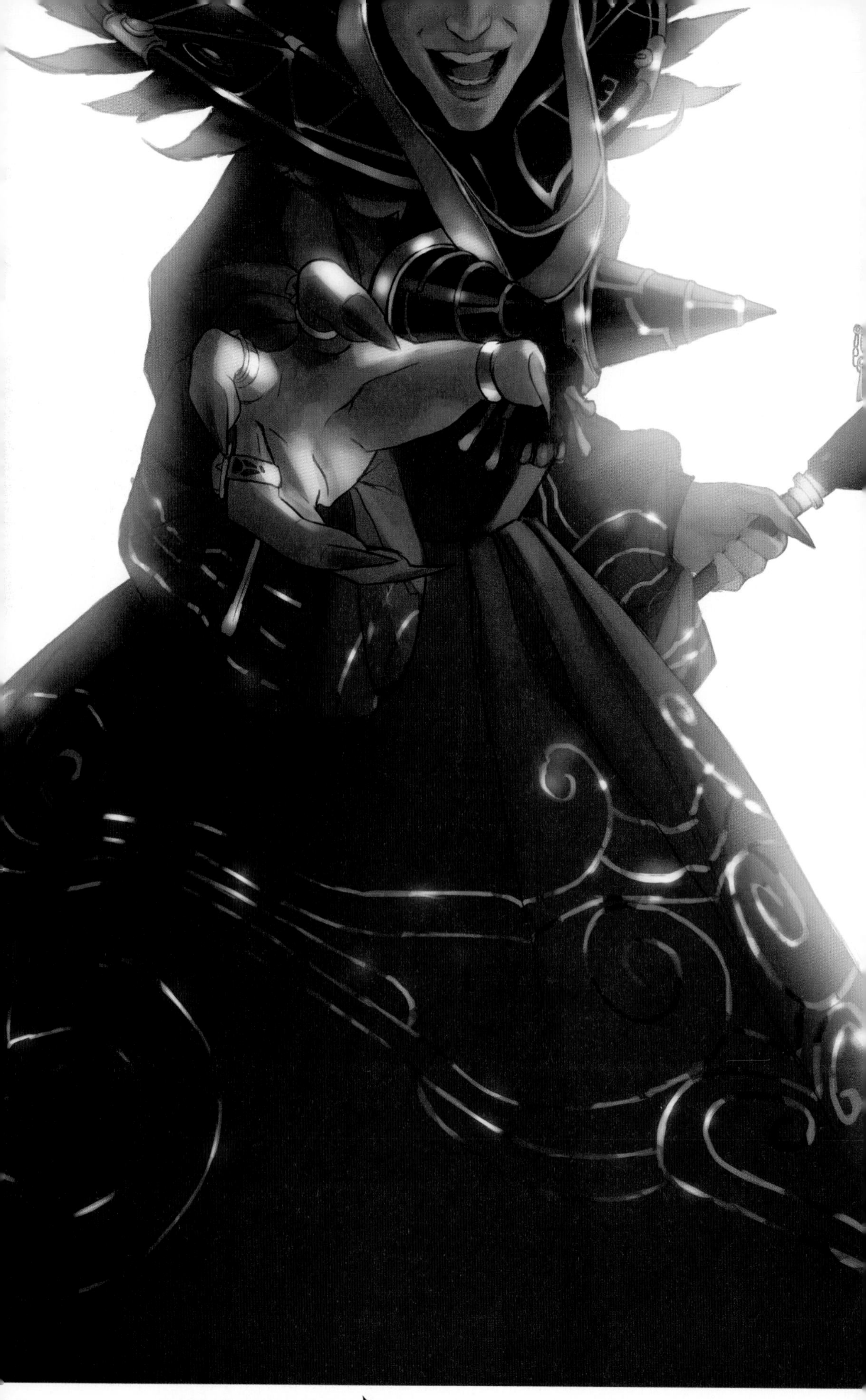

MIGUEL MERCADO ISSUE NINETEEN CHARACTER VARIANT

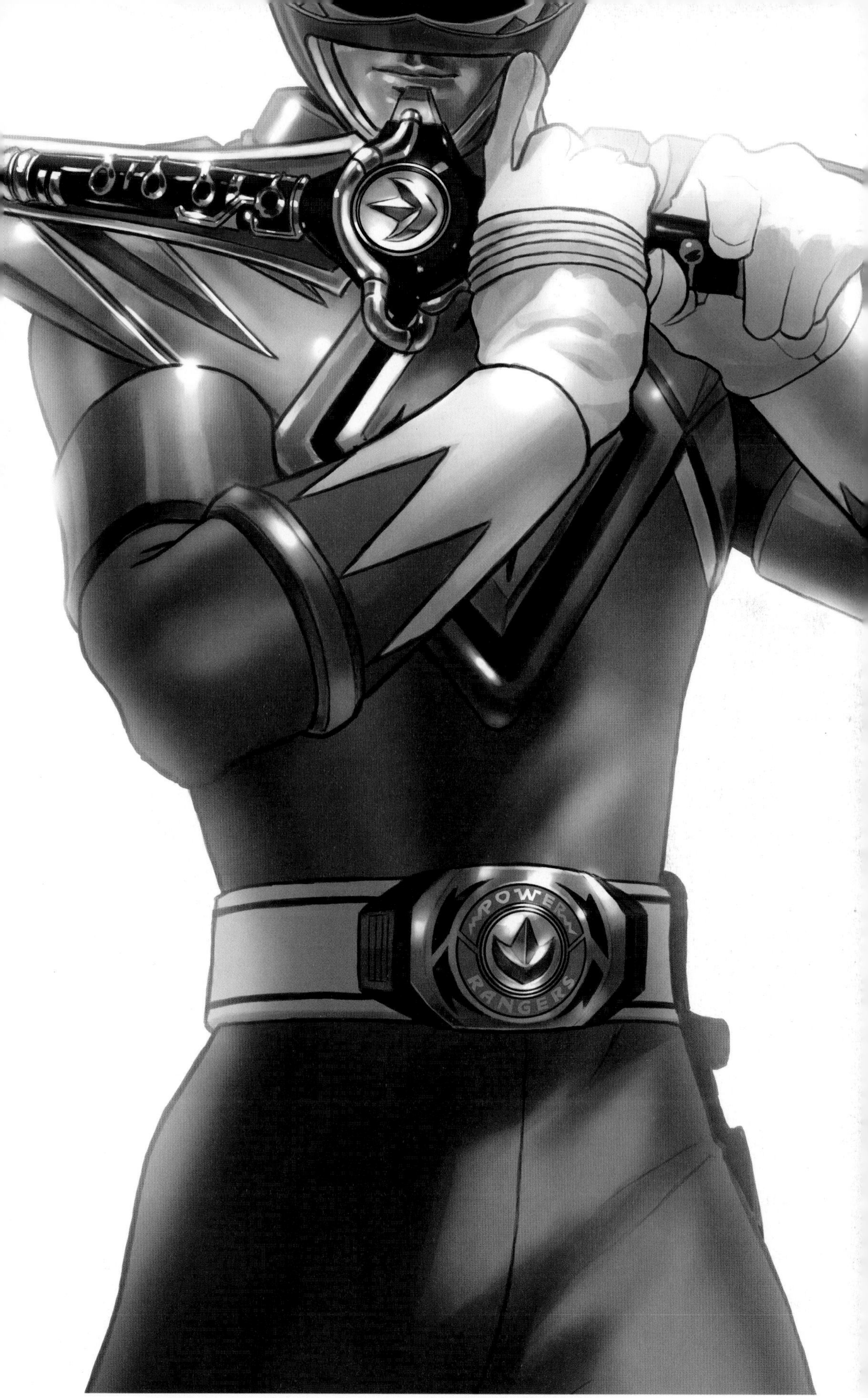
POWER
RANGERS

MIGUEL MERCADO ISSUE TWENTY RANGER VARIANT

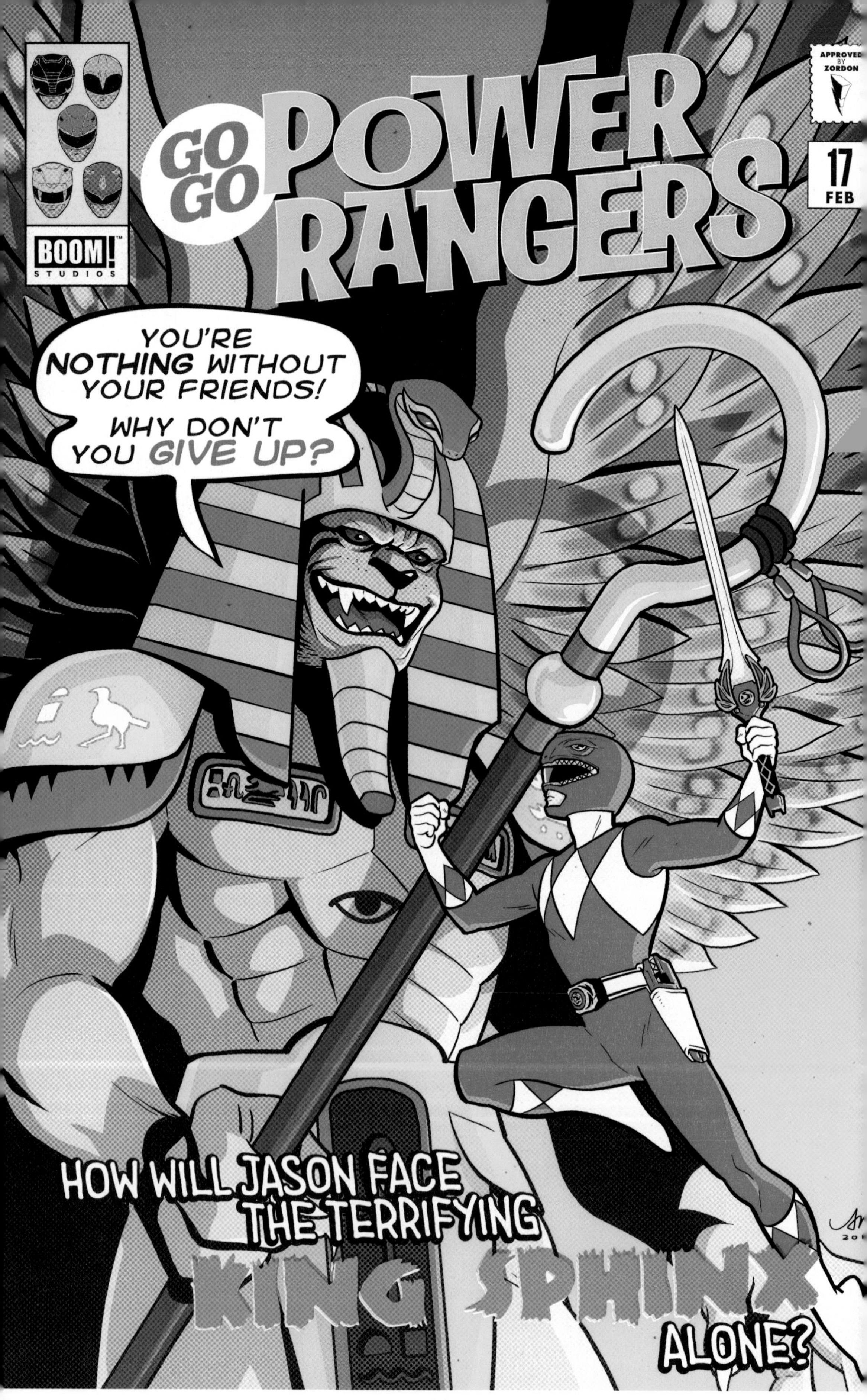

BOOM! STUDIOS
GO GO POWER RANGERS
APPROVED BY ZORDON
17 FEB
YOU'RE NOTHING WITHOUT YOUR FRIENDS! WHY DON'T YOU GIVE UP?
HOW WILL JASON FACE THE TERRIFYING KING SPHINX ALONE?

AUDREY MOK WITH DESIGN BY DYLAN TODD ISSUE SEVENTEEN SUBSCRIPTION COVER

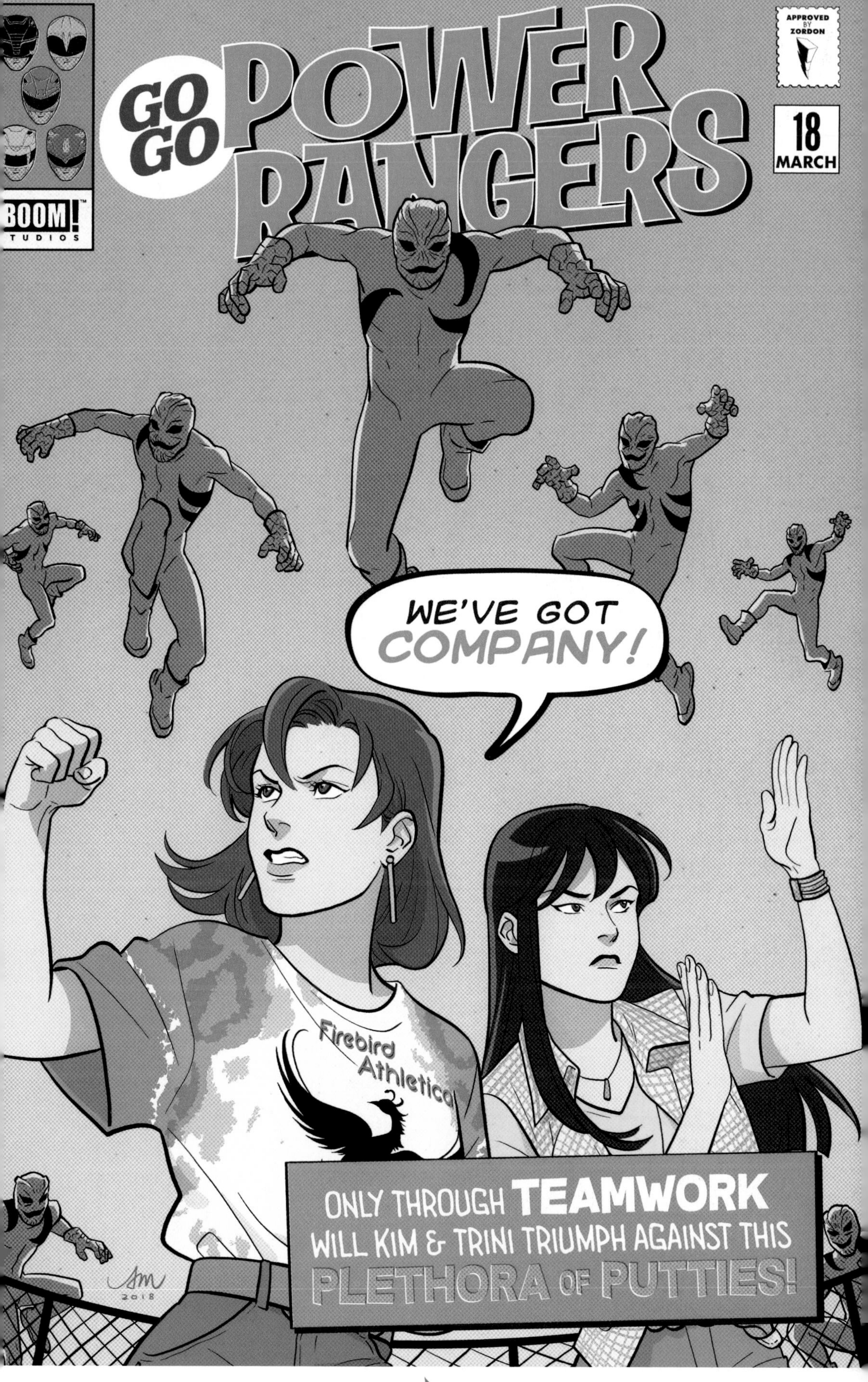
BOOM! STUDIOS
GO GO POWER RANGERS
APPROVED BY ZORDON
18
MARCH
WE'VE GOT COMPANY!
Firebird Athletica
ONLY THROUGH TEAMWORK WILL KIM & TRINI TRIUMPH AGAINST THIS PLETHORA OF PUTTIES!
AM 2018

AUDREY MOK WITH DESIGN BY **DYLAN TODD** ISSUE EIGHTEEN SUBSCRIPTION COVER

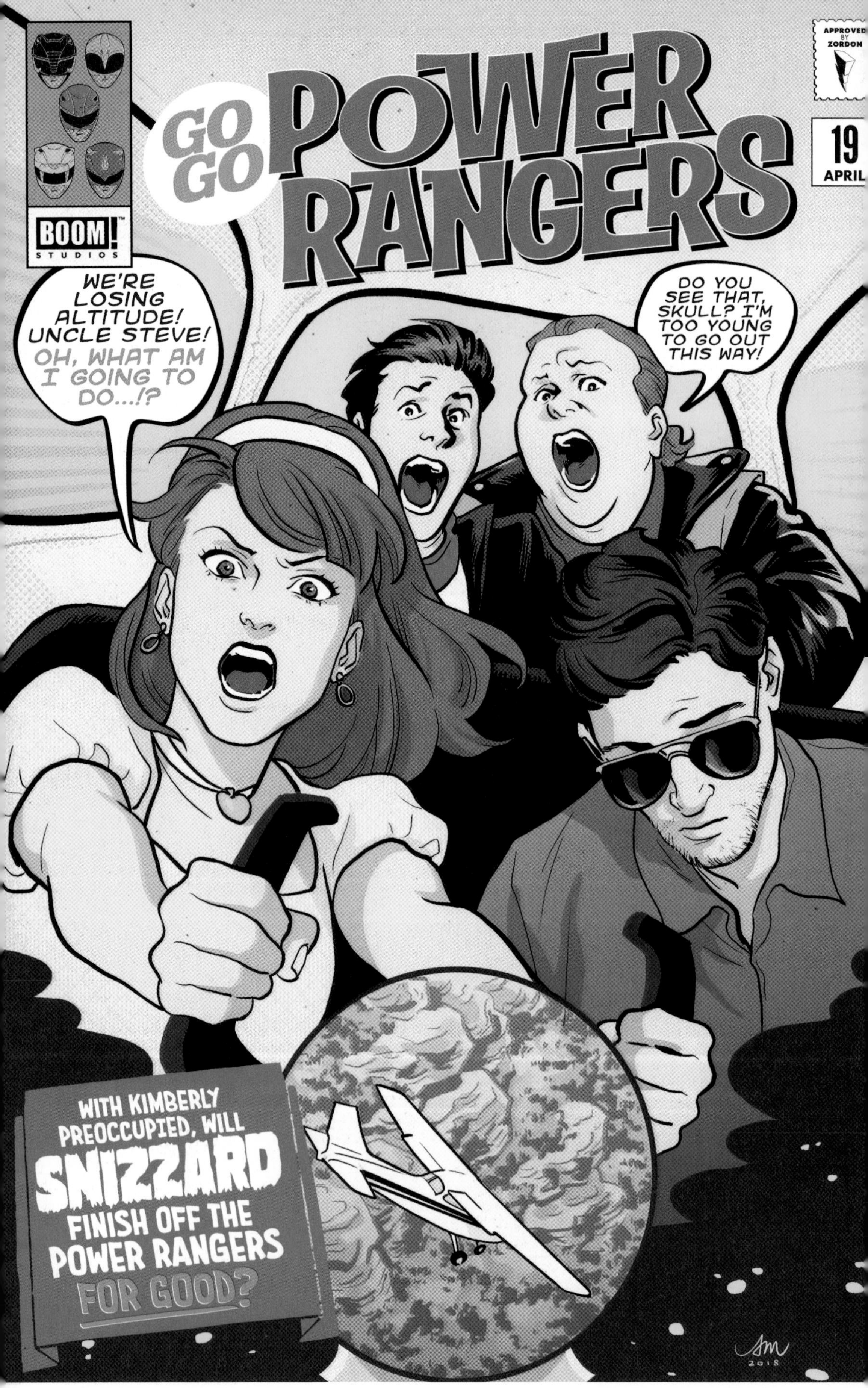
GO GO POWER RANGERS
19
APRIL
APPROVED BY ZORDON
BOOM! STUDIOS
WE'RE LOSING ALTITUDE! UNCLE STEVE! OH, WHAT AM I GOING TO DO...!?
DO YOU SEE THAT, SKULL? I'M TOO YOUNG TO GO OUT THIS WAY!
WITH KIMBERLY PREOCCUPIED, WILL SNIZZARD FINISH OFF THE POWER RANGERS FOR GOOD?

AUDREY MOK WITH DESIGN BY **DYLAN TODD** ISSUE NINETEEN SUBSCRIPTION COVER

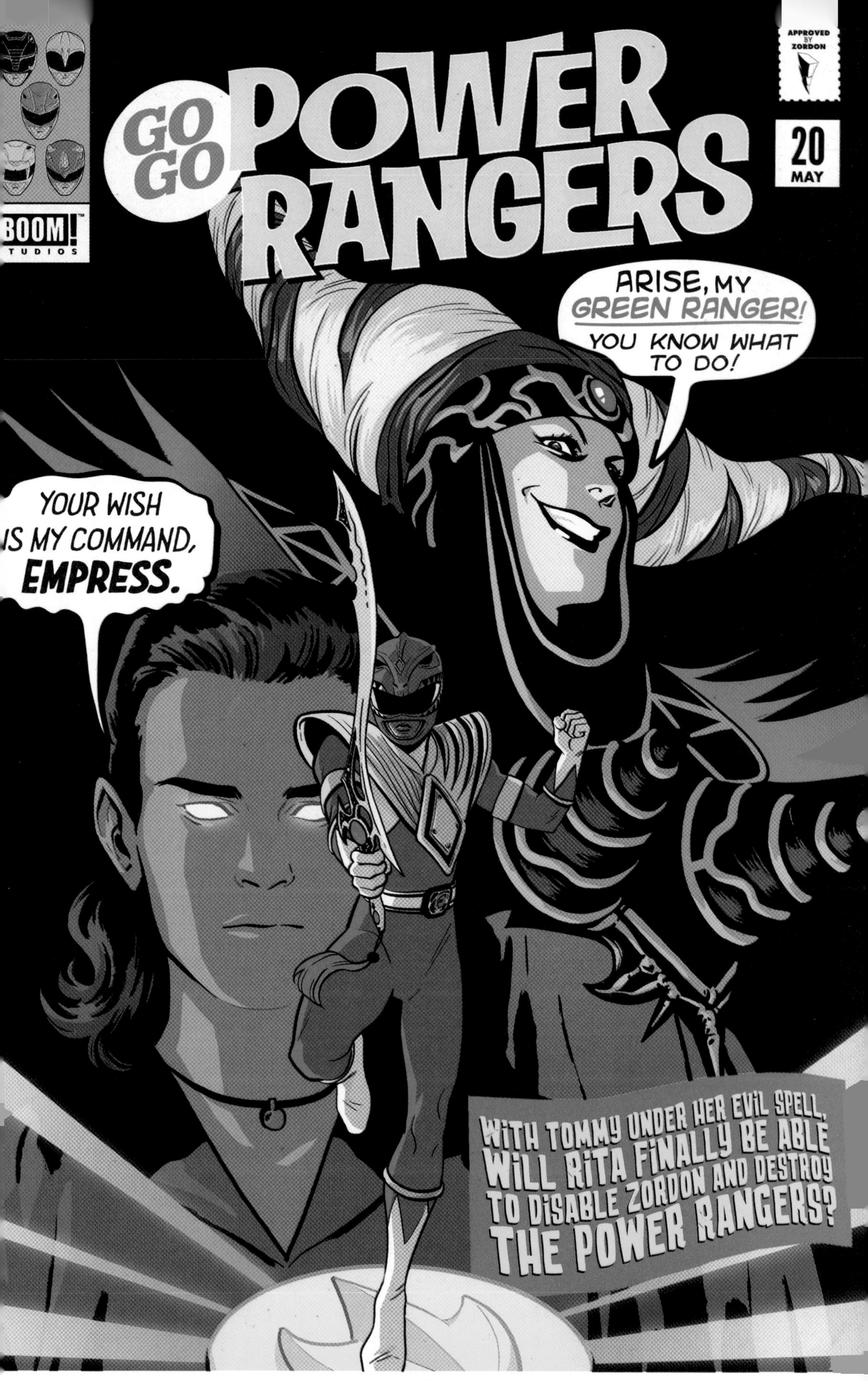

GO GO POWER RANGERS
BOOM! STUDIOS
APPROVED BY ZORDON
20
MAY
ARISE, MY GREEN RANGER! YOU KNOW WHAT TO DO!
YOUR WISH IS MY COMMAND, EMPRESS.
WITH TOMMY UNDER HER EVIL SPELL, WILL RITA FINALLY BE ABLE TO DISABLE ZORDON AND DESTROY THE POWER RANGERS?

AUDREY MOK WITH DESIGN BY **DYLAN TODD** ISSUE TWENTY SUBSCRIPTION COVER

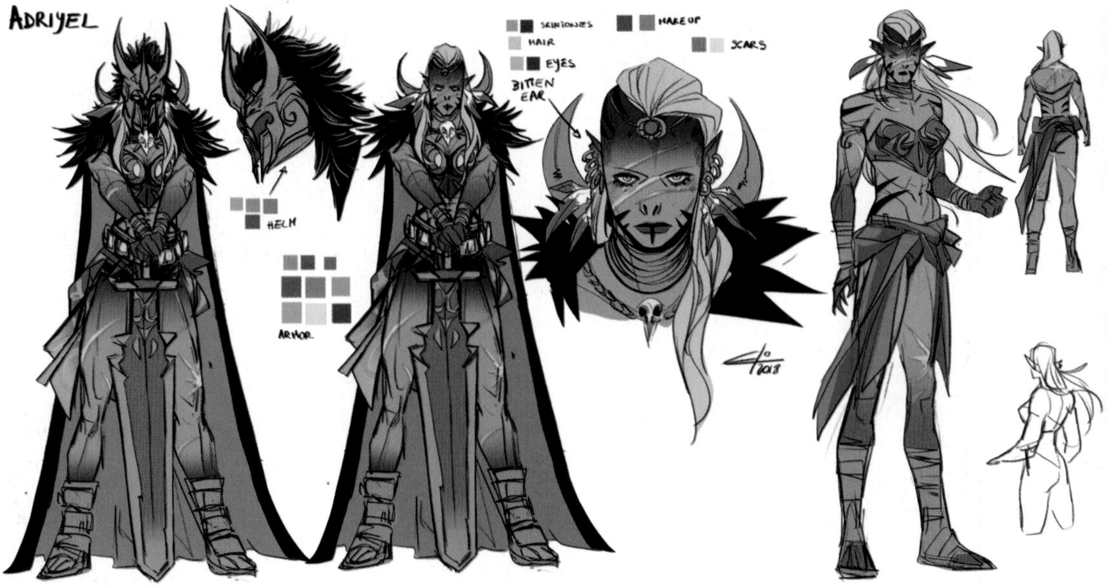
ADRIYEL
SKINTONES
HAIR
EYES
BITTEN EAR
MAKE UP
SCARS
HELM
ARMOR

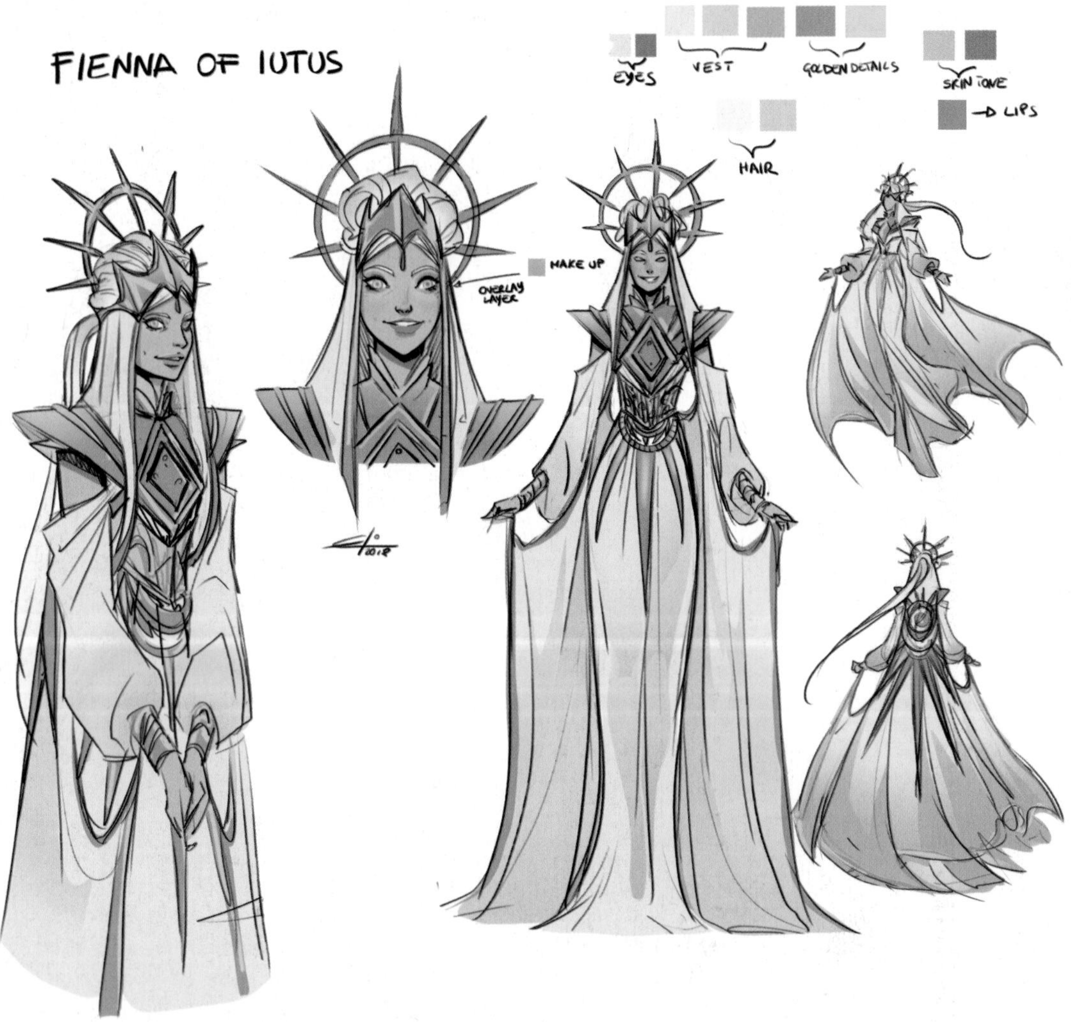
FIENNA OF IUTUS
EYES
VEST
GOLDEN DETAILS
SKIN TONE
LIPS
HAIR
MAKE UP
OVERLAY LAYER

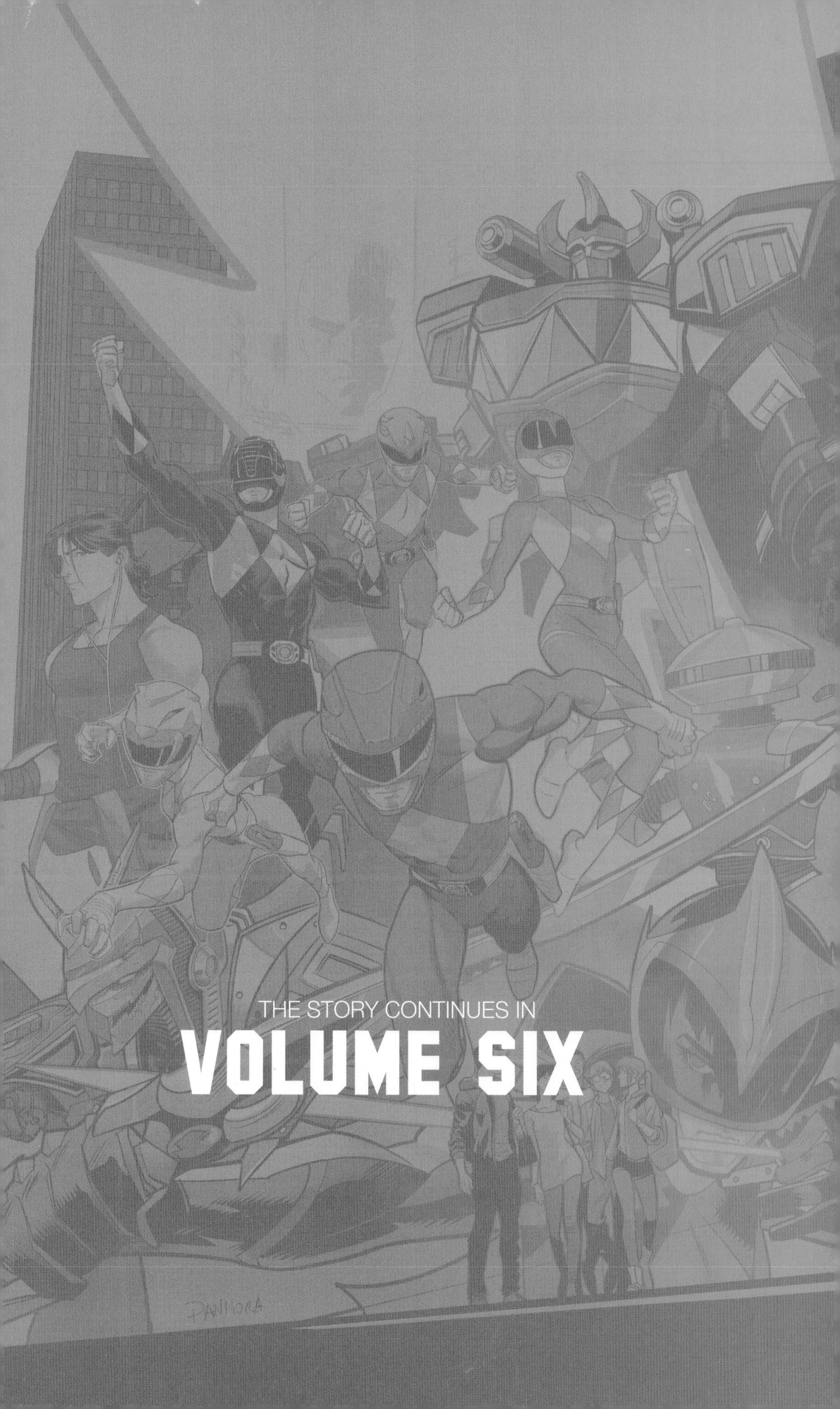
THE STORY CONTINUES IN
VOLUME SIX

DISCOVER
MORE POWER RANGERS!

HIGGINS • PRASETYA • HERMS
ORLANDO • HOWELL • LAWSON
MIGHTY MORPHIN POWER RANGERS
VOLUME ONE
INTRODUCTION BY POWER RANGERS EXECUTIVE PRODUCER JUDD "CHIP" LYNN

HIGGINS • PRASETYA
SILAS • HERMS
VALENZA • ORLANDO
HOWELL • LAWSON
MIGHTY MORPHIN POWER RANGERS
VOLUME TWO

FLETCHER
THOMPSON
HOWARD
DI NICUOLO
STERN
MIGHTY MORPHIN POWER RANGERS
PINK
INTRODUCTION BY AMY JO JOHNSON KIMBERLY HART, THE ORIGINAL PINK RANGER

SABAN'S
POWER RANGERS
AFTERSHOCK
RYAN PARROTT LUCAS WERNECK JOANA LAFUENTE

MIGHTY MORPHIN POWER RANGERS
POSTER BOOK
FEATURING 20 REMOVABLE POSTERS

PARROTT • MORA • ANGULO
SABAN'S
GO GO POWER RANGERS
VOLUME ONE

Mighty Morphin Power Rangers
Kyle Higgins, Hendry Prasetya, Matt Herms
Volume 1
ISBN: 978-1-60886-893-3 | $19.99
Volume 2
ISBN: 978-1-60886-942-8 | $16.99
Volume 3
ISBN: 978-1-60886-977-0 | $16.99
Volume 4
ISBN: 978-1-68415-031-1 | $16.99

Mighty Morphin Power Rangers: Pink
Kelly Thompson, Brenden Fletcher, Tini Howard, Daniele Di Nicuolo
ISBN: 978-1-60886-952-7 | $19.99

Saban's Go Go Power Rangers
Ryan Parrott, Dan Mora
Volume 1
ISBN: 978-1-68415-193-6 | $16.99

Saban's Power Rangers: Aftershock
Ryan Parrott, Lucas Werneck
ISBN: 978-1-60886-937-4 | $14.99

Mighty Morphin Power Rangers Poster Book
Goñi Montes, Jamal Campbell, Joe Quinones
ISBN: 978-1-60886-966-4 | $19.99

Mighty Morphin Power Rangers Adult Coloring Book
Goñi Montes, Jamal Campbell, Hendry Prasetya
ISBN: 978-1-60886-955-8 | $16.99

Mighty Morphin Power Rangers Year One: Deluxe HC
Kyle Higgins, Hendry Prasetya, Steve Orlando
ISBN: 978-1-68415-012-0 | $75.00

BOOM! STUDIOS

AVAILABLE AT YOUR LOCAL COMICS SHOP AND BOOKSTORE
Find a comic shop near you at www.comicshoplocator.com
WWW.**BOOM-STUDIOS**.COM

Licensed by: Hasbro

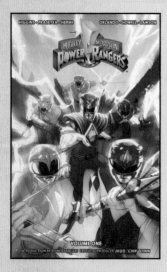

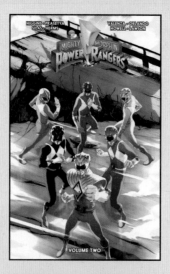

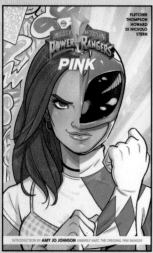

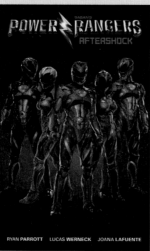

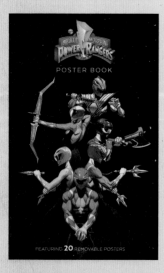

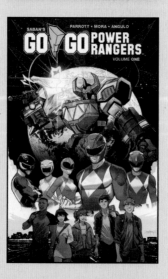

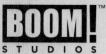